The Turquoise Suitcase

Six Odysseys to Oz

For Mary,
love from
Helen.

Helen Womack

Published by

MELROSE BOOKS

An Imprint of Melrose Press Limited
St Thomas Place, Ely
Cambridgeshire
CB7 4GG, UK
www.melrosebooks.co.uk

FIRST EDITION

Copyright © Helen Womack 2016

The Author asserts her moral right to
be identified as the author of this work

Cover designed by Hannah Belcher

ISBN 978-1-911280-49-1
epub 978-1-911280-50-7
mobi 978-1-911280-51-4

Printed and bound in Great Britain by:
Airdrie Print Services Ltd
24-26 Flowerhill Street
Airdrie, North Lanarkshire
Scotland, ML6 6BH

About the Author

Helen Womack was born in the UK. Most of her career as a foreign correspondent was devoted to the former Communist world, particularly Russia, but she also developed a passionate interest in Australia. Hence *The Turquoise Suitcase*, which is her second book. Her memoirs of life in Russia were published by Melrose Books in 2013 as *The Ice Walk: Surviving the Soviet Break-up and the New Russia*.

To Mateship

This book is for all my friends in Australia

'In a mean little flat on the other side of the earth, an extraordinary feat of remembering took place...'

(Robyn Davidson, *Tracks*)

Contents

Dreaming

Once upon a time there was a woman who lived in the frozen North. Her life was icebound and she was trapped like an Arctic fox in a cage. Early on Easter morning, when the Christian white fellas say their God rose from the dead, she had a powerful dream. She dreamt that if she went to a red desert, she would find water; in the driest place on earth, she would find a new source of life.

The woman had always trusted her brain and used it to make plans. Now she decided to try something new – to follow her heart and her instincts, the signs and omens of the road, and see where they led. She bought a ticket to the Other Side of the World. She would walk alone and accept whatever came her way. Whatever came her way would be what was meant to be.

She was a foxy lady who used to stay in five-star hotels. For the first week, she had fine accommodation, arranged and paid for. After that, she would fall off the edge of the known world. Then her experiment would begin. Her old life would be over, as if she had really died, and she would find out if there was life after life.

On the morning her old life ended, she left her city hotel and wandered down to the Yarra River. There she met a man called Yaroslav. She was happy because he spoke a language close to the one she used to speak in the Frozen Country and they could understand each other. He gave her a leaflet about some crazy bus company and told her to try it. She had promised that she would accept whatever came her way, so she bought a ticket to ride on the boisterous bus.

The driver was a wild girl with orange plaits, who gave her passengers a roller-coaster ride all along an ocean road. The woman from the Frozen

Country was in heaven. She loved the cliffs and beaches because she had been born on an island. She swam in the sea, near a place where there were seals, and considered making her new home there.

But then she remembered the dream about the desert. And in a bar that night, she met a man from her own country, who told her that up in the red wilderness, there was a certain black fella who had a five-billion-star hotel. She had promised that she would accept whatever came her way, so she bought a ticket to A Town Like Alice.

The woman had no plans. She was not expecting anything in particular. But when she saw the blackish fella, handsome with greying curls, she recognised him. Her brain said: *This is impossible. You have never seen him before in your life.* But her heart said: *No, you have known him for a million years.* His name was Muthabadah. She knew she could trust him to lead her down tracks where there might be serpents.

Her dream came true. In the heart of the desert, she found water. In a red canyon there was a black pool where she swam as joyfully as in any ocean. Afterwards, it was very hot. The woman dressed in a long purple skirt to protect herself from the sun and went walking around a big red rock called Luluru. On the rock, she saw a perentie lizard. Nobody else saw it because they were not paying attention but Muthabadah heard the scuttle of its feet.

Later, in the camp, she fell in love with Muthabadah. The woman had no plans. She was not expecting anything in particular. The last thing on earth she was expecting was to fall in love. It just happened in a twinkling. Her brain said: *Don't be stupid. Only in fairy tales do people fall in love at first sight.* But her heart said: *Shut up, brain!* In an instant, the woman saw right through Muthabadah's fattish body into his soul. She saw him as God made him. And she gave him a chance to see her in the same way.

She told herself: *What will be, will be. Whatever will be, will be good, and there is no other way that things can be.* This is a true story for bedtime. And the woman's name was Udjerlah.

*****

Once upon a time there was a man who'd had some bad experiences. He'd lost his first love; she'd died young. He didn't think he could ever love again. He did marry another woman and he had a beautiful daughter. But then he got divorced. He decided that in future, he would play with all the women of the world. The only woman he really loved was his daughter, since the death of his first love, the love of his life.

The man, who was blackish, had had some other bad experiences too. In his youth, he had been a wild boy and he had paid for it under the law. When he was a little child, the bush had been a good teacher to him but he did not have much schooling. He was rotten at spelling. And his feet stank. He knew all this. Only a woman with bad taste would love such a man, he thought, so he played with all the women in the world. And he drank whisky and he went to the casino.

There was a white woman who did not care about any of this. She simply loved him as he was. She loved him because he was a fine man. Her name was Udjerlah and she was a fine woman herself. But he said he was the boss, so she let him have it his way.

Although he had little book learning, he was no fool. He was strong, brave and positive. He gave out energy like a battery. He was gentle and kind as well. And he was very funny. But he was afraid. He was afraid to love because he knew that love hurts. You love a person and then you lose them. He could not bear to experience that agony again.

So he played with all the women in the world. That was his protection against the terrible fire of love. He also believed variety would keep him young and women would not notice his fattish body, his greying hair.

He was a Kangaroo Dreaming man. It was an odd thing but he sometimes looked like an old kangaroo when he lay on his back, asleep. Other times, he looked like an ancient king. To Udjerlah, he always looked very beautiful when he lay on his back, asleep.

One night he was sleeping alone in his swag near the big red rock called Luluru. An old red kangaroo came to him in his dreams. "Hello brother," he said, "let's have a yarn about men's business."

The old kangaroo told him about love. "Life without love is a poor, sad business," said the roo.

"But love hurts," said the man, talking in his sleep.

"True," said the roo, "but if you love in spirit, there can be no loss, and you are always connected to the one you love."

"But love is a trap. I want to be free," persisted the man, still talking in his sleep.

"Listen brother," said the roo, "do you think Mrs. Kangaroo can stop me bounding over the bush? No woman can restrict a man's freedom. Any woman who truly loves knows this because she is free herself."

"There is one other little thing that is worrying me," said the man, whispering in his sleep.

"I know what it is," said the kangaroo. "Here is some medicine."

The man took the bottle. On the label, it said: "Love. Love is the best way to keep your tail up. Guaranteed."

That's funny, thought the man when he woke, *because I am always saying to myself that 'every day, it only gets better'.*

And so, as the sun rose, the man fanned the fire to boil the billy for breakfast tea. And the man's name was Muthabadah.

*****

The man whose name was Muthabadah was a travelling sort of fella. His ancestors had walked across the landscape but he went around the modern way, driving, driving. He was always at the wheel of some sort of vehicle. The woman whose name was Udjerlah had also travelled a good deal in her life. She listened for the wind and when it blew, she knew it was time to go. Now the wind had blown her to A Town Like Alice and she was making her home there. She was waiting for the man whose name was Muthabadah.

Late one night, a strong wind with rain in it blew Muthabadah to Udjerlah's door. He smiled his cheeky smile, threw his travelling bag on the floor and out of it, as if it were nothing, produced a gift for Udjerlah.

It was a beautiful tablecloth, made by black women of a tribe related to Muthabadah's mob. Udjerlah did not have a table, so she wrapped the cloth around herself like a dress. Then she decided it looked better hanging on the wall. It brought warmth to the beige box that was her rented home.

The wall hanging was a picture of life itself. It was in the same earth tints as the desert; the same ochre colours as Muthabadah's people used to paint their bodies. There were hundreds of little yellow dots on brown, hundreds of little brown dots on yellow. There were black dots on red and white dots on black.

Red lines ran like roads and grey, wavy lines flowed like water. Circles were camp sites or water holes and arrows were animal tracks; kangaroo tracks for the hunter. The wall hanging was a map as well as a picture. Udjerlah was as happy as a child at Christmas.

The hour was late. Muthabadah was not hungry for food; he was ready for bed. The next morning, after he had eaten bacon and egg and smoked a cigarette, he was off again on the road, bumping along dusty tracks to the big red rock called Luluru. He was going walkabout in his modern way, down tracks that were like the map that was a picture of life itself.

Of course, it was really only a tablecloth, but Udjerlah didn't have a table. She swept his crumbs and tobacco from the breakfast counter and washed his greasy plate. She was missing him already but she was also glad that he had gone. She was proud of the work that he did. He had to go in order to return and she would wait. It was the pattern of life itself.

For while Muthabadah had his business, Udjerlah had hers. The black people said that if men stuck to men's business and women kept to women's business, there grew the wonderful possibility of human business.

There was also the business of individuals. With Muthabadah busy, Udjerlah was free to do her business of weaving words. Like cloths, she wove stories about love and freedom. She knew that love and freedom were really the same thing.

When she finished writing for the day, she went for a ride on her bike. A light breeze was blowing and two hawks circled high in the sky.

*****

The man whose name was Muthabadah was beginning to trust the white woman, Udjerlah. He knew she had great power but he saw that she did not use it to restrict his male freedom. She was a white witch. He began to relax.

It was natural that Muthabadah had been wary of Udjerlah. She would have been suspicious of him too, were it not for that first moment when she had seen him in his essence. They came from different worlds, on different sides of the world. But more importantly, they were human. He began to trust her with his life story.

Muthabadah grew up on ancient land, near a river which sometimes sprang suddenly but more often disappeared into the sand. It was not easy for Udjerlah, who had always had a roof over her head, to imagine what life must have been like for Muthabadah, growing up under a gum tree. Its grey-green leaves were often his shelter when he was a boy. But he didn't feel sorry for himself because of this; on the contrary, he considered himself rich to have had a childhood in nature.

Although Muthabadah's roots went deep and far into the past, he lived in the modern world and he could use computers as well as the next man. One day, while he was away on the road, he sent Udjerlah an email entitled 'Some Story Time' and this is what it said:

My first eight years of life were untied without caution as we, my family and I, grew up longside a river. In those days, we were made to live outside towns as fringe people, not to be seen or spoken too by white people. All black people had an area of their own, a tree or clearing they called home, while mainstream city folk made decisions for uneducated blackish people, pondering their future

We didn't know much different at the time, as we were kids growing up in the bush without knowledge, except the freedom of ourselves on the land which gave us freedom. Myself, brother and two sisters, mum and dad and grandpop, dad's father. During this period of our lives, we excelled in our skills to survey, understand and respect the land that gave us so much energy without noticing. How does one person describe freedom? One word I guess, 'Happy', barefoot, high on life.

Udjerlah was moved by this letter and asked for another instalment, but Muthabadah preferred to tell her more when they next met. She would have to be patient and wait for the flower to unfurl.

The sun was shining brightly in the cloudless desert sky. Udjerlah decided to drive to Caterpillar Gap from where, during the Dreamtime, ancestor beings had swarmed out to form what the white fellas call the Macintosh Mountains. There she found an old ghost gum and sat beneath its branches, feeling herself into Muthabadah's skin when he had had such a home in the open air.

The trunk of the tree supported her back as she sat, looking out at the grasslands and red rocks beyond. Tourists came and went in their camper vans. Some of them only stayed five minutes before driving on to Middle Gap, Meeting Place Rock and Farthest Gorge. If they kept up a brisk pace, they could see them all in a day and be back in town in time for tea. But Udjerlah just went on looking at the grass and rocks.

The sound of the breeze blowing through the grass reminded her of the sea in her own northern country. Here were no seagulls but green budgerigars and bar-shouldered doves calling 'cookawook'.

She continued to sit as the sun slid down in the sky. Eventually, she was rewarded by the sight of a black cockatoo. At first, she thought it was a crow, dark harbinger of death, but then she saw the vermillion feathers under its tail when it took off in splendid flight.

What a fine home to have, thought Udjerlah, *under the branches of a gum tree. You would get to know every stone and blade of grass around you and all the creatures that were your neighbours. And you would never have to worry whether your tan-coloured sofa toned well with your apricot curtains or your dinner plates matched the dessert dishes.*

It was, however, turning chilly. As the sun disappeared behind the gap, all warmth went out with the light. Muthabadah had told Udjerlah not to drive at night. He had been insistent on this matter, stern almost. An outback gunman was at large, but the greater danger was that she would simply run into a huge kangaroo in the dark. She got into the car and drove straight home.

When she arrived, the telephone was ringing.

"Where have you been? The stars are already twinkling," said Muthabadah. But he was not chiding her; he was laughing. He told her he would be late home and not to wait up for him.

*****

Fast asleep under the duvet, Udjerlah stirred when Muthabadah slipped into bed beside her. They were not having a 'relationship'. He hated that word, which smacked of dreariness and arguments. She tried not to badger him with, "Do you love me; do you love me?"

The next day he took her camping in the bush.

"There's one condition," said Muthabadah.

"What's that?"

"I'm in charge."

"Fine," said Udjerlah. She was happy to obey a man whose authority she could respect. They were not going to tourist campgrounds but out into the desert, where her life would be in his hands. Jokingly, she saluted him, but in all seriousness, she put her trust in her captain.

They were not walking naked, like tribesmen in the tourist posters. He was a modern Aboriginal; he drove a jeep. No doubt he could kill a kangaroo with a boomerang, but he had bought the kangaroo meat for their supper in the supermarket and marinated it at home in red wine. He was a good cook.

Still, there was an element of danger, being out in the middle of the desert in the heat of the day. It was a hostile environment in which an inexperienced person could easily walk to a grim death.

Before they set out, Muthabadah asked Udjerlah if she knew how to change a tyre. Liberated woman though she considered herself to be, she was forced to admit that when it came to technical problems, she had always resorted to batting her eyelashes at men. He snorted and made her jack up the jeep on the drive. For good measure, he made her get under the vehicle and change the oil.

Once they were out in the desert, the first lesson he taught her was how to drink water; not to gulp it, ice-cold, from the esky but to sip it, lukewarm. "Take little sips," he said. "The more you drink, the more you want to drink." For himself, he carried no water at all but chewed a twig that made him salivate.

They walked across a red, sandy wilderness that to Udjerlah seemed to contain nothing at all. A white fella would only be able to see the ridges and undulations from the air but black fellas could see them all clearly at ground level. Their dot paintings, said Muthabadah, were like three-dimensional pictures – if you knew how to look at them, you entered the third dimension.

He showed her a group of humpies, or twig shelters, left by an Aboriginal family that had walked that way. The main humpy was for the women and children. The old man would have sat off to the side. They would all have waited for his signal, telling them it was time to move on.

Muthabadah spoke little to Udjerlah but gestured to her, requiring her to learn his body language. When he did use his voice, he spoke briefly and softly, refusing to repeat himself. It was up to her to hear. She loved this form of communication. After all, so little needed to be said. They moved across the landscape in companionable silence.

His eyesight was as sharp as a hawk's and he had an animal's sense of smell. He found bush tucker while Udjerlah was fiddling about, wiping the lenses of her spectacles on her shirt.

"Here, taste these plums," he said but warned her off the yellow globes that looked like melons. "They're paddy melons. They'll bloat you and give you a raging thirst." Elsewhere in the bush were plants that acted as natural contraceptives but Muthabadah didn't know too much about them.

"That's women's business," he said.

There was a possibility that the first snakes might be emerging from their holes after winter. He did not fear them and neither should she. "If you see a snake, just stand still. It will slither past you," he said. Nevertheless, just in case one of them got bitten, he carried a bandage that could be used to bind a limb and slow the attack of the venom.

The sun was sinking in the sky. He held up his hand and with his fingers, measured the distance between the sun and the horizon. The gap came to exactly the depth of four fingers. That meant there was only one hour left to sunset.

He gestured to her to gather firewood. He broke the heavy mulga branches himself while she followed him, carrying the smaller pieces. Her shirt, knotted at the sleeves, made a good sling for the wood.

He chose the camp site with care. "Not there," he said. "See those fresh dingo tracks?" They avoided low bushes that might attract animals but settled near a tree, out of the wind. He sat listening until he was acquainted with all the normal sounds of the area. If there was any abnormal sound in the night, he would be alert to it in an instant.

Using sticks, he barbecued the kangaroo meat. It tasted delicious, washed down with tea from the billy can. Then they rolled out the swag and went early to bed, fully dressed for warmth.

Udjerlah lay gazing up at the stars. Muthabadah had taught her to see not only the constellations but forms in the spaces between the stars. The space to the side of the Southern Cross was called the Emu. She felt herself flying with the Aboriginal ancestors, up there in the Milky Way.

Eventually she came down to earth and snuggled against his back. He smelt deliciously of sweat and smoke. Silently, she thanked him for treating her to his five-billion-star hotel.

After a week in the desert, they reached Victoriaville, both reeking like savages. Udjerlah reckoned they deserved a night in a five-star hotel, so they checked into the best place in town, complete with swimming pool and spa. They rang room service and ordered oysters, which they ate in bed while watching inane movies.

"It is important," said Udjerlah, flashing her credit card, "to be able to move from the five-billion-star hotel to the five-star hotel, from the swag to the king-size bed and back again."

"Indeed," said Muthabadah, perhaps with a touch of sarcasm in his voice, "I do declare, one should do it with the greatest of ease."

*****

All this happened in a rare season, when rain washed the desert and brought forth an Eden of wild flowers. Long, long ago, it was a time before baggage became heavy and the spiders wove their webs of mistrust. If only Muthabadah hadn't started humbugging her; if only Udjerlah hadn't taken up the missionary position…

They split up at Luluru. It was there that Udjerlah lost patience and told him to take a hike. "You can't find a rock anywhere," he said bitterly. He was standing with his back to the biggest bloody rock in the world and he couldn't see the irony of that complaint.

Now the drought returned with a vengeance. The once-happy couple were again king and queen of separate realms and all that was left to them was sweaty, hard yakka on the bone-dry land.

- Udjerlah and Muthabadah are Aboriginal words for man and woman.

Midway upon Life's Journey

It really was a dream that called me to Australia, which is funny because Oz had never figured much in my thinking in the first half of my life. As a child growing up in Yorkshire, I'd loved one particular jigsaw of Australia, with a merino ram, a metal windmill and the Royal Flying Doctors taking off on a mercy mission over the outback. But there were few other hints that life would take me again and again to Oz, or that Australia would so burn and burnish me in its regenerating inferno.

When I finished school and university, I went to work as a journalist in Eastern Europe and became a specialist on Russia and the former Soviet Union. By chance, many of my friends in Moscow in the 1990s happened to be Aussie colleagues – Deborah Snow of the ABC, Robert Haupt and Robyn Dixon of Fairfax newspapers and Geoff Winestock and Lindy Sinclair, expatriate Australians working for *The Moscow Times*.

Lindy, who against a backdrop of Russian shortages wrote a column called 'The Wistful Gourmet', hosted the best dinner parties. And Geoff, on a summer afternoon out at the dacha, saved me from drowning in a fast-flowing Russian river. "We had Aussie life-saver training; never struggle against the current," he told me when I was back, panting on the bank.

Thanks to this cheerful Aussie influence, I started to have little fantasies about Oz. On days when I felt dissatisfied with the life I had, I would imagine myself running away to Australia. I remember having a disagreement with my Russian husband, Costya, and thinking to myself: *Right then, I will go to Australia!* On the 'green continent', the grass was bound to be greener and there all my problems would be solved.

But that was the extent of my Australia thinking for years. Still I lived between my first home, England, and my adopted home, Russia.

On trips back to visit my parents, we would have outings to the Yorkshire Coast. I particularly loved Whitby, with its ancient abbey, Dracula myth and, yes, memorial to Captain James Cook, who was born nearby. I fancied the idea of buying a house in the area.

I began to read about Captain Cook, who discovered the East Coast of Australia as an afterthought, having completed a mission to observe a transit of Venus in 1769, and who was killed by Hawaiian islanders in a disastrous end to his third voyage in 1779. The *Endeavour*, the *Discovery* and the *Resolution* – the names of his ships inspired me.

But work kept me in Russia. I was in the 'right place at the right time', covering the painful free-market reforms being introduced by President Boris Yeltsin. The Russians knew they had to reform their stagnant economic system but the post-Communist changes were not easy for them. Then Yeltsin launched his war in Chechnya and things started to go to hell in a handcart. The transformation of Russia that we all hoped for was clearly not going to happen overnight.

Things started to go sour in my private life too. I was married to Costya on paper but we had long ago drifted apart. My new relationship with a guy called Vitaly was not working out either. When, in the year 2000, the Russian submarine Kursk sank with the loss of all 118 hands onboard, something sank in me. I was desperate for a break from Russia. Truth to be told, I was heading for a full-scale mid-life crisis.

My parents came to the rescue; my magical parents, who over the years gave me so many opportunities and supported me in everything I tried to do. As a millennium present, they gave me 2,000 pounds, one pound for every year since the birth of Christ. I didn't spend the money immediately but banked it until I could think of a worthy way of using it.

One night in Moscow, I had a vivid dream. I dreamt that if I went to the desert, I would find water – drip drop, drip drop, drop, drop, drop; under the shadow of a red rock, I would find a new source of life.

T.S. Eliot's rock was in 'The Wasteland' but from the dream I understood mine was Ayers Rock or Uluru, to give it its proper Aboriginal name. I felt the Rock was calling me.

Perhaps the explanation was simpler. Sydney had just successfully hosted the Summer Olympic Games, so Australia was in the news and being actively marketed as a desirable destination. Uluru was in all the tourist brochures and adverts.

I talked to my Aussie friends about Oz. On Skype, Robyn Dixon, who by that time was working in South Africa, said in a laid-back drawl: "The great thing about Australia's the lifestyle's great." She couldn't have put it better. I rushed out and booked a holiday Down Under.

Preparing for this trip, I read Bill Bryson's book *Down Under*. It was witty and affectionate and, although he hinted at the down sides one could encounter Down Under, it was clear he loved Australia. I was particularly struck by this passage:

> *In a single generation, Australia remade itself. It went from being a half-forgotten outpost of Britain, provincial, dull and culturally dependent, to being a nation infinitely more sophisticated, confident, interesting and outward looking.*
>
> *By coincidence, a few nights earlier I had watched a television documentary about the immigrant experience in the 1950s. One of the people interviewed was a man who had arrived from Hungary as a teenager after the uprising there. On his first full day in the country he had gone as instructed to the local police station and explained in halting English that he was a new immigrant who had been told to register his address. The sergeant had stared at him for a moment, then risen from his seat and come around the desk. The Hungarian recalled that for one bewildered moment he thought the policeman might be about to strike him, but instead the sergeant thrust out a meaty hand and*

said warmly, 'Welcome to Australia, son.' The Hungarian
recalled the incident with wonder even now, and when he
finished there were tears in his eyes.

I read other books too. I was just starting to get into New Age spiritual literature; you know, all the stuff about 'feeling the fear but doing it anyway'* and 'following your heart to find your treasure'**. I was sceptical of this self-help psychobabble but decided to give it an honest try and, like the journalist I am, come back in due course with a report for my readers. I became a 'spiritual guinea pig'; deliberately, I turned myself upside down and set off on a pilgrimage to see how my life might change.

I went to Oz for a three-month break and ended up being accepted as a migrant and making six extended working visits to the Southern Hemisphere. Altogether, if you add up the time I spent there, it was three years, two months – a respectable length for a correspondent's posting.

Some people are lucky to have one 'trip of a lifetime' to Australia. I had six life-changing trips – twelve long-haul flights, in the course of which I certainly cured my fear of flying. For if you can maintain the grip of fear for a couple of hours on a short flight, you simply have to let go when you're stuck in an airline seat for 14 hours or more.

Along the way I learnt many things. I came to understand that the days when someone like Captain Cook could go out and make discoveries in the outer world are pretty well over. The map of the earth is complete. The only new discoveries are to be made within oneself. Or, as Mitzi Del Bra sings at the beginning of my favourite Australian film, *The Adventures of Priscilla, Queen of the Desert*, 'I've been to paradise but I've never been to me.' Mad as it sounds, I was going to try and find this continent of me.

Moscow, March 2014
Feel the Fear and Do it Anyway, Susan Jeffers
** *The Alchemist*, Paulo Coelho

The First Voyage
Magic Happens

As you set out for Ithaca
hope your road is a long one,
full of adventure, full of discovery.
Constantine Cavafy

The sun set over Uluru. My three-month holiday in Australia, financed by my parents, was coming to an end. It was time to start thinking of turning for Europe but I wasn't ready. There was too much unfinished business between me and Oz. Instead of heading for Cairns and the Great Barrier Reef, which was the planned grand finale before my flight to London, I was going down to Adelaide to pick up a large navy suitcase I had left there, and returning to Alice Springs, where I fully intended to dig in and stay.

I'd fallen in love, you see; in love with the red desert and with a particular itinerant guy who came and went from Alice Springs. If I wanted to see him, the best thing for me was to base myself in Alice and wait for the wind to blow him in. For the sake of argument, let's call him Adam. I was naïve; I thought he would make me whole.

There were logistical problems, though. I needed somewhere to live and I would have to apply to the immigration department for an extension of my tourist visa. But my will was strong.

I was paying 60 dollars a night for a room in the Larapinta Lodge motel. Obviously, I couldn't go on doing that. Moving to a backpackers' hostel, with all the students on their gap years, wasn't really an option, as they were not intended for long stays. But the woman at Larapinta reception told me about somewhere called the Sienna Apartments, which offered low-cost, semi-permanent accommodation to people like nurses and miners on short work contracts. That sounded as if it might suit me.

It was April and the weather was cooling off a bit. I looked on the map and reckoned I could walk out to this Sienna place, which was on the southern edge of town, through Heavitree Gap, the natural gateway to Alice Springs. I was wearing my white canvas hat and carrying a bottle of water. Still, the sun felt like a hot iron pressing down on me.

I hadn't even made it to Gap Road before my water bottle was empty. Passing Piggly Wiggly's supermarket, a cheap store that seemed to serve mainly Aboriginal customers, I bought a second, bigger bottle, which saw me all the way to my destination.

Sienna Apartments was a complex of one-storey units, rather like prisoner-of-war huts, grouped around lawns, in the shadow of the MacDonnell Ranges. It was hardly Changi, though. For the use of residents, there was a swimming pool, a launderette and a little shop selling basics such as bread, milk, canned soup, crisps and bars of chocolate. Behind the units, more people were living in caravans.

The couple at reception, who introduced themselves as Dean and Sue Nankivell, were very friendly and when I explained my situation, they said I could have a unit, 'no worries'. Noticing I was a woman on my own, they put me on the 'quiet' side of the complex. If my memory serves me correctly, they charged me 120 dollars a week, but in any case I was paying less than by clocking up days at the motel.

I moved into unit 64, which like all the others had beige walls and spartan furniture. There was a bedroom, shower and kitchenette, plus a patch of carpet with a sofa and television that passed for a living room. The walls were thin and I could hear my neighbour practising his guitar. The door opened straight onto the front step and I noticed that in the evenings, after a hot day, the residents would open their doors and sit on their steps, drinking tinnies of VB (cans of Aussie beer) and chatting.

I was thrilled. It was all I wanted; a place of my own.

The first night, I tried out the swimming pool. Autumn was coming to the Southern Hemisphere and the Aussies found the water a bit chilly but to me it was balmy. I floated up and down, scooping up and chucking out the bodies of moths that had been drawn to the water during the heat of the day. As I swam, I cleaned the pool for everyone. Then I went to the launderette and afterwards hung out my washing. Five minutes later the washing was dry, such was the aridity of the desert air.

The shop was closed by the time I thought of supper but I had some fruit and cereal, which I laid out on the kitchenette counter. In a cupboard, I found a teabag and a sachet of instant coffee. If I had the tea now, the coffee would be there for breakfast. The kettle was furred and the only pan was made of aluminium but none of that mattered, as I would go shopping for supplies and equipment. I went to bed happy.

The next morning I made a delightful discovery. Across the road from the Sienna Apartments was the Alice Springs Date Farm and Gardens. Over several acres, date palms had been planted and in the café you could have freshly-baked date scones with your coffee, sitting out under the trees.

I didn't know then but was to learn that date palms grew around here thanks to Afghan cameleers who, in the 19th century, helped to bring the railway to Central Australia. The palms grew from the dates they munched along the way, spitting out the stones. When the railway was finished (the famous trans-desert train is called 'The Ghan'), the Afghans released their camels into the wild, creating the largest population of feral camels in the world.

There were no camels in the garden but rather a male red kangaroo, nearly the size of a man. Rather unimaginatively, the owners had called him Skippy. He'd been rescued as a joey (baby) from the pouch of his mother, who'd been run over on the highway. I knew it was quite common for Australians to rear such joeys – they hung them up in shopping bags to recreate the gentle movement of the pouch – but they were supposed to return them to the wild when they grew up. Poor Skippy, though, had been castrated. This explained why he was docile and lolled under the tables of customers enjoying their snacks. He was so tame that you could stroke his face and long ears. He was elegant as a gazelle, but with extraordinarily powerful back legs.

Once I discovered Skippy, I became a fixture in the Date Palm Gardens café and went at every opportunity to sip drinks and read. The garden was a good outlet for me, meaning that I did not have to spend all my time cooped up in my unit. I was starting to appreciate the fact that life in Oz could be lived to a very large extent outdoors.

The weekend was coming and I was waiting for Adam. We had a tentative arrangement to meet at sunset on the top of Anzac Hill, the highest point in Alice, from where you get a fantastic view of the MacDonnell Ranges. Half nervous, half excited, I waited on a bench under the Aussie flag but Adam didn't turn up. Hope was wilting into disappointment. I sat on the lookout until it was almost dark and there was only one other visitor left on the hill with me.

"Hi," I said, "it's just you and me up here now."

"Hi," he answered.

The stranger, a thin guy in a green tee shirt and brown felt hat, introduced himself as Anthony Clift. He said he'd just moved from Sydney to work as a nurse at the Alice Springs Hospital. We walked back down to town together, chatting along the way.

We met again – in the Date Palm Gardens, at my suggestion. In the course of our next few meetings, I gathered that Anthony was not very happy in the nurses' quarters at the hospital. I showed him my unit. He started staying with me some nights, sleeping on the sofa while I had the bedroom. He brought his guitar and I sang, and we gave my guitar-playing neighbour a run for his money.

It all happened quite fast but felt very natural. I was at ease with Anthony, whom I soon started calling Ant. I had my first friend in Alice Springs.

Now I urgently needed to sort out my paperwork with the immigration authorities, as my tourist visa was running out. I applied for an extension, which would allow me to continue my holiday in Australia until the end of the year.

Again I climbed Anzac Hill and sat on the lookout. The town lay, like a peach in a bowl, encircled by low red mountains except for a break in the hills at Heavitree Gap. The ranges made Alice a fortress, for the only way in from the south was through this narrow gap.

The chink in the solid wall of rock reminded me of the Biblical teaching that a camel can pass through the eye of a needle sooner than a rich man enter the Kingdom of Heaven. I focused on that cleft. I visualised myself flying through the air like an arrow from a bow. I flew with deadly accuracy, passed through the gap and landed on the other side, somewhere on the southbound Stuart Highway. And I willed myself to stay in Oz.

Ridiculous, you will say, but a few days later I got the green light from the immigration department to stay for another nine months. It was probably a routine decision but to me it felt like a miracle.

Lacking a work permit, I wasn't able to apply for any jobs in my profession. The *Centralian Advocate*, which was the local rag, and the Alice Springs studios of the Australian Broadcasting Corporation (ABC) were closed to me. But I still had some savings and I did occasional odd jobs for pocket money or other benefits.

One person to give me a big leg-up as I tried to make a new life in town was Andrew Langford, the owner of the Sounds of Starlight Theatre, who put on a didgeridoo show for the tourists. Andrew, originally a Sydneysider, had come up into the outback to work as a horticulturalist on Aboriginal communities. That was where he learnt to play the didgeridoo.

There were politically correct types who said white people shouldn't play the Aboriginal instrument. But the Aboriginal musician and artist Tommy Crow once famously said: "If Aboriginal people can play the guitar, why shouldn't white fellas play the didge?" Andrew Langford was a white fella who had learnt to play the didge like a rock star.

I went to his show a couple of times and then he offered me a little job, selling tickets in his box office for an hour or two, twice a week. In exchange, he gave me a bicycle. Suddenly I had the freedom to pedal out to places like Emily Gap and Jessie Gap, a few miles east of Alice.

At Emily Gap, I saw strange, striped Aboriginal rock art. At Jessie Gap, I watched topknot pigeons and even once saw a black cockatoo, much rarer than the pink-breasted galahs that gathered at dusk on the telegraph wires in town.

One weekend, Andrew invited me to go out with him, his wife Samantha and son Zak to 'fossick' for 'rubies'. Prepared for a picnic, we piled into Didge-One, Andrew's 'troopie' (troop carrier) which, extraordinarily, or so it seemed to me, had a snorkel on the front in case the off-road vehicle became submerged in a flash flood. (I was to learn that flash floods were a hazard in the desert and, indeed, a common way of dying in one of the most arid places on earth was by drowning.)

We drove east, past Trephina Gorge and half way to the old gold-mining town of Arltunga before we stopped in a dry river bed and started looking for the 'rubies', which were in fact garnets. We didn't hit it rich but Andrew spotted a lizard, which fascinated Zak.

Another weekend, the Langfords took me for an outing to Rainbow Valley, south of Alice. I was enchanted by the Sphinx-like rock that rose above the flat clay pan and was to make many more visits to this magical spot. My chief memory from that first visit was how well-behaved young Zak was. He sat in the back of the 'troopie', placidly playing cards, as we bumped over the rough terrain and never once did he whinge. He was only about seven at the time.

"How are you going with that bike?" Andrew asked me one day, not long after the Rainbow Valley outing.

"Great, thanks," I said.

"Wouldn't you rather have a car?" he asked, and to my astonishment he gave me the keys to a hatchback that still went, despite being a bit of a banger. It had cream bodywork, a carpeted dashboard and a jingling elephant hanging from the mirror. On the back window was a purple sticker that said 'Magic Happens'. I called this utility vehicle Alan and to me, Alan was the cutest ute.

Proudly, I parked Alan in the car park at Sienna Apartments. A cowboy, clambering out of a shiny black jeep, looked down on me and said: "There are two kinds of cars, real cars and cars that have names." I noticed the sticker on his back bumper. It said: 'Shit doesn't happen. It comes out of arseholes.' I knew which sticker philosophy I preferred.

Crazy with excitement, I rang my friend Ant. "You won't believe this," I said, "but we've got a car. It's a Datsun called Alan." Ant came straight over to have a look. The passenger door didn't open, so Ant climbed in through the hatchback. (Over time, we developed quite a comic routine, folding ourselves in and out through the hatchback.)

That first evening we took Alan for a spin, even though the light was failing and we knew it was not wise to drive on desert roads in the dark. We went to Corroboree Rock, a traditional Aboriginal meeting place east of Alice.

The cracked, red surface of the rock looked like the skin of a perentie lizard. The moon came up in an indigo sky. Ant got out his guitar and I softly sang a few ancient ballads of the Northern Hemisphere. We trusted the spirits of the Eastern Arrernte people, for whom Corroboree Rock is sacred, would hear our music in the spirit of goodwill in which it was intended.

On the way home, kangaroos bounded in front of the headlights. Signs warned of the danger of cattle wandering onto the road. It was quite frightening and we drove at a snail's pace. Even that was not enough to prevent a dreadfully upsetting accident. A beautiful owl flew straight into our windscreen and broke its neck. We had no chance to avoid it. We had killed not any bird but the bird of wisdom. We were deeply sorry. It was a warning we couldn't ignore.

After that, we only went out in the safe hours of bright sunshine, sticking to the bitumen and never going off-road. Taking these sensible precautions, we regained our confidence and went on to have many happy excursions into the outback.

Meanwhile, Alice Springs opened up to me like a flower – a pink desert rose, perhaps, or a scarlet Sturt pea. The little place was so friendly that it was impossible to walk down the main Todd Mall without a dozen people smiling at me and saying: "G'day, how 'ya going?" Except, the funny thing was they kept calling me Kate. "G'day, how 'ya going, Kate?" I just laughed and told them my name was Helen.

Unbeknown to me, there was a woman who was having a similar experience. When she walked down Todd Mall, people smiled at her and said: "G'day, how 'ya going, Helen?" They were surprised to discover she was in fact Kate.

It seemed I had a doppelganger, which frankly worried me because in German folklore, if you see your double it is an omen of your death.

Eventually, at a dinner party, I did meet my doppelganger, Kate Lawrence. She was a splendid woman who'd come up from Adelaide to work for an organisation called Waltja Tjutangku Palyapayi – a bit of a mouthful but in short, an Aboriginal corporation that did good work for families. Kate looked eerily like me.

True, I was slighter fatter but we both had short, dark hair, narrow faces and wire-rimmed glasses. Our taste in clothes was similar. Kate said she had a brother called Michael, as I do. Her birthday was the 25th January, one day before mine, although in the year before I was born. We shared a love of singing. Her grandmother had come from Yorkshire. So the list of similarities went on. It was a relief when we finally established some differences. Kate was not a journalist but a social worker. And our meeting foretold friendship, not early death for either of us.

Having said that, I did have a rather narrow escape, at home in Sienna Apartments, of all places. I'd been out and bought a desk, computer chair and laptop, as I intended to start writing a book. I'd been working happily at the desk for about two weeks and noticed nothing untoward.

One evening, as I was sitting at the desk with my back to the open door, Adam surprised me by walking in. I'd waited for him for so long that I'd almost forgotten about him. He didn't phone or anything. He just turned up.

"Don't move," he said quietly. I sat, frozen.

He raised his hand and brushed the wall, just above my head.

"That was a Redback," was all he said. I'd been sitting for a fortnight, blithely oblivious to the fact that one of Australia's deadliest spiders had been hanging from a web a few inches from my face.

Adam was like that, a man of action and few words. He was unpredictable and if I wanted to catch up with him, I would have to be patient and go with the flow.

Perth, Sydney, Melbourne...

I was glad to settle in Alice Springs and take stock of the considerable journey I'd made to that point. I'd been on the road for three months since leaving the UK and needed to wake up in the same bed, eat home-cooked meals and not move, at least for a while.

Before setting off from England, I'd tried to buy a house at the seaside in Yorkshire. I reckoned a property would be an anchor for me; a reason to return to the Northern Hemisphere. But things didn't work out and I set off on my journey across the world without that safety net. I was in free fall and that was how it was meant to be.

I flew via Thailand. On my first couple of days in Bangkok, I did the obligatory tourism. I went to see the Grand Palace, with its gold and jewel-encrusted temples. In a strange way, it reminded me of the Kremlin in Moscow. But I wasn't there to see the sights.

I was going up the River Kwai to do some research for a book I wanted to write about an uncle, who'd been a POW on the Thai-Burma Railway of Death. After that, I was going on to Perth in WA to see another uncle, who'd also been a prisoner of the Japanese. It was pretty unusual, I reckoned, that two men from the same Yorkshire family had both been captured and enslaved by the Japanese. After the war, one had stayed in Britain while the other had migrated to Oz.

In Perth, I found the second uncle, whose name was Arthur, living in a bungalow in the suburb of Scarborough, not that it was anything like the Yorkshire Scarborough. We went swimming together in the Indian Ocean before Uncle Arthur opened up to me about his war experiences. Before we parted, he lent me a little black oilskin diary he'd kept throughout his imprisonment, and for which he could have been executed, if caught. With great care, I put it into a safe pocket inside my rucksack to read on the road.

And so I set off on my first exploration of Oz from Uncle Arthur's house and since I was already in Perth, I reckoned I might as well begin by having a bit of a look at WA.

The state of Western Australia is enormous. It covers half the continent; it really is a whole country in its own right. I was only going to be able to scratch the surface and see a tiny area around Perth and its trendy port of Fremantle. I wouldn't have time for the wonderful corner of southwest WA, famous for its giant trees. Neither would I make it up the Coral Coast to swim with dolphins, watch dugongs or see the stromatolites, the earliest life form on earth, which made all other life possible simply by breathing out oxygen for eons.

But to start with, as I had seen nothing at all of Australia, Perth itself was exciting enough for me.

I stayed in a hotel with a Wild West feel. London Court, a half-timbered shopping arcade on Hay Street, was Perth's attempt to recreate Elizabethan England. Only when I came down to the banks of the Swan River, famous for its black swans and lined by magnificent, mature palms, did I feel I had found the authentic Perth. I was moved.

Here on the edge of the desert, in splendid isolation from the rest of the world, was a fine city, with a mini-Manhattan of several skyscrapers and some gorgeous parks. I was particularly struck by the modern bell tower on Riverside Drive, a grouping of red-brick sails from which rose a thin glass spire. I would have loved to hear the Swan Bells ring out but only the parrots were squawking that day.

Naturally, I was keen to see some of the legendary wildlife that lives only in Australia, so the next day I booked a trip for myself to Yanchep National Park, 30 miles north of Perth. Here I not only saw koalas in the gum trees but got to hold a koala called Millie while a park ranger photographed me. I know it sounds childish but I cannot begin to convey the utter thrill of this experience; the unbelievable softness of Millie's grey coat. Eventually, of course, I was to become as blasé about koalas as I am about rabbits in Yorkshire but I will never forget that first magical contact.

The tour to Yanchep also included a drive out to the Pinnacles, an area of ancient limestone rock formations that stand like sculptures in the desert. Under the baking sun, I sat on one rock and photographed another that looked like a contemplative kangaroo. Across the yellow sands, beyond the hundreds of weird rocks in all shapes and sizes, I could see a strip of green vegetation, the azure line of the Indian Ocean and a huge, cloudless blue sky.

On the way back to the city, the tour bus drove along the edge of the Indian Ocean and stopped for fifteen minutes on the beach. Fifteen minutes! I couldn't believe it. I had crossed the world, come all the way from the frosty Northern Hemisphere in winter, and they were giving us fifteen minutes at the Indian Ocean.

The other passengers stood meekly, fully dressed on the white beach. "I don't care what you say," I called to the driver, "I want half an hour and I'm going in the water." At that, I stripped off my skirt and tee shirt and ran into the warm, glittering shallows. In retrospect, perhaps it was unwise. Who knows what sharks might have been lurking there? (For sharks do, apparently, swim in surprisingly shallow water.) But it was pure ecstasy, 'heaven on a stick' as the Aussies say. The driver didn't seem to mind the delay. He just had a smoke and chatted to the more obedient passengers until I came back, dripping and satisfied.

On another of my outings from Perth, I went to Rottnest Island or Rotto, as the locals call it. The island was discovered in the 17th century by the Dutch, who mistook the marsupial quokkas they saw there for giant rats and named the place Rotte Nest, or Rats' Nest in their language. The Aboriginal Noongar people knew the island as Wadjemup.

The catamaran for Rottnest left from the quayside at the Swan River, so I had another opportunity to admire the avenue of majestic palms and the beautiful white-clapboard boat houses.

We sped off down the Swan, passing the posh villas of the Perth elite. Among them, our guide said, was the palatial home of Alan Bond, the disgraced business tycoon, who was jailed for four years for fraud for his involvement in the biggest corporate collapse in Australian history. Clearly, there were some skeletons in Perth cupboards but I hadn't come looking for them.

When we docked at Rottnest, I hired a bike and cycled through landscape that reminded me of the Yorkshire moors, with its bare hills, low trees and heather-like ground plants. The only difference was the heat, and the minor matter that at one point I almost rode over the tail of a long, black and no doubt deadly-poisonous snake that was sunning itself on the bitumen. I was an inch or two from crushing the tip of its tail with my wheel and certainly, if I had done, the injured snake would have doubled back, lashed out and bitten me on the bare leg, if it was the last thing it did.

It was a good lesson that in arriving in Oz, I had come to a wild and potentially dangerous place. 'Here be dragons', as the old maps said. I was an innocent abroad, in savage lands.

On my last day in Perth, I had a coffee in Kings Park with Eric Harrison, the founder of the Perth Meditation Centre, whose books on meditation I'd found very helpful. I'd been trying to meditate for a number of years but found it almost impossible to sit still and stare at a single point, like Buddha musing on a lotus. From Eric's books, I'd learnt that it could be effective to listen to the sounds around oneself, from traffic to birdsong to the gentle in and out of one's own breath.

Now I was meeting the author in person, and I was in awe. If Eric had been ready to take me on as his assistant-disciple, I might have stayed in Perth. But he said to me: "You must find your own path."

And indeed, on the plane to Sydney the next day, I had a revelation that brought me to tears. I was reading *The Songlines*, Bruce Chatwin's classic book about the Dreaming tracks of Aboriginal people. They 'sang up' the land as they walked and walked themselves to a 'good death'. Eureka! It was OK to be a nomad, then. I had always walked; that was my way. Step by step, I would expand my consciousness by the simple, joyful means of walking.

The passengers on the plane with me must have thought I was bonkers, weeping and laughing over a book, but I was very open to everything then, both vulnerable and receptive, as if I had shed a skin.

"Chicken or beef?" asked the stewardess, bringing me down to earth, although we were still 30,000 feet in the air. It was over four hours to Sydney, across the whole of Australia, not much shorter than the flight from Singapore to Perth.

In Sydney I was booked for two nights into the expensive, central Menzies Hotel, overlooking Wynyard Park, paid for as part of my parents' generous holiday package. I made full use of the short time, going down to the harbour and walking in the botanical gardens. The weather was perfect, hot but with a refreshing sea breeze.

I strolled between the Opera House and the Harbour Bridge, enjoying the acts of the street performers – a Chinese girl playing a slender stringed instrument, a fire eater in tight, white leather shorts. Across the sparkling water, I could see the laughing clown's mouth that was the entrance to the Luna Park fairground.

The harbour was full of commuter ferries and tourist boats. I was attracted by the Mississippi-style paddle steamers, with their red wheels, but in the end I took a more modest craft for a short cruise that gave me a different angle on the city from up on deck. Behind our wake, the bridge and Opera House faded into the distance and we turned into a bay with fine waterfront properties, the homes of Sydneysiders who had achieved their highest aspirations. On the way back, we passed Kirribilli House, the prime minister's residence, flying the Australian flag.

What can I say? Sydney was great, of course. But I felt like a provincial Pom, who'd been up to London to see the Queen. What was left for me to do? Only to ask a passerby to take a photo of me, grinning stupidly, in front of the famous white sails of the Opera House. And to have a banquet-for-one in a Chinese eatery, as I'd been told that Sydney was a more Asian city than 'English' Melbourne, to which I was heading next.

The summer heat in Melbourne was hardly English and I revelled in it as I walked along the bank of the Yarra River, admiring the modern sculptures and watching local kids in bathing costumes splashing in the fountains. From the riverside, I got a good view of the skyscrapers of the business district, the dome and tower of Flinders Street Station and the spire of St. Paul's Cathedral.

I'd been told that Melbourne was a foodies' paradise – the restaurant capital of Australia – but I was on a budget and looking for a simple dinner, so I settled on an inexpensive Greek place that gave me a hearty welcome and even heartier lamb *kleftiko* with salad, wine and honey dessert.

Lunch next day in the café of the botanical gardens was in another league of splendour. Eating with the Melbourne ladies who lunch, I felt I could have been at the Chelsea Flower Show or the Cheltenham Literature Festival. The quiche and meringues were fit for royalty.

The gardens themselves were very fine, despite the fruit bats that had become something of a pest. I sat among exotic white flowers that looked like giant lily of the valley – Yucca gloriosa, as my botanically-minded mum would have known – entranced by the repeated crystal notes of the little bellbird.

Enjoying the gifts of Melbourne, I spared a thought for a former colleague of my father's, a man called Bob Addison. His was, I think, one of the saddest stories I ever heard. He worked at the building society where my dad had his career and was jokingly called Bobby Adding Machine, as he was good with figures. He postponed his travels until he retired, when he set off with his wife on a 'trip of a lifetime'. He had just landed in Auckland and bent to pick up his suitcase from the airport conveyor belt when he felt a pain in his back. New Zealand doctors diagnosed cancer and advised him to return to England immediately, which he did, without seeing anything of the Southern Hemisphere.

Every time I thought of him I thanked my lucky stars. As my dad used to say, if I fell off the Woolworth Building, I'd fall on my feet. Here I was, on lawns near the Melbourne war memorial now, sitting on a sunny day in the shade of a stately eucalyptus tree. The plaque said it had been planted on Australia Day, the 26th January 1956, in memory of the nation's war dead. It was 45 years old, the exact same age as me; it had been planted on the very day I was born.

Lolling under the tree, I was listening on my Walkman to an English baritone singing a Handel aria, set to lines from Psalm 128:3. I misheard the words, despite the singer's perfectly good diction. He was actually singing, 'Thy wife shall be as the fruit of the vine', but what I heard was, 'Thy *life* shall be as the fruit of the vine'.

The music spoke directly to me. One did not necessarily have to have children – and I did not – but one did have to be as creative as possible in life. That was all that was required. I rose from under the gum tree, feeling at peace with myself and the world.

Great Ocean Road

Melbourne was luscious but I was eager to get out of the city and hit the open road. Not any old road, you understand, but the Great Ocean Road, built by Australian men returning from the First World War and hugging the incredible Shipwreck Coast all the way from Melbourne to Adelaide. I was going on a four-day tour with a small private company that I'd chosen because of its promise to take a steady pace; its slogan was 'Wayward Bus: Let the Others Rush'.

At the appointed hour, I met the jolly little white minibus at the side of a main road leading out of Melbourne and introduced myself to my fellow travellers, mostly young backpackers half my age. The driver was a sporty young woman with ginger plaits, called Jen.

We drove out through the town of Geelong, passing Bells Beach, home to the world's longest running surfing competition, and arrived in the resort of Lorne in time for morning tea. At the Kennett River, we saw koalas, while Cape Otway boasted Australia's oldest lighthouse. Guarding the hazardous confluence of the Bass Strait and the Southern Ocean, it was the light of hope to thousands of migrants in the 19th century, sighting land after their long voyages from Europe.

Walking back up the path from the lighthouse, I heard the tall, handsome young man from the back of the bus, who had been silent and mysterious up to this point, breathing rather than saying, "Hangaroo, hangaroo". He was right. There was a small kangaroo in the bushes. "Markku, Markku," he said in his strange, breathy voice.

Back on the bus, Markku showed me his passport and I saw that he was Finnish. He was deaf and dumb. I don't know why – there were better-looking, younger lasses on the bus – but he chose me as his travelling companion and moved forward to sit next to me. Markku made the whole trip special. He couldn't say much, of course, but he was a hundred times more observant than the other chattering backpackers.

We spent the night in Apollo Bay. I was stunned by the scale of it. We have bays on the Yorkshire Coast, but they are narrow inlets compared with the deep scoops and wide sweeps of the Australian coastline. Thunder clouds darkened the sky and water before a shaft of evening light turned the scene into a Turneresque study in peach and pink.

The gap-year students had bunk accommodation but I paid extra for a small cabin to myself and turned in for an early night. I was glad to see Markku go to the pub with guys his own age but he was sitting next to me on the bus again the following morning.

Overnight, the weather had cleared and we had a fine, sunny day for our visit to the famous Twelve Apostles, offshore rocks that stand like sentinels, guarding the southern approaches to Australia and marking the start of the deadly Shipwreck Coast. Markku and I photographed each other in various poses with the Apostles in the background. We held hands in front of the London Bridge rock, which had collapsed some years earlier, causing embarrassment to one Australian couple.

The adulterous pair had been having a dirty weekend, having told their respective spouses they were away at conferences. They were standing, canoodling, on the far end of London Bridge when the middle section of the eroded rock collapsed into the sea, leaving them stranded on a newly made island. Helicopters had to be scrambled to rescue them and, of course, the media were waiting with their cameras when the exposed lovers were delivered back to the mainland.

From the Twelve Apostles, we drove to Port Campbell National Park and Loch Ard Gorge, scene of one of dozens of disasters that struck 19th century sailing ships trying to reach Australia on this most dangerous stretch of coastline. In 1878, the Loch Ard, built in

Glasgow, had almost brought its 37 passengers and assorted cargo safely to Melbourne when it got lost in fog and was wrecked on reefs near Mutton Bird Island. Two survivors made it to the shore of the mainland.

The ship's apprentice, Tom Pearce, clung to an overturned lifeboat and drifted to the beach. There he heard the cries of a young lady called Eva Carmichael and plunged back into the sea to pull her out. In the process of saving her, he caught a glimpse of her underwear and felt honour-bound to offer to marry her, but she declined because of the class difference between them, or so the story goes.

The only other thing salvaged from the wreck of the Loch Ard was a large, decorative porcelain peacock, intended for the Melbourne International Exhibition of 1880. It was completely undamaged and can be seen to this day at Flagstaff Hill Maritime Village, Warrnambool.

In the old cemetery at Loch Ard Gorge, we saw the graves of those who had travelled in hope, no doubt enduring seasickness and many other hardships on the way, only to lie in sandy ground on the other side of the world. It was touching, but didn't prevent me and other girls from the bus from taking a swim and frolicking on the beach where Tom and Eva had come ashore.

We were walking back to the coach when I felt Markku tug on my sleeve. "Hidna, hidna," he almost snorted.

"What is it Markku?"

"Hidna."

And sure enough, to the side of the path, he pointed out an echidna, Australia's funny little spiny monotreme, which is very shy and therefore rarely sighted. In fact, in all my time in Oz, this was the only occasion I ever saw an echidna. Loud and inattentive, we would all have walked straight passed it, if it hadn't been for Markku's sharp eyes.

The rest of the tour, which was excellent, giving the right balance between education and entertainment and enough time to stand

and stare, included a cruise from Port Fairy to see a colony of New Zealand fur seals and a wild afternoon of sandboarding on the dunes of the Younghusband Peninsula, by which time we were already in the Coorong lagoon region of South Australia.

The tour came to an end and we were left to our own devices in Glenelg, the resort town attached to Adelaide. By this time, we who had been total strangers had all bonded and become the best of friends. We went together to the New Zealand ice cream parlour to discuss our accommodation options. The backpackers' hostel was the best bet, although I cheated a bit by getting a single room. In the evening, I walked on the pier and watched the sunset with Markku. We were saying goodbye, as he was off on another tour the next day and due back at work in Finland a week later.

"Hangaroo, hangaroo!"

"Hangaroo, hangaroo!" we hollered and hugged each other. I hoped he went well and saw mobs of bounding kangaroos as he continued on his travels.

After the backpackers had all dispersed on their next adventures, I lingered a while in South Australia. I took the tram up from Glenelg into Adelaide, a twenty-minute ride that delivered me to a square where Queen Victoria reigned in stone and bronze. In Adelaide I discovered another pleasant Australian city, with cathedral, shopping precinct, pubs, restaurants and fine parklands to north, south, east and west.

I spent an interesting afternoon in the Tandanya National Aboriginal Cultural Institute, which gave me a sense that Adelaide was the gateway to something remote and less explored. But Adelaide itself didn't hold me. The city hotels were expensive and I found myself drawn back to Glenelg. The little seaside town reminded me of Filey in Yorkshire; Filey with a Mediterranean climate.

Luckily, the school summer holidays were coming to an end and I was able to find a reasonably-priced self-catering holiday flat. It was at the back of its block, with a view of a car park from the living room window. But I could walk straight out from the flats to the promenade. What more could I want?

I took long walks along the beach, noticing that the Australian seagulls were smaller than the fat herring gulls at home. To my northern eye, the Norfolk Island pine trees looked like upside-down Christmas trees with their differently arranged needles and branches. I also spent a happy afternoon at the Rodney Fox Shark Experience, a museum honouring a local film maker and conservationist who survived a shark attack. Here I learnt, among other horrifying facts, that the great white shark has multiple rows of self-replacing teeth.

When I got bored with Glenelg, I took myself off on a trip to Kangaroo Island, discovered in 1802 by the explorer Matthew Flinders, who reported that the kangaroos were tame and trusting because they had never encountered human beings. After Flinders' near-starving crew had stewed half-a-hundredweight of kangaroo heads, forequarters and tails to make soup and also wolfed as many kangaroo steaks as they could consume, the marsupials no doubt changed their view of mankind.

The weather was glorious and I was up on the deck of the SeaLink ferry for the whole ride from the mainland port of Cape Jervis to Kangaroo Island. Strangely, I didn't actually see any wild kangaroos there, just some cute joeys in a rescue centre. But a koala peed on me from a great height when I pointed my zoom lens up at him in the gum trees. And I saw a flock of pelicans in the harbour at Penneshaw.

The highlight of the trip to Kangaroo Island was a swim at pristine Snellings Bay. One of the reasons I had come to Australia was that I wanted to swim as much as possible. The white beaches and turquoise waters were irresistible and the thought of the great white's self-replacing teeth, while a shadow on my pleasure, to be sure, was not enough of a deterrent to stop me.

Back in Glenelg, I sampled every imaginable flavour of frozen yoghurt at the New Zealand ice cream parlour. I also had plenty of coffees in the cafes around town. I had discovered a kind of coffee I particularly liked and hadn't found outside Australia – the flat white. It was neither a frothy cappuccino nor an ordinary coffee with milk but something in-between.

At the same time I was dissatisfied. I had not crossed the planet to measure out my life with coffee spoons. Everything I had seen in Australia had been wonderful and yet nothing had been very far outside my European experience. Nothing had really fired my heart. Nothing had made me ache at the thought that I might not see it again.

I remembered the red rock that had called me and was still calling. It was February and the wrong time of year to go to Uluru, where the heat would still be intense. But it was the only time I had.

I took the tram into Adelaide again and went to the office of the Wayward Bus Company, which had looked after me so well on the trip from Melbourne. They were offering two tours to Uluru. One, called 'Face the Outback', was an eight-day camping trip from Adelaide, going through the badlands of South Australia and the red desert of the Northern Territory, and ending up at the Rock. The other, called 'Just the Red Centre', was four days of camping, starting and finishing in Alice Springs, and taking in Kings Canyon, Uluru and the Olgas.

The only camping I had done before was as a Girl Guide in a wet British woodland, when I had eaten raw fish fingers because I couldn't get a fire going. I wasn't too sure how I would cope with camping. And anyway, it was the Rock I wanted to see, not the rest of the vast outback. So I opted for the shorter tour and booked a flight to Alice Springs. For the night before the expedition, I would have a comfortable bed in Toddy's Backpackers on Gap Road.

I asked the owner of the Glenelg holiday flats if I could leave the large navy suitcase I had dragged across the world in his storeroom for safekeeping. I promised to return for the case when I'd taken in the Rock and was ready to move on to the last stop on my planned route, the Great Barrier Reef.

And so, like many an outback explorer before me, I left Adelaide and set out into the searing wilderness. The explorers of the past had had horses and guns; some of them even entire field kitchens. I was carrying nothing more than a rucksack and was ready for adventure.

Rock of Ages

Our group for the Red Centre trip was small, just five backpackers from various countries and me, all crammed into an off-road jeep driven by a laidback guy in khaki shirt and shorts called Geoff.

"We're going to be camping, in case you haven't been warned," he grinned as we set off.

But the start of the tour, at least, was hardly arduous, as we hadn't been on the road out of Alice for more than half an hour before we stopped at a roadhouse called Jim's Place at Stuarts Well for morning tea. The roadhouse had a rather pathetic little zoo, with a couple of kangaroos and an emu. "The symbols of Australia," drawled Geoff.

The eponymous Jim gave us a warm welcome as he invited us to help ourselves to the instant coffee or tea bags and offered us scones if we wanted them. He was followed everywhere he went around the roadhouse by a tame dingo.

"This is Dinky," he said, explaining how he'd rescued the dingo as a young pup and kept him as a pet.

Dingoes don't bark; they howl. And Dinky was no exception. He was well known at Stuarts Well as the Singing Dingo. One of the girls from the tour spotted Jim's upright piano and began tinkerty-tonking on the keyboard. The piano was out of tune. Dinky jumped up on the seat beside her and started howling his little canine heart out. The music was interestingly dissonant, to put it charitably.

After the roadhouse, things got a bit rougher. Geoff turned off the bitumen and we were bouncing for an hour or two over a dirt track, churning up a great cloud of red dust behind us. The colours of the desert were the red of the earth, the green of the bushes and the blue of the sky. They could have been the tricolour of Central Australia.

Eventually we came to a stop by a dry river bed. Geoff squatted down in the sand and gave us an elementary lesson in Aboriginal sign language, drawing the circles and arrows that represent water holes and animal tracks in indigenous geography, storytelling and art.

Then he sent us out in the heat of the day to collect firewood while he prepared lunch. "Don't forget your sunscreen and water," he called. There was hardly any vegetation, let alone trees, but we managed to find dry twigs from the low bushes. We soon learnt not to touch the spiny spinifex grass, which grew in yellow clumps on the red earth.

When we returned, Geoff had laid out a spread of Vegemite sandwiches, salad with beetroot, and tinned pineapple. After our exertions, it tasted delicious. While we ate, a wedge-tailed eagle patrolled the sky overhead. Geoff pointed out a little thorny devil lizard in the sand at our feet. "The desert is full of life," he said before we moved on.

We set up camp, ready for the night, at the Kings Canyon campgrounds and then went hiking at the canyon in the relative cool of the late afternoon. We walked for quite a while through a landscape of low rocks that looked like griddle cakes. Where was the famous canyon, where in the movie *Priscilla, Queen of the Desert*, the drag queens had stood in their sequins and feathers, each of them a proud 'cock in a frock on a rock'?

Suddenly we came upon it, the surprising plunge of the canyon, its smooth red walls dropping down hundreds of feet. We stayed up on top, walking gingerly around the edge. At a safe distance, the backpackers horsed around, playfully threatening to push each other over into the abyss. I sat, looking out at the vast desert, which struck me as an arid ocean, far from the haven of the sea.

What thrilled me most about Kings Canyon, though, was my discovery of deep black pools, accessible when you scrambled down the narrow path into the valley. People were swimming here. The fresh water was cold but there were no sharks, no crocodiles and no toxic jellyfish for that matter. I made a mental note of this. Perhaps, paradoxically, I was going to get my greatest swimming satisfaction in Australia not at the coast but in the middle of the desert. There was no time for a swim that evening, however, as we had to get back to camp.

While we'd been walking, Geoff had prepared for us a nice hot chicken curry with rice. I began to realise what an amazing job this modest bloke was doing. He'd driven all day, entertained and educated us as best he could, got us settled into the camp and done all the cooking for us. All we had to do was enjoy ourselves, and help with the washing up, while Geoff must have been completely knackered. I'm not sure any of us appreciated this enough at the time.

If I'd been worrying about camping, all my anxieties turned out to be laughable when I saw the splendid facilities at the campground. There was a shop, swimming pool, barbecue area, toilets and showers. If you wanted, you could go camping in Australia in full makeup, which one of the Essex girls on the tour did. That evening, she emerged from the showers with washed hair, heavily perfumed.

We were sleeping in small, individual tents, which at first seemed like a good guarantee against snakes, spiders and all other conceivable long-leggedy beasties. But inside the tent, I couldn't see the marvellous canopy of the desert sky, with its myriad stars. It was still very warm, so I moved outside and lay on my groundsheet, gazing up at the constellations, like diamonds strewn across black velvet.

Outside, I could hear the irritating chatter of the Essex girls, which was obviously going to go on half the night. I had not come camping in the wilderness to listen to two silly chavs popping beer cans and discussing boyfriends and shades of lipstick. So I moved my groundsheet a good distance from the group until all I could hear was the buzz of insects, under the dome of the night sky. The new moon had been and gone, so the stars were particularly bright.

I lay awake in a state of wonder for most of the night. I learnt the truth of the saying that 'the darkest hour is before the dawn'. It did indeed get darker and colder in the hour before the first crack of light appeared on the horizon. Although I hardly slept at all, I got up feeling deeply rested.

"Where did you get to?" asked a concerned Geoff when I showed up in camp for breakfast.

"Oh, you know, I'm a big girl," I said and he understood I was not going to let him shepherd me like the youngsters.

Now the time had come for us to head to the Rock. We had camel rides at Curtin Springs roadhouse on the way. Some of us were fooled by Mount Conner, which rises up, flat-topped like a table, on the way to Ayers Rock and is known as 'False Uluru'. Eventually the real Rock, the biggest monolith in the world, appeared like a sleeping giant on the horizon. What we were seeing was the tip of a desert 'iceberg', Geoff said. Most of the Rock was under the ground. It was a heart-stopping sight.

Local Anangu people manned the ticket booths at the entrance to the national park. The World Heritage-listed sacred site, discovered in 1873 by the surveyor William Gosse and named after the Chief Secretary of South Australia, Sir Henry Ayers, was given back to Aboriginal people by the Australian government in 1985. To preserve the delicate desert environment, the Rock was cordoned off and you could only approach it by certain paths and roads.

We spent the afternoon in the Aboriginal Cultural Centre, which explained the local creation myths – the Rock was the site of an epic fight between ancestral snake beings, Kuniya and Liru. We were specifically asked not to climb the Rock, although the Anangu admitted they couldn't stop us, if we insisted on being what they called 'mingas' (ants) and desecrating what was effectively their cathedral by tramping up it.

I couldn't understand why the soft-spoken Anangu didn't simply ban the climb. The foolhardy and inconsiderate were allowed to go up, hanging on to a chain so they didn't fall. The traditional owners feared tourist income would drop if they stopped the practice completely. Nobody in our group opted to do the disrespectful climb. Rather, we all chose to take the recommended base walk around the six-mile perimeter of the Rock, which we would do the following morning.

At the campground in Uluru that night it was the same story as at Kings Canyon – too much civilisation and too many noisy, happy campers. We weren't going to 'do sunset' on our first evening because that was the grand finale of the tour. A troupe of dancers and didgeridoo players had been booked to entertain us round the campfire instead. In despair, I left the group straight after our barbecued dinner and wandered off on my own to the Naninga lookout, from where I caught the last rays of the sun, turning the Rock, brick-red by day, into a long, pink lozenge.

It was up here that I met Adam.

"Good evening," he said quietly. "How 'ya going?"

I explained to him my frustration with the communal camping. He nodded.

"I could lend you a swag," he said.

He was doing some job at the campgrounds. In his truck, he had a spare swag, the rollup bed carried by Aussie bushmen.

"Yeah, great," I said, and after we had chatted a bit more he went to his vehicle, fetched the swag and rolled it out for me on Naninga Hill.

"I'll be down below if you have any problems. Otherwise, catch 'ya in the morning."

Perhaps I took a bit of a risk but I felt no threat from Adam.

Out of courtesy, I told Geoff where I would be spending the night and then retreated to my private hill. The swag, with its padded base and tarpaulin cover in case of bad weather, was incredibly comfortable and I had the night of my life, stargazing, alone in nature. I discovered that the right kind of camping was very much for me. I unlocked a hitherto unrealised part of myself. I was a bushwoman.

Early the next morning, before the rest of the camp woke up, Adam and I shared tin mugs of instant coffee and got to know each other a little better. He asked me out to the bar of the Sails in the Desert, the smart hotel for well-heeled visitors to Uluru, and we agreed to meet there in the evening. Then he went off to work and I rejoined my tour group.

The sun was up and they were all having breakfast. "Saved you a pancake and some bacon," said Geoff kindly. After that, before the day got too hot, we went for our base walk around the Rock.

I must say it was the best way to see the great Australian icon. If we'd climbed, from the top all we'd have seen would have been the desert, but at ground level we saw the details of the Rock itself. It was an inversion of the old Polish joke about the best way to see Warsaw – from the top of the skyscraper imposed on the city by Stalin. Because being on top of the ugly building was the only way to avoid seeing it.

The Rock was fascinating. Most of the time, when the weather was dry, it was red but when occasional rain clouds gathered, it was known to turn the colour of liver and run with waterfalls. I was seeing it in its usual red mode, pockmarked with craters including one that looked like a human brain. The numerous little caves at the base were like side chapels to the main cathedral.

Uluru didn't disappoint me, except that I was puzzled not to see more indigenous people in this most Aboriginal of places. True, there were guides, ticket sellers and a few others helping the tourists but where were the Aboriginal people who lived there?

Nobody else on the tour seemed much interested in the question. By midday, it was far too hot to explore further anyway, so we returned to the camp for a siesta.

In the evening, I watched the sun set over the distant Olgas before going to find Adam, as arranged, at the hotel bar. He stood up to greet me with a radiant smile; he was very attractive.

"How was your day? Did you like the Rock?" he asked.

"Yeah, except I didn't really see many Aboriginal people. Where are they all?"

He avoided the question but did, in the course of our conversation, reveal that he was himself of partly Aboriginal origin. He wasn't a desert Aboriginal but came from a more urban background interstate.

We talked of this and that and laughed a fair bit. There was some chemistry between us. At the end of the evening, I asked him again where the Aboriginal people at Uluru lived.

"There's a community behind the Rock called Mutitjulu," he said.

"Can I go there?"

"Nah, too difficult."

My curiosity was aroused. I'm dangerous when my curiosity is aroused. And even though – or perhaps because – Uluru hid its secrets, I was feeling the excitement that had been missing in other blander parts of Australia. Yes, this was why I had crossed the planet, for this humming, vibrating, ancient and thoroughly foreign red desert.

Adam and I parted but agreed to meet again the next evening, up on Naninga Hill.

The last day of the Red Centre tour was devoted to the Olgas, or Kata Tjuta as the strangely rounded mountains are known to the Aboriginals. As we hiked through the Valley of the Winds, I felt I was on the set of some obscene Woody Allen movie, pursued by giant red bottoms and boobs. Well, that's my impure and frivolous mind for you. The place is, of course, incredibly powerful and full of meaning for the Anangu.

I stayed with the group for our last-night sunset viewing of the Rock. Coach loads of tourists lined up to watch the sun go down, the wealthier ones with fancy picnics and bottles of champagne, those on a budget like us with trail bars and tins of soft drink to celebrate the moment. As the setting sun started to turn the red Rock pink, thousands of cameras – professional and amateur, Japanese, European and American – whirred and clicked. I stood well back and photographed the photographers taking their pictures.

Then, while there was still a gleam of light left in the sky, I hurried to the Naninga lookout to find Adam, have a last chat with him and return the swag he'd lent me. He was waiting for me and we talked for a long time in the moonlight. We arranged to see each other again when we both got back to Alice Springs.

At the end of the tour, tireless Geoff delivered us all safely to our various lodgings in Alice. I extended my stay at Toddy's Backpackers and waited for Adam to come into town. In the meantime, there was plenty to keep me interested – the Telegraph Station, the museum of the Royal Flying Doctors, the Reptile Centre and Panorama Guth, an extraordinary rotunda of landscapes created by Dutch artist Henk Guth (this was before fire devastated the irreplaceable 360-degree panorama in 2005).

By the weekend, Adam was back in Alice and he took me to a house where he lived with some mates. Their kitchen was a bit of a mess, so I cleaned up for them and made something nice for tea.

"What am I going to do with you?" Adam asked. "I'm away on the road most of the time."

"It's OK," I said. "I can occupy myself."

He phoned a friend of his, a nurse, who kindly put me up at her place for a few days. I didn't want to overstay my welcome, so after about a week, I moved to the Larapinta Lodge motel and then found the semi-permanent solution of the Sienna Apartments.

"House warming present," said Adam a day or two after I'd moved in, and he surprised me by giving me his swag.

"I can't…"

"It's OK, it's an old one. I've got a new one for myself."

And so my first acquisition at the new place was a battered green swag, which I kept rolled up on top of the wardrobe. I was a real bushwoman now and whenever I felt the urge, I could go out on my own into the desert and sleep under the stars.

From the Inside Out

You have to be mad, a misfit, a mercenary or a missionary to come to the Northern Territory, or so the locals say. If you stay in Alice Springs long enough to see the normally dry Todd River flood with rain three times, you will become a permanent resident.

My motives weren't mercenary but I was mad enough and unconventional, with some ideas that perhaps I might do a bit of good in a country that desperately needed reconciliation between its oldest inhabitants and its newer settlers.

I instantly loved the little town – the houses with verandahs strung with fairy lights; the jacaranda trees around the Uniting Church; the Sunday markets on Todd Mall. I found a place in the community that embraced all kinds of people from academics to cowboys, artists to mine workers. Indeed, the full diversity of the town was to become clear to me when I attended a protest against the US invasion of Iraq (backed by the Australian government), when everyone gathered on the council lawns – Catholic priests, lesbians, Aboriginal elders, truck drivers, dress shop owners, ecologists and publicans; a rainbow of peaceful humanity.

Starting in Alice, I began to explore Australia not from its coastal rim, where the vast majority of the population live, but from the inside out. Alice Springs was at the very heart of the continent and, it seemed to me, at the heart of the matter. I was inspired by the story of Rev. John Flynn, founder of the Royal Flying Doctor Service, who had dedicated his life to creating a 'mantle of safety' for the people of the Inland. Note he did not speak of the outback, with its suggestion of 'out of sight, out of mind', but of the inland, the whole point of the country.

Little incidents were very revealing. One day I was sitting in my unit at Sienna Apartments when there was a timid knock on the door. I opened it to find two Aboriginal people standing there, an old man and a slightly younger woman, perhaps his wife.

"Painting?" the man said, and I didn't quite understand until he unrolled a picture he wanted to sell. It was about two feet square, on a strange piece of canvas that had the texture and colour of an Elastoplast. The dot painting was in black, showing water holes with animal tracks and human feet.

"How much?" I asked.

"Twenty dollars," he said.

"OK," I replied, because I quite liked the work and I needed something to hang on the beige walls of my apartment.

It was a fair trade. The man wasn't begging and he didn't try to scrounge alcohol, as I knew Aboriginal people sometimes did. The couple reminded me of the gypsies who used to come to the door, offering to sell clothes pegs, when I was a child growing up in Yorkshire.

"Can we have a lift home?" the woman asked then.

"Where's home?"

"Just down the road."

I had the car Andrew Langford had given me and I hadn't been out for a drive for a while, so I said, "Why not?"

We piled into the hatchback and I took directions from my passengers.

"Right, left, right again here."

Not long afterwards, we reached one of the town camps, flyblown shanty towns on the edge of Alice, where many Aboriginal people either live permanently or stay if they have come in from the desert. I caught a glimpse of litter, camp dogs and a black-skinned, fair-haired snotty-nosed child.

"Here," they said, "here, thanks, be seeing ya."

I drove back to Sienna Apartments, where I ran into the manager,

Dean Nankivell, doing some job in the yard. I told him my little story.

"You were lucky they didn't live at Imanpa," he laughed, referring to an Aboriginal community 170 miles southwest of Alice, "or you'd have had a long drive out into the desert."

Dean and his wife, Sue, were a kind couple. I had other friends – the Langfords; Ant, the nurse at the hospital; and Kate Lawrence, my dear doppelganger. I was starting to meet and get to know people in town. Soon my life was to become an intense social whirl.

One morning I was browsing in the Arunta Bookstore, run by a famously eccentric woman called Iris Harvey, who not only sold a wonderful range of geography, history and art books but also supplied art materials to Aboriginal people and bought their paintings from them to sell to the tourists. She probably ripped off both Aboriginals and tourists but she had to make a living herself. The bookshop closed when she retired but in its day, it was a vital part of Alice life.

Behind the counter on the day I was looking at postcards was a silver-haired man in the kind of knitted cap known in Alice as a beanie – for it was winter in the desert now and time to wrap up warmly.

"That's a nice set you've chosen," he said. There was nothing about his Australian accent to give him away as a foreigner and yet for some reason I immediately recognised that he was East European.

"Not Russian by any chance?" I asked.

"Yugoslav. The name's Dinko Tomasich."

"Oh, I've worked for many years in Moscow."

At that, we were off, deep into a long Slav conversation. Dinko told me he'd been born in Belgrade but come to Australia when he was three years old. He'd grown up in Sydney and had a career in Canberra but lately he'd been out in the bush. He'd just finished working on a remote Aboriginal community and was now assisting at the bookstore while he decided whether he wanted to stay in Alice Springs. He closed the shop for lunch and we continued our talk in a café round the corner.

"You must come to my place for a meal," he said hospitably.

I did, on more than one occasion.

Through Dinko, my network of friends grew. At his lavish dinner parties, I met members of the local intelligentsia. With them, I went to see foreign movies at the Araluen Arts Centre. My social life snowballed.

In particular, I became friendly with Meredith Campbell, a former ABC journalist who had become a local politician and was running for the town council as a Labour candidate; also with academics who taught at the local college of further education for Aboriginal students.

At the suggestion of one of the college staff, I started to do a bit of voluntary tutoring with a couple of mature students, both women. They were not desert Aboriginal ladies but had come to Alice Springs from Queensland, where they were well integrated into modern, urban life. If I remember rightly, one of the women worked as a dinner lady at a primary school.

At college, they were catching up on the education they had missed earlier in their lives. Both were doing projects on their family history, which I read with interest because they spoke of painful matters such as the loss of tribal languages and how indigenous children of the 'Stolen Generation' had been forcibly taken into state care.

Both projects were full of well-researched information but they were unstructured and therefore not easy to read. This wasn't the women's fault; nobody had ever taught them about form and content. So I took a piece of paper and a pencil and drew a vase.

"See here," I said, "your introduction's like the narrow neck of the vase; you establish what you're going to talk about. Then you fill out the vase with all your facts and figures; your quotes and anecdotes. And at the end, you bring it all to a neat conclusion, like the base of the vase."

"Wow!" said the women and I could see that a light had gone on in both their minds.

A week later, they came back with their work restructured. It was now both interesting and readable. They were thrilled and I was very proud of them. They put the work in to be marked. I was sure they were going to get A grades.

But what came back was a complaint to me that I had done the women's homework for them; that I had 'disempowered them'. The women had never written so well before and it was impossible they could have made so much progress in such a short time.

I was stunned. The women were upset but still grateful to me.

"You showed us. We know now," they said, and as a gift they gave me a beautiful piece of cloth.

Needless to say, I didn't do any more tutoring work. Perhaps it was just one teacher at the college whom I had rubbed up the wrong way, rather than a problem with the institution itself. But I began to suspect there was something of an 'Aboriginal industry' in the Northern Territory – whites earning high salaries to shepherd Aboriginals – and the system had a vested interest in indigenous people only progressing so far.

"It's complicated," said my new friend Meredith Campbell. "Let's go camping out bush to take your mind off it."

I had the old green swag that Adam had given me. Meredith had a pink one of which I was rather envious. We packed an esky with tucker and set out for a girly trip, spending our first night at the Hugh River before going on to camp at Rainbow Valley, which I already knew to be, without exaggeration, a Wonder of the World.

These days there are special walkways at Rainbow Valley to preserve the delicate environment, and rightly so, but back then you could simply walk out onto the vast clay pan under the rainbow rock, and we did. We danced on it, as on a stage, chasing each other's shadows in a desert ballet. We ate our supper on it and, finally exhausted, rolled out our swags to sleep on its welcoming flat expanse.

The clay pan was dry, of course, as it is most of the time, but occasionally it fills with rain water, forming a shallow lake in which the rock is reflected. It is indeed a heavenly place.

Lying out on the clay, Meredith and I gazed up at the stars. No alien spaceships came down to abduct us; neither did we find snakes in our swags the next morning. I woke first to see Meredith's ruffled hair and peaceful face peeping out of her pink swag.

"Tea?" I asked when she opened one eye.

After breakfast, we explored the rock that looked like a crouching beast; in its red and ochre fissures we reckoned we saw ancestral faces. We found caves and lolled in their shade to watch swallows and painted finches. We couldn't tear ourselves away and stayed on past lunchtime.

For posterity, I took a photo of our picnic table, which Meredith had covered with a white lace cloth and spread with fruit, nuts and sparkling pink drink. It contrasted fabulously with the red, craggy landscape around us. Meredith had style, and already in those days she was developing a business as a marriage celebrant, offering ceremonies and celebrations in the great outdoors. The little party she laid on for me at Rainbow Valley was unforgettable.

Rainbow Valley was so beautiful – indeed there was so much beauty and positive stuff going on in Central Australia – that I couldn't understand why the local Murdoch-owned newspaper, the *Centralian Advocate*, focused exclusively on the grim, bleak and negative. Every issue was dominated by stories about Aboriginal people abusing grog and bashing each other, which did happen, certainly, but surely there was more to the picture than that.

Although my lack of a work permit prevented me from practising journalism, I was meeting colleagues in my profession and was particularly glad to run into a man called Dave Richards, who at the time was a producer for local ABC radio. He was very much on my wavelength and dreamed of finding a way to reflect the region's glory, not just report the gory stories.

Being a fan and loyal customer of the Date Palm Gardens, I invited Dave to drink coffee with me there. In return, he introduced me to the restaurant in the lovely arid-zone botanical gardens named after botanist and Aboriginal rights campaigner Olive Pink. Over numerous coffees, scones and cakes, we thrashed out the idea of starting our own outback magazine. Dave was very interested in the possibilities of the internet and envisaged a webzine while I championed paper, glossy paper. Dave said he knew fantastic local photographers who would join us.

Nothing came of our talk at that point but we had sown a seed.

I needed work, serious work, if I was going to make a new life in Oz. Meanwhile, my routine of helping Andrew Langford at the didgeridoo theatre twice a week gave some shape to my life, while leaving plenty of time for play.

The crisp winter weather drew me outdoors. At the height of summer, when daytime temperatures can reach plus 45C (113F), desert Aussies seek relief in darkened rooms. But in winter, while the nights are nippy, the days are a delicious plus 20C (68F), perfect for sports and physical activities.

The sky was never anything but blue. Most days I would cycle out on the road running east of Alice, admiring the horses in the paddocks and the oranges and grapefruits ripe on the citrus trees. After my bike ride, I would dive into the outdoor swimming pool at Sienna Apartments, where many of the residents thought me crazy.

The water was minty fresh but not really freezing for someone inured to Russian cold.

"Can we join you?" asked a couple of women one day.

"Sure," I said. "We'll do it the Russian way."

So we all jumped, screaming, into the pool, after which we dashed to my unit, downed shots of vodka and shared a hot shower, laughing maniacally.

That July, I even had a Christmas dinner. Dave Richards, who was involved at the local Steiner School, told me some Aussies believed their Christmas should not be marked in December but celebrated when it was properly cold, in the Southern Hemisphere winter.

In this spirit, the school was holding a party to which I was invited.

It was a starry, frosty night – or as the Aboriginals would say, 'a two-dog night' (because you need to snuggle up with two camp dogs to keep warm). We gathered round a fire to sing carols and ate turkey with all the vegetables and trimmings, followed by Christmas pudding and mince pies for good measure.

I was having so much fun that I hardly missed Adam, although I was happy when he phoned or dropped by to see me. The developing relationship with Adam made me think it was time to talk to my husband Costya back in Russia. When I discovered he wasn't really missing me – in fact he'd moved his girlfriend into our place in my absence – I suggested we get a friendly divorce and he agreed. It took me a while to get over the grief and let go of that emotional baggage.

I was less sure what to do about Vitaly, a musician I'd been seeing in Moscow as my marriage to Costya deteriorated. He did seem to be missing me but our relationship had been quite complicated and I decided he could go on the back burner for a while. Meanwhile, Adam was welcome.

He drifted in one evening, bearing the gift of a table cloth with an Aboriginal pattern in strong desert colours. He rolled a cigarette and started telling me how he'd been held up on his way into Alice Springs at a police roadblock.

"There's a gunman on the loose," he said. "Cops are after him."

We read later in the papers that police were searching for a man who held up British backpackers Peter Falconio and Joanne Lees near Barrow Creek, on the Stuart Highway north of Alice. Joanne escaped and hid in the bush but Peter was missing, presumed dead.

The case was rather mysterious. The press thought Joanne was suspiciously cool about the fate of her boyfriend, whose body was never found. But in 2005, a court in Darwin convicted a drifter called Bradley John Murdoch of Falconio's murder and his appeals were rejected, so evidently justice was done.

Outback Drives in a Datsun
Called Alan

Out and about in the desert, as I was, I left a message on my telephone answering machine for those who failed to catch me at Sienna Apartments: 'Hello, I've gone walkabout and can't speak to you right now. Please leave a message and I'll get back to you.' To my surprise, this upset one white woman, who told me the expression 'walkabout' was offensive to Aboriginal people.

It's true that white employers used to use the term derogatorily when complaining of the 'unreliability' of their Aboriginal workers, failing to understand that black labourers didn't simply walk off the job but disappeared when they needed to conduct important ritual business in the desert. But there was a famous film called *Walkabout*, starring Aboriginal actor David Gulpilil, so I didn't see how the term could be that racially insulting; at least it wasn't when the movie was made in 1971.

And in a way, to the consternation of people close to me, I really had gone walkabout – walkabout from my main life in the Northern Hemisphere – while I did seemingly odd things in the desert that made sense to me, in search of myself. In the same way, my friend Ant had gone walkabout from a life that no longer fulfilled him in Sydney. He was my partner in walkabout; we went wandering together.

Except that we didn't hike all that much; rather we drove out for numerous trips in the borrowed Datsun called Alan.

Inch by inch, we explored the Macdonnell Ranges from Trephina Gorge in the east to Glen Helen in the west. We were particularly drawn towards the setting sun, into the country of renowned Aboriginal painter Albert Namatjira. Born in 1902 at the Hermannsburg Lutheran mission west of Alice, Namatjira was introduced to watercolours by artist Rex Battarbee but quickly overtook his white mentor in skill and accomplishment and went on to win prestigious Australian and foreign awards for his evocative landscapes and studies of gum trees.

'That must be a Namatjira tree,' we would often say, as we spotted white ghost gums outlined against the red caterpillar-like formations of the undulating ranges. (The Dreamtime ancestors in this region were the hairy, processionary Yeperenye caterpillars, or itchy grubs.)

On one of our early outings along the Larapinta Drive, passing Mount Gillen on the edge of town, we got no further than Simpsons Gap before we were overcome by the beauty of the scenery and felt the need to make a stop. I was grateful for Ant's slow pace; his love of detail.

We walked up a red dirt track to the top of Cassia Hill which, millions of years ago, had been the bed of the ocean, and looked out over the bush. We shared a packet of biscuits and then sat in companionable silence for the rest of the afternoon, listening to the birds and insects, until we nearly merged ourselves with the shimmering landscape. A tiny striped lizard ran across my foot.

Eventually Ant gave a nod and by unspoken, mutual agreement, we continued on to Simpsons Gap, where we watched the rock wallabies skitter down the scree to feed by the waterhole in the evening light. The pool was an unblinking black eye. Driving home in the dusk, we saw rabbits, the curse of Oz since they were introduced from England in the 19th century and their omni-nibbling population exploded.

Ant had quite a stressful job. He'd moved from the hospital where he'd been nursing to work as a drug and alcohol counsellor at an organisation called CAAAPU (Central Australian Aboriginal Alcohol Programmes Unit). We used to laugh at the silly-sounding acronym but Ant saw tragic cases that were no laughing matter and the work was emotionally draining.

The antidote was always to go out for another outback drive, further along the road into the Western Macs. It was not so much the 'road less travelled' as the 'road hardly travelled at all'. As soon as you left Alice, you had the way pretty much to yourself and the glorious red land spread out in invitation.

On another of our trips, we stopped to pay our respects at Rev. John Flynn's grave, a round boulder in the shadow of Mount Gillen, before driving on to Standley Chasm, 30 miles west of Alice. The chasm is named after Mrs. Ida Standley who, in 1914, became the first school teacher in Alice Springs.

Ant and I had a little snack in the kiosk café on the bank of Angkerle Creek before heading up into the chasm, a stopping point for trekkers on the 140-mile Larapinta Trail.

The going was easy at first. We crisscrossed the creek and clambered over small rocks, noticing to right and left small trees that looked like palms.

"What are they?" I asked.

"Cycads, I think," said Ant. "There are more of them, and bigger ones, at Palm Valley in the Finke Gorge. Because, you know, at one stage in the past, the desert used to have a tropical climate."

"Oh," I said. I'd read somewhere that the Finke River was the 'oldest in the world', meandering on a course that existed even before the ancient ranges were pushed up. But I was no expert on geology.

The signpost for the Larapinta Trail pointed left up a very steep track, so we continued on the main path into the chasm. It was as narrow as The Shambles, the medieval street in York where householders on opposite sides could reach out of their open windows to shake each other's hands.

At the far end of the chasm, we waded through a thigh-deep pool before coming out in bright sunshine on the other side. We stretched out on adjacent rocks and warmed ourselves, watching a pair of wedge-tailed eagles wheeling overhead. A crow cawed drily from a nearby branch.

We loved Standley Chasm and visited it several times. On one such occasion, it had been raining and the water at nearby Jay Creek washed up over the road to a depth of about an inch. We slowed down and to our astonishment saw a line of small silver fish crossing the road. They were swimming in the shallow water, of course, but it looked for all the world as if they were walking over a pedestrian crossing.

"See their tiny umbrellas?" I joked.

"What have you been smoking?" said Ant.

We had found aquatic life in the arid zone – which brings me to the subject of swimming. Ever since I'd seen the deep black pool at Kings Canyon, I'd suspected the best swimming in Australia was to be had not at the shark-prone coast but ironically and paradoxically, in the middle of the desert. This was confirmed when Ant and I discovered Ellery Creek Big Hole, 20 miles west of Standley Chasm.

Unlike some waterholes that appear and disappear depending on the cycles of rain and drought, Ellery is permanently filled with creek water that flows through a narrow gap in the ranges and pools in a small lake, ringed by reeds and red river gum trees. Aboriginal people knew for tens of thousands of years about the water sources that sustained life in the desert, but white explorers came upon them in a hit and miss way and when they found them, sometimes allowed their cattle to defile them.

The Aboriginal name for Ellery Creek Big Hole is Udepata and it was a special meeting place for Arrernte people following the fish and honey ant Dreaming trails. Nowadays, it is cared for as part of the West MacDonnell National Park and has a car park, barbecue area, toilets and warning signs for the mostly white visitors.

'The water is extremely deep and has been measured at 28 metres in some parts', said an information sheet provided by the Northern Territory government. 'Due to its depth, the temperature of the water can be very low and can be hazardous. When swimming, it is best to stay in the shallow edges of the waterhole until you are used to the temperature and then make your way out to the deeper sections. Prolonged exposure, even in summer, can result in hypothermia. Beware of submerged logs and rocks. Do not jump, dive or swing into the water.'

Bearing this in mind, Ant and I entered the water carefully. It was a sunny day. I soon felt confident and swam further out. I could feel the cooler currents caressing my body but I wasn't alarmed, used as I am to the bands of cold water in Russian lakes. Ducks flew overhead and a cormorant dried its wings on a rock.

Ant was doing fine too and we both managed to swim through the gorge, coming out on the other side onto a strip of warm sand.

"This is it, this is it, no sharks, no crocs, no rips, just cool currents," I said.

"Yeah," said Ant, "heaven on a stick."

So after that, trips to Ellery Creek also became a regular part of our repertoire. Nothing untoward ever happened, except that we once bogged Alan the Datsun in a drift of sand and had to have help digging out the back wheels from another visitor who thoughtfully kept a shovel in the boot of his car.

Alan was not a four-wheel drive vehicle but good only for sealed surfaces, so certain wild places like Serpentine Gorge were off limits to us. We took care on the road and never stayed out after dark. After wet weather, we waded through flooded patches to make sure the water was not too deep before driving through. Compared with crazy bushmen, who forced and sometimes abandoned their bangers on rough terrain, we were the maiden aunts of the desert.

Beyond Ellery Creek, we saw on the map an accessible place called the Ochre Pits and thought that looked interesting. There we discovered cliffs of soft rock in rust-red, yellow and cream colours and realised we had come upon the palette from which local Aboriginal people took pigments to paint their bodies for rituals and ceremonies.

Traditional Aboriginal colours are red for the earth, yellow for the sun and black and white for the charred wood and ash of the campfire. You do see modern Aboriginal paintings in shades of pink, blue, purple and green but they break convention. It is no coincidence that the

Aboriginal flag is a yellow circle on a red and black background.

In the light of the afternoon sun, clumps of spinifex glowed like golden crowns on top of the cliffs and trees cast dramatic shadows. Ant, who in the days before 'selfies' loved taking pictures of his silhouette, got some great shots of his shadow, looming against the walls of ochre.

Deeper and deeper we penetrated into the West MacDonnell Ranges until we got as far as we could go on the bitumen – the end of the road, for us, and the highlight of all our journeys – Glen Helen Gorge. We were drawn to visit and revisit this haunting spot; to marvel at the expanse of red cliffs and the gorge and waterhole in all their grandeur.

Before returning to Alice, we would refuel the car and ourselves at the Glen Helen Homestead and sit out with coffees on the back verandah, drinking in the view. At the front of the homestead was a broken-down, out-of-tune piano, with a pair of boots on its lid. Not much of a place for classical music, I gathered, but the homestead had a reputation for great folk and bush ballad evenings.

We were always on the road home by sunset, however. Oh, those juicy pink desert sunsets, softening all the colours of Namatjira's land.

I understood, of course, why tourists pressed for time did all the obvious things; why after seeing the Sydney Opera House and Harbour Bridge, they took in Uluru before hurtling on to the next 'icon', the Great Barrier Reef or the Big Banana or whatever. But they were not seeing the country; they were not seeing it at all.

The Western Macs convinced me that Australia deserved much more attention than that.

North and South

Depending on how you look at it, Alice Springs is either at the heart of everything or in the middle of nowhere. From the centre of Australia, it's hundreds of miles across desert in any direction before you come to the 'civilisation' of a city. Alice's remoteness explains its friendliness but knowing everyone in town can also make you feel a bit claustrophobic. At a certain point, you have to get out, if only for a break.

Ant and I had been east and west, so I started thinking of making trips north and south. It was the right time of year to do it. The cool winter weather would be good for camping in the outback south of Alice, while up in the North, before the start of the terrible, humid 'build-up' to the tropical wet season, it would be pleasantly warm and dry.

I opted to go with the Wayward Bus Company again because their small group tours enabled me to take in broad swathes of the country that I couldn't see under my own steam, while giving me more freedom than I would get on a big coach excursion.

The first available bus was going 950 miles south to Adelaide, via Uluru, which I had already seen, but it never harms to have another look at Uluru. I would go on that for a week and then return to Alice, from where I would take a second week-long trip, 930 miles north to Darwin. When I finally got back to Alice, I would have done a figure of eight, taking in the whole central part of Australia from north to south; from south to north.

Uluru again showed its classic red face against a blue sky, as the weather was dry. I wondered whether I would ever see it, as in desert photographer Steve Strike's famous picture, purple against grey rain clouds, with waterfalls cascading down its flanks. Whatever the weather, it was a powerful place.

From Uluru, we drove south, crossing the Northern Territory border at Kulgera, and headed down to the opal-mining town of Coober Pedy in South Australia, where we spent the night in an underground hotel. Yes, underground. Coober Pedy's on a different planet; it's no coincidence films about Mars have been made here.

Alice Springs does get some rain that spills down from the tropical Top End but Coober Pedy is dry as a bone and so scorching hot in summer that it is close to the limit of human endurance – sometimes nearing 50C (122F). The answer for the locals is to live in underground dugouts, where the temperature is always a comfortable 25C (77F). Homes, hotels and even churches are underground. The Aboriginals call the place *kupa-piti*, which means 'white man's burrow'.

Inside the hotel, it was surprisingly comfortable. There was no natural light but the hewn stone of the walls, contrasting with the rather chintzy bedding, was a clever design solution and made the place feel as homely as Fred and Wilma Flintstones' cave.

The next morning, because it was winter, we were able to walk easily above ground and I strolled down the main street, where I noticed many of the businesses were run by either Greeks or Yugoslavs. At lot of the shops were selling opals, of course. While other passengers from the bus went shopping for bargain jewellery, I slipped away to have a look at the Serbian Orthodox Church, an underground gem that gave new meaning to the expression 'catacomb church'. (Here worshippers were escaping the rigour of the sun, not the harshness of Communism.)

"Beautiful," said a quiet voice behind me.

It was a Canadian woman from our group. Her name was Bev Montgomery and she was a teacher, spending a year in Oz on an exchange programme. She made a good companion for the rest of the trip.

We had lunch together and walked around town, noticing the saloon bar, the clapped-out cars, the camp dogs and the brightly coloured Aboriginal graffiti against uranium mining at nearby Roxby Downs.

Not a place where we would like to live long-term, we agreed.

But we were staying in Coober Pedy for another night because later that afternoon, we were going to go fossicking for opals ourselves. Out in the desert, in a moonscape of small hills, we scrabbled in the earth and kicked the dust but none of us found anything except 'potch' or common opal, which is dull and worthless. The precious opals, with their bewitching play of colours from turquoise to pink, eluded us.

You don't need a licence to prospect for opals in Australia; anyone can try their luck, which is how the community of Coober Pedy grew. Cheek by jowl, and apparently in neighbourly harmony, poor folks who have searched all their lives in vain live next to rich people, who have made millions from opals. It makes for an interesting social mix.

"You get cases," said our guide, "where someone hits it rich, loses it all in the casino in Adelaide and is back here, digging for opals again in no time."

We consoled ourselves for our fossicking failure with steak and chips in a Greek café and beers in an underground bar before hitting the sack in our cave hotel.

Bright and early the next morning, we drove 100 miles east down a back road to William Creek, which is on the famous Oodnadatta track. The bus company asked me to take some photos for their publicity, so I did a few classic shots of rusted vehicles lying out in the desert and our little bus churning up the red dust as it bumped along the road. To get a shot of a small stone at the right angle to make it look as if it were a giant like Uluru, I lay flat on my stomach on the ground.

"A real professional," laughed Dan and Kerry, a couple of jokers from England. I took a few pictures of them too, clowning around in the red dirt, and for a season they became the new faces of Wayward Bus.

There wasn't much at William Creek except a petrol pump, a campground and the William Creek Hotel, hung to the rafters with hats, scarves and other objects left by tourists who had passed through. In a room that served as a small museum, however, there was an extraordinary exhibit – a feral cat that had been dissected to reveal the contents of its stomach. The greedy beast had consumed dozens of small native hopping mice, now an endangered species.

"I hate cats," said an Aussie bloke, peering at the display. "Beautiful on the outside but full of shit."

You could say the same about all living creatures, I thought.

Outside there was further evidence of ailurophobia – a tree known locally as the 'Pussy Willow'. It's not there anymore because sensitive European tourists complained about it, but back in 2001, the tree was still festooned with the corpses of more than a dozen feral cats that had been shot and strung up as a warning to other cats. It looked like a medieval execution. I was moved to write a short ditty:

Have you seen the Pussy Willow on the Oodnadatta Track?
The ferals went a-hunting but they won't be coming back.
They're strung up in the branches, an example to the rest,
For whether tiger-striped or marmalade, they're just a furry pest.

Oh the ferals went a-hunting for the little hopping mice,
The numbats and the bilbies; that wasn't very nice.
But the man who keeps the roadhouse at a place
called William Creek
Said: "By crikey! Someone's shot 'em!"
You should have heard the squeak

Of the little Aussie critters as they partied 'neath the tree
Where the ferals were a-hanging for the other cats to see,
Tiger-striped and marmalade, tabby, grey and black,
And all as dead as dead can be. They won't be coming back!

The poem went down well in the pub that night. Afterwards, we tottered and zigzagged back to the campground. The others snuggled up in tents while I had my swag in which I lay, fully dressed, for the temperature dropped below zero that night; I even had a woolly hat pulled down over my ears. But I had to be roofless to see the stars.

Out on the Oodnadatta Track next day we came upon some springs that over the centuries sustained both Aboriginal traders and trackers and white explorers in the merciless desert. The 'mound springs' of Wabma Kadarbu, in land traditionally belonging to the Arabunna people, bubble up from the Great Artesian Basin underground to form small, jewel-like ponds that provide habitat for water birds.

We were able to splash around ourselves in a little thermal spa there before we continued on to Lake Eyre, Australia's largest lake – when it contains water, that is. It glinted promisingly on the horizon but when we reached the shore, we realised the flash of white we'd seen was salt. We could only imagine the despair of 19th century pioneers, travelling without the advantage of a well-equipped bus.

At every turn, the badlands of South Australia seemed to have defeated men, or at least white men. Marree had become an irrelevance since the Ghan railway had been diverted along another route; Farina, envisaged as a grain settlement until would-be farmers cottoned on to the lack of rainfall, was a ghost town. But the badlands were beautiful, if you saw them for what they were: Nature.

We made it to Wilpena Pound, a vast natural amphitheatre in the Flinders Ranges, and hiked up to the top of one of the mountains, guarded by eerie rocks with laughing or forbidding faces. All around grew sturdy specimens of a strange spiky plant that looked like a cactus crowned with a bulrush. I was reliably informed that it was a Xanthorrhoea quadrangulata.

But that was not the worst of my worries. For our next thrill, we were supposed to go up in a light plane to get a bird's eye view of Wilpena Pound and I was going to chicken out.

"You can do it," said Bev, Dan and Kerry, putting friendly arms around me, as we stood on the summit, looking out over the desert.

I sat on a rock and thought about it. A butterfly fluttered down and settled on my tee shirt; it sat on my shoulder for the longest time.

Yes, I can do it, I thought quietly, and that afternoon I went flying with them, over the pound, over millions of years of Australian geology, finally laying to rest a fear of flying from which I'd suffered since covering a nasty little war in the former Soviet Union. I was over it.

After the Flinders Ranges, the landscape softened and everything became a bit of a blur as we passed through wineries on our way to Adelaide. I do remember the town of Hahndorf, settled by Germans and home to Hans Heysen, famous for painting gum trees. I was amused and disturbed in equal measure to learn that, when everything German went out of fashion at the time of the First World War, the Australian government had changed the town's name from Hahndorf to Ambleside.

The tour ended and we were dropped off and left to our own devices in Adelaide. I didn't linger long but immediately started checking out the options for getting home. A flight would have been quick but I fancied a trip on the legendary Ghan and as luck would have it, a train was leaving the next afternoon for the overnight ride to Alice.

The upright seats in economy were a bit uncomfortable but I was mesmerised by the desert passing outside the window. The colour was predominantly yellow in South Australia but I woke the next morning to the red of the Northern Territory and my heart was singing. I'd been bitten by the bug and was already a 'Territorian'. I had a couple of days in Alice to do my laundry and rest before I set off again, this time taking the Stuart Highway north, all through the Territory to its capital, Darwin.

Again I was in a bus group. "Get ready to rock and roll," said the driver, an instruction he was to repeat annoyingly after each stop. All the other passengers were Dutch, speaking Dutch among themselves, which suited me fine, as it gave me the perfect excuse to be unsociable.

Twenty miles north of Alice, we crossed the Tropic of Capricorn but the desert landscape hardly changed at this line and the red earth looked as if it would go on forever. By mid-morning and just in time for tea, we were at Wycliffe Well, the 'UFO capital of Australia', a lonely spot where sightings of flying saucers are regularly reported. The doors of the roadhouse toilets were painted with aliens in gender-appropriate colours.

On the forecourt outside, an Aboriginal lady in a flower-print dress, who had walked from God knows where to buy a loaf of white bread, only to find it sold out, asked me if I had any. I gave her a sandwich from my lunchbox. She no doubt thought we had come from outer space.

From Wycliffe Well, it was a short jaunt to the Devil's Marbles, an area of about ten square miles covered with granite boulders, perfectly rounded by the weather. 'This is the Devil's country; he's even emptied his bag of marbles around the place!' wrote John Ross, a member of the expedition that laid the overland telegraph line in Victorian times, and thus the place got its English name. The Aboriginals call it Karlu Karlu and believe the sacred rocks were formed when the Devil Man passed through, dropping balls of hair as he made a traditional hair-string belt.

I've seen one of those balls before, I thought and remembered that the Rev. John Flynn's grave on the outskirts of Alice looked just like a Devil's Marble. In 1952, a boulder was removed from the reserve to create a memorial to the founder of the Royal Flying Doctors but this upset Aboriginal people so much that it had to be given back and a similar-looking but non-sacred boulder found to replace it on the grave.

The land was burning on the road up ahead. I couldn't tell if this was controlled 'back burning' by locals to get rid of dry grass that could cause a major fire or whether something or somebody had ignited the bush, but the smoke was thick and even after we passed the flames, the charred ground went on for miles. From the blackened trunks of some trees, I was fascinated to see the bright green shoots of new leaves appearing. Far from destroying the trees, the fire had regenerated them.

After Tennant Creek, an old gold-mining town, the vegetation gradually started to become more tropical. Frangipani and flame trees filled the air with their fragrance and colour. We stayed a night in cabins at Mataranka and swam in the glorious thermal pools there. I wasn't so keen to go in the nearby Roper River where, apart from barramundi fish, crocodiles could also be lurking.

In Katherine the next day, we had a marvellous cruise down the famous gorge that is the jewel of Nitmiluk National Park. While we were in the gorge, it came on to rain torrentially and I got soaked to the skin. I didn't think it mattered, as the hot sun soon came out again. This was a mistake, as my clothes had not dried properly when I boarded the air-conditioned bus and rode for two hours to Kakadu in damp knickers.

In the World Heritage-listed wetlands of Kakadu, I saw cormorant-like birds called darters, water lilies bobbing on the Yellow River and cunning crocodiles pretending to be floating logs. By evening, I had a raging case of cystitis and felt as if the crocodiles had invaded my urinary system. This unfortunately ruined my visit to Ubirr the following day and made it completely impossible for me to concentrate on the wonderful Aboriginal rock art there. All I could think of was reaching Darwin and getting a doctor's prescription for some antibiotics.

In Darwin, I said goodbye to the bus tour and shortly afterwards, thanks to the help of an Indian doctor, to my torment. Now I was going to have a whale of a time. After my sojourn in the desert, it was a delight to reach the palm-fringed coast, which looked like paradise.

I tucked into breakfast at Cullen Bay yachting marina before going off to explore the markets, which had a distinct Asian flavour, Darwin being a relative hop over the Timor Sea to East Timor, Bali and the rest of Indonesia. The stalls were piled high with bananas, lychees and smelly durian fruit. At sunset, I visited the craft market on Mindil

Beach, where young women in sequins and chiffon entertained the crowd with a display of belly dancing.

I found the city itself rather modern and soulless but then one had to make allowance for the fact that Cyclone Tracy more or less wiped old Darwin off the map in 1974. Some of the suburbs were graceful and there were fine tropical houses in up-market Nightcliff, where I paid a visit to some friends of friends.

They were kind to me and took me out for a seafood dinner, after which we went to a quiz night. As time went on, I was to discover that the Aussies are rather fond of quiz nights, not necessarily in pubs, accompanied by beer, but also in community halls, where you bring your own bottle. I was rather glad that although I managed to show off a smattering of knowledge at the Darwin quiz, I did not win it, as the first prize was a load of garden topsoil.

Darwin was going to have to raise its game, I felt, if I was to be tempted into extending my stay. But surely the sea swimming would be unbeatable, so I packed my tackle and headed for the beach.

'Danger, box jellyfish can be deadly', read the sign.

'October to May: DO NOT ENTER THE SEA

'June to September: Take precautions when swimming
  • Take vinegar with you to the beach. Children are especially at risk in the water
  • Serious stings from jellyfish have been recorded in all months of the year

'FIRST AID – Resuscitation + Vinegar poured liberally on affected area + Transport to Hospital = LIFE.'

So that pretty well put the kybosh on swimming, except in man-made swimming pools. I think tantalising is the only word to describe Darwin, into whose gorgeous-looking turquoise waters you basically cannot dip a toe. I knew then that I could never live there. And I started to have a better understanding of why the city had a reputation for tropical ennui and alcoholism.

Not to be totally defeated on the wild-swimming front, I did have a trip out to Litchfield National Park, where I splashed joyfully in the lake under Wangi Falls. A group of beautiful Aboriginal children swam with the ease of otters in the clear water. Afterwards, they crowded round me, took my hand and showed me a perentie (monitor) lizard in the grass.

That experience helped to redeem the Top End for me. And I had not, after all, been eaten by a crocodile, unlike two poor German tourists who came to Darwin after surviving the Bali bombing, only to be taken by crocs when they went swimming in reptile-infested waters. That true story from the local press, where every other headline seemed to concern crocodiles, certainly made one think about the mysteries of fate.

From Darwin, my overland options back to Alice Springs were limited to sitting upright for 19 hours on the Greyhound Bus (since the Ghan railway had not at that time been extended to the Top End). At least the bus was cheap.

"Don't put your feet on the seats and don't eat snacks on the bus," was the driver's welcome, as we boarded. As I say, it was cheap.

I was mightily pleased to be back in Alice, and not just because the journey had been rough. I realised that the little desert town felt like home. Wherever I roamed in Oz – and I was to roam a good deal more – I always found myself drawn back to Alice. For me, there was no other place in Australia that exerted quite the same magnetic pull.

Spring

Perhaps it was Adam's periodic presence in town that made Alice Springs so seductive. "Where have you been?" he asked when I got back from my trip, for he had returned to Alice before me.

"Ah, well, I can go on the road too," I replied enigmatically.

"Come over to the house," he said. "The mulberry tree is covered with fruit."

I went with him to the house he shared with mates and saw that indeed, the mulberry was dropping rich, dark berries all over the drive and lawn. I made a mulberry crumble with custard that was consumed with approval at dinner, and ended up staying over at their place.

Morning coffee I enjoyed out in the garden, under the mulberry tree. I was puzzled that all this fruitfulness was happening not in autumn, as you would expect in the Northern Hemisphere, but in spring. Australia – or at least the desert – really was a topsy-turvy place. Autumn was the refreshing time, after the rigours of summer; winter was mild, a joke really; and spring bore fruit but also carried with it the renewed threat of summer's hot iron. The daytime temperatures were already climbing up into the 30s of Celsius.

The warmer weather was ideal for a fantastic outdoor event that was coming to Alice: the Yeperenye Festival. Being held in the centenary year of Australia's federation, the celebration was a showcase of Aboriginal culture, for what would the country be without the contribution of its indigenous citizens? Twenty thousand Aboriginal people from all over Oz were going to converge on Alice Springs for what was billed as 'the biggest ever corroboree'. And Adam had got us tickets.

The party went on all day and well into the night. We floated round, choosing snacks from different kiosks and admiring the dot paintings of desert tribes, before settling on the grass to watch the dancers and yidaki (didgeridoo) players from way up North in tropical Arnhem Land. We stayed on for the fun fair after dark.

Unfortunately, after the festival I fell ill or 'got crook', as the Aussies say. I was poorly with a flu as virulent as anything I'd ever experienced in wintertime Moscow.

"You can't go out now," said Adam. "You'll have to stay here, at least for a while." And so, because I was crook, I sort of ended up living with him, in a brick bungalow, on a housing estate that looked as if it had come out of an episode of *Neighbours*. I kept my unit at Sienna Apartments, though, as I liked my independence.

While I was ill, we watched a lot of stupid American movies, hired from the video store because there was no internet downloading then. Adam and I were on the sofa, watching television together, when we saw two planes hit the Twin Towers in New York and we understood the world had changed forever. Probably everyone remembers where they were and what they were doing on 9/11. I remember feeling a great urge to protect all my loved ones. I missed my family back in Europe.

Perhaps it was the shock of 9/11 that made Adam open up about his family. He told me he had a daughter from an earlier marriage, which he hadn't mentioned before.

"Her name's Jessie," he said. "She lives with her mum in Darwin. You can meet her if you like. Half term's coming up."

And so we arranged that when the school holidays started, we would drive to Darwin to pick Jessie up and the three of us would go on a week-long trip through the Kimberley Mountains to Broome. That was something to look forward to. Meanwhile, Adam was getting ready to go back to work; his holdall was already packed.

I still wasn't very well. My Yugoslav friend Dinko dropped round to see me and I introduced him to Adam.

"G'day mate," they greeted each other.

"Not feeling so good?" said Dinko.

"Getting over it," I replied. We chatted and I told him about the bus trips I'd been on.

"Bus trips are for tourists," said Dinko. "I'm going to Canberra next week to stay with some friends. Want to come for the ride?"

"Yeah," I said. "I should be better by then."

"Mind if I borrow her?" asked Dinko.

"Be my guest," said Adam.

Thus Canberra was added to my schedule. I was certainly going to get to see the country, from its capital to its wildest frontier. I must admit if Dinko hadn't suggested it, I probably wouldn't have gone to Canberra. I thought of it as a 'compromise capital' – chosen so that neither Sydneysiders nor Melburnians got their noses out of joint – and a boring seat of government. Perhaps I'd been influenced by Bill Bryson, who in his book *Down Under* described how he'd searched in vain for night life in Canberra and been reduced to drinking in the bar of his own hotel:

> *I glanced at my watch, appalled to realize it was only ten minutes after ten, and ordered another beer, then picked up my notebook and pen and, after a minute's thought, wrote: 'Canberra awfully boring place. Beer cold, though.' Then I thought a bit more and wrote: 'Buy socks.' Then I put the notebook down, but not away, and tried without much success to eavesdrop on a conversation across the room. Then I decided to come up with a new slogan for Canberra. First I wrote: 'Canberra – There's Nothing to It!' and then 'Canberra – Why Wait for Death?' Then I thought some more and wrote: Canberra – Gateway to Everywhere Else!', which I believe I liked best of all. Then I ordered another beer and drew a little cartoon. It*

*showed two spawning salmon, halfway up a series of lively
cascades, resting exhausted in a pool of calm water, when
one turns to the other and says: 'Why don't we just stop
here and have a wank?'*

Dinko laughed at this but said I was quite wrong.

"Canberra's a great place," he said. "You'll love it."

And I did, perhaps because Dinko had the good sense not to show
me any of the government buildings.

Our trip to Canberra was really a road movie, a case of the journey,
all 1,662 miles of it, being more important than the destination. We
listened to music and joked a lot as we rode down the Stuart Highway
in Dinko's blue ute.

South of Alice, the desert was a tapestry of delicate wild flowers.
Every few miles, I kept shouting at Dinko to stop the car so I could
leap out to photograph and pick them. Soon the dashboard was covered
with handfuls of white paper daisies, Australian bluebells and hairy
mulla mullas, the desert equivalent of pink clover. Dinko must have
thought I was mad but I was experiencing a Pom's nostalgia for the
spring flowers of the Northern Hemisphere.

"Stop the car!" I yelled again. This time, what had caught my eye
was a bleached kangaroo skeleton, lying on the red earth among the
flowers, the epitome of the desert, I thought.

"At this rate, we'll have to spend the night at Erldunda (a roadhouse
still within the Northern Territory)," said Dinko, so I allowed him to put
his foot down on the accelerator. We made it into South Australia by
nightfall and stayed instead at Coober Pedy. But not before I made Dinko
stop another half dozen times to photograph the red flowers of the rosy
dock against the pink of the setting sun. It was all new to me, you see.

The next day, we turned from the Stuart Highway to the Sturt
Highway, the main road between Adelaide and Sydney. I was glad Dinko
was at the wheel because I could see one could easily get confused by

Australian highways named after explorers with near-identical names. We passed through Renmark on the Murray River which, as ecologists know, is cursed with a problem of increasing salinity, but I found the country town pleasant, at least for a coffee stop.

On the A20, we dipped briefly into the state of Victoria before crossing into New South Wales (NSW). At the South Australia-Victoria border, I was shouting to Dinko again to stop the car because I had just seen an outrageously funny road sign, with a red diagonal line seeming to ban flies from the road.

'DEFEND YOUR COUNTRY! BE A FRUIT FLY FIGHTER', it said, warning of spot fines of 200 dollars if you brought contraband fruit from one state to another. Of course, I knew it was important to preserve the purity of Australian fruit and not spread disease but I still found it amusing that the Aussies seemed to be more concerned about apples and pears than guns and narcotics at their internal borders.

The landscape now was lovely, reminding me of Yorkshire in April or May. Yellow fields of flowering rapeseed stretched as far as the eye could see and the pink cherry blossom was out. It breathed new life into me to see these southern states in springtime, after the harshness of the desert.

We passed more pretty country towns – Mildura in Victoria; Balranald, Hay and Wagga Wagga in NSW – before finally arriving in Canberra. We were staying not in the city itself but out in a little town called Bungendore, half an hour's drive away, where Dinko's friends Liz and Tim had a wooden home among the gum trees.

From Bungendore, in NSW, we made day trips into Canberra, heart of the tiny Australian Capital Territory (ACT), which I suppose is to Australia what the Vatican City is to Italy. But as I say, I wasn't much interested in the governmental side of the place. Rather, we were going to see the Floriade.

I wished my flower-arranging mum and garden-loving dad could have been with me to see the magnificent beds of tulips, irises, hyacinths, narcissi, pansies and primulas at what was described as 'Australia's biggest celebration of spring'. A million flowers were blooming in Commonwealth Park and entry was free.

Weeping willows mourned into the waters of Lake Burley Griffin while all along the banks red and orange lilies spread out in joyful carpets. There was a show of fashion made out of plant material. I particularly liked one dress, the bodice made of velvety moss and the skirt a swirl of grasses.

Back in Bungendore, we had hearty roasts around the log fire and stout walks in the eucalyptus woods. Liz and Tim had 26 acres of land and the wildlife in their 'back garden' was plentiful and varied. Bonzo the dog chased the kangaroos while I found a blue-tongued skink (lizard) that let me pick it up. It lay the full length of my forearm and seemed quite comfortable on the sleeve of my fleece.

Horses grazed peacefully in the paddocks. Mimosa was in flower, reminding me of International Women's Day in Russia and the unimaginative men who buy dried-up little yellow bunches on the one day out of 365 when they notice their wives. The Australian mimosa grew thick, furry and fragrant and I wouldn't have minded a bouquet of that.

Sadly, we had to leave the next day. I hadn't understood but Dinko was leaving the blue ute at Bungendore; he'd been delivering it for Tim. We got a lift to Adelaide, from where we took the Ghan back to Alice. I was getting used to commuting on the Ghan.

It was great to be in Alice again but the brief escape to Canberra had done me good. I returned to the desert rejuvenated and full of the joys of spring. Evidently, it's important for a person with roots in the Northern Hemisphere to feel the sap rising and once a year, to see the golden daffodils.

Out West

I woke on an iridescent morning to an aurora of possibilities. Adam was arriving in Alice that evening and the next day we were heading to Darwin to pick up his daughter Jessie, after which we would have a whole week to romp through the Kimberley Mountains to the pearl of northwestern Australia, Broome.

"Can Jane come too?" asked Jessie when we arrived in Darwin, so we ended up taking her school friend too. There was just room for the four of us in Adam's battered old Toyota, which he called Outback Betsy. The car was hardly more roadworthy than Alan the Datsun but Adam was confident we would make it through to Broome and back to Alice via the punishing Tanami Desert.

"Might have to do a bit of bush mechanics on the way," he joked.

"Or I might have to push?"

But though she looked almost ready for the scrap heap, Outback Betsy went like a rocket.

The two girls travelled easily; there was no fighting on the backseat, as with siblings. We made camp for the first night in the bush somewhere west of Darwin. Before it dropped dark, we all lay out on blankets and played the game of spotting likenesses in the passing clouds: camel, duck? Then we got a fire going and toasted marshmallows in the embers. We had sausages and baked potatoes too.

At the state border with Western Australia the following day, an officer in khaki confiscated the bag of remaining potatoes that he found in our car boot. He let us go with a friendly warning but I gathered the fruit and vegetable controls were as tight here as they had been down South. Not for the nothing the popular TV series *Border Security* shows quarantine officers stopping apricot smugglers at Sydney Airport. The rules are strict, whether you're travelling from overseas or interstate.

Once in WA, we made for the town of Kununurra and camped by Lake Argyle, Australia's largest reservoir. Thanks to the Ord River Dam, the lake has a good level of water and we spent a happy afternoon messing about in a little boat. It was a bit like the Lake District, only the temperature was plus 35C (95F) and there was no Beatrix Potter cottage.

From Kununurra, we went west on the legendary Gibb River Road, a stony track through the rugged Kimberleys, taking in spectacular gorges and sites of Aboriginal rock art. Not for us the five-star El Questro station homestead, where fishermen and honeymooners pay over 2,700 Aussie dollars per night for a room, but a modest motel with corrugated iron outhouses and frogs in the showers. But the mangoes were ripe in the orchard and I was thrilled to see the strangely bulbous baobab tree, which I thought, in my ignorance, only grew in Africa. Adam said there was a 1,000-year-old, hollowed-out baobab tree that was used as a prison cell in pioneering days but that was further west, near Derby.

Adam was an experienced outback driver, so I was content to sit back and be a passenger. Humpbacked Brahman beef cattle, raised in the region because of their ability to tolerate extreme heat, wandered frequently into the road and one even stood at the petrol station, expecting to be revered like a holy cow in India.

Along the way, Adam also seemed to know where it would be safe to go river swimming.

"I wouldn't go in there if I were you. There might be freshwater crocodiles," he said at one place, referring to a small type of croc that wouldn't put you in a death roll, like the terrible saltwater or estuarine crocodile, but that could still give you a nasty bite if you swam too near to its nest.

At another spot, though, he was happy to let me swim. Having said that, he and the girls didn't seem keen to join me in the water; rather they sat on the river bank, under the paperbark trees, and photographed me waving from mid-stream.

We had reached Mount Barnett, the gateway to a series of dramatic gorges – Manning Gorge, Galvin Gorge, Bell Gorge, Lennard Gorge and most thrilling of all, Windjana Gorge, with 100-metre high cliffs that 350 million years ago had formed a barrier reef under the sea.

In Windjana National Park, I was hoping to see Aboriginal cave paintings of the Wandjina creator spirits, or sky gods, dating back thousands of years. One tour operator, Brolga Healing Journeys, said: 'The Aboriginal people treat these sites with respect and caution, indeed often approaching Wandjina sites with a wariness bordering on fear. The Aboriginals tend not to stay at the sites for long, for they believe that the Wandjina are present and you don't want to anger them by outstaying your welcome.'

But unfortunately, or perhaps luckily, I never got to Windjana or indeed any of the other gorges beyond the first one. Adam parked the car at Mount Barnett Station and we set off on foot over rocky terrain. The girls ran on ahead and Adam went after them, leaving me trailing behind. We climbed for about an hour until we came to the falls at Upper Manning Gorge.

I saw the girls leap off the top of the rocks and dive over the waterfall into a plunge pool below. Adam dived in after them. All three of them were splashing and bobbing happily in the dark water. I stood on the top of the falls, unsure what to do. Adam was waving at me. I continued to dither over the 15-yard drop.

Adam seemed to lose interest and turned away to swim with the kids. I could see I wasn't going to get any help from them but would have to help myself. My main worry was what to do about my glasses. Still I was dithering.

Luckily, it being the dry season, there wasn't too much water flowing over the falls. I plucked up the courage to sit on the top rock and ease myself about six feet down to the next rock shelf. But after that, there were no more gradual shelves. There was no way I could climb back up the slippery rocks. The only way forward was to jump down the remaining 12 or 13 yards.

Adam was waving at me again. I had to go for it. I held my nose and jumped straight down into the water, coming up for air with my glasses miraculously unbroken and still on my face.

I realised afterwards that that was not the only miracle. If I had hit a rock, I could have broken my back or neck and floated up as a corpse. Then mine would have been the fate of the hapless Japanese businessman in the film *Japanese Story*, starring Toni Collette and Gotaro Tsunashima, about an outback romance that ended tragically in just such a way.

I don't know what I expected from Adam – a dig in the ribs about my physical prowess or an inquiry as to whether I was OK, perhaps – but certainly not the stony silence in which we left Manning Gorge.

"We're driving straight to Broome," he announced, meaning that we would be missing all the other gorges and the rock art I had been so keen to see.

Adam glowered for hours until he finally explained why he was so angry with me. "It would have upset the girls," he said, "if we had had to helicopter your body out." For me, this was an unexpected way of looking at things and made me reflect for a while on my own capacity for stupidity and selfishness.

"You were waving at me," I said weakly.

"I wasn't waving. I was telling you to stop. There was a path you could have taken and walked down to us."

I was supposed to read his hand signals and know the topography of a place I was visiting for the first time. This made me reflect a little on Adam's capacity for caring.

We seemed to get over it, though, and rode on to Broome, where we had a fun day with the girls, watching captive crocodiles jumping for chicken carcasses at a wildlife park. We were even allowed to hold the baby crocodiles and Jessie snapped a picture of me with my hand safely around the throat of a tiny, snapping 'croquette' that we christened Gucci.

We paddled at Cable Beach in bright sunshine. By night, we admired the ladder the moon made on the water. While I visited the Japanese Cemetery, with its graves of pearl divers who came from Japan in the late 19th and early 20th centuries, Adam slipped off to the pub and relieved the residue of his annoyance by playing on the pokie machines.

Thus, we were in high spirits again for the return journey to Alice, going across the blistering and merciless Tanami Desert. All along the route, we saw the rusted wrecks of abandoned cars but Outback Betsy did not let us down as she ploughed on, raising huge clouds of red dust behind us.

I was struck by the delicacy of the pink desert roses and little lizards we stopped to photograph. Then a huge, three-or-four-wagon road train would thunder past and I was struck all over again by the monstrosity of some of the desert traffic.

At Yuendumu, I was very shocked at the squalid conditions of the Aboriginal community, which reminded me of the poorest villages of rural Russia, if not the bombed-out settlements of a war zone. There were flies everywhere, although in fairness you often feel you could do with a giant swatter against the insistent insects of the outback.

"Yeah, well now you know what some of these communities are like," said Adam.

The sky ahead was darkening and it looked as if there might be a drop of rain. We reached Rabbit Flat, not far from the Granites gold mine, and arranged our swags for the night in a circle around the car.

Suddenly the wind whipped up and the sky turned the livid colours of a bruise.

"Quick, into the car," said Adam and we just managed to pack everything away again before the storm hit. We spent the night squashed together but glad to be dry as the rain pounded, pelted and eventually came to a patter on Outback Betsy's roof.

The next day we made it through to Alice, where we put the girls on the Greyhound Bus for the long ride back to school in Darwin. Adam returned to work and I went home to my little unit at Sienna Apartments.

Floating at the Reef

Keep Ithaca always in your mind;
arriving there is what you're destined for...
Ithaca has given you the beautiful journey...
And if you find her poor, Ithaca has not deceived you,
Wise as you have become, with so much experience,
You will know what these Ithacas mean.
Constantine Cavafy

Out at sea off the Queensland Coast, I was swimming in the open ocean, without aqua-lung, without even snorkel and flippers and without the slightest fear, for all the forces of the universe were holding me up.

I was at the Great Barrier Reef, where I should have been several months earlier, if I had not taken a detour from my planned route, a time-out from my usual life, and lingered and played around in Alice Springs.

A boat from Cairns took me and a small party of other tourists out to the reef. The ginger-haired instructor offered to kit us out with diving equipment but the turquoise water was so beautiful that I did not want a rubber barrier between myself and the corals.

"Take a snorkel and flippers then, instead," he said, but I didn't want to be bothered with even such modest paraphernalia. I had a pair of goggles that my brother Michael, an optician, had made for me, fitted with my own lenses. I slipped from the boat into the water in just these goggles and my bathing costume and held my breath as I gazed down at the shoals of multi-coloured fish, darting in and out among the cliffs of the reefs.

Perhaps I should have been frightened. If the instructor had forgotten me and the boat had left me behind, I would have been helpless in the Pacific. But I just floated on the waves and had then, for a few minutes, what mystics call the 'oceanic experience' of total trust that all is well, and of interconnection with everything. I emerged from the water and clambered back onto the boat in a state of bliss.

I'd been having a rough time in the weeks immediately before this Queensland treat. After I'd returned to Alice from the jaunt through the Kimberleys, I'd started to have second thoughts about going out with Adam. The waterfall that might have broken my neck seemed symbolic of an abyss I was in danger of going over. The relationship had been good while it lasted but there were problems I could not ignore and it was time to end it.

I phoned Adam and told him I was sorry but it was finished.

"Thanks for the big fat let-down," he said angrily and slammed the phone down.

Immediately, I fell victim to the well-known rule of psychology that 'the dumper becomes the dumpee' and began to regret my decision. Adam and I got back together briefly over Christmas and then he dumped me. That felt a lot better. I find it very hard to dismiss others but if someone tells me in clear language that I am not needed, I can depart with a light heart. Then I am the freed spirit Ariel, living merrily under the blossom bough.

My one-year Aussie visa was running out. If I wanted to fit in the Great Barrier Reef before returning to the Northern Hemisphere, it was time to pack up in Alice Springs. I had few possessions. The only important thing to take was the nearly-finished manuscript of the book I'd been writing about my uncles at war, which went to show I'd not entirely wasted my time while enjoying a mid-life gap-year in Central Australia.

My money was also starting to run out but magically, just at that moment, Auntie Phyllis, my fairy godmother in England, sent me a gift that gave me liquidity and enabled me to book tickets for Queensland.

The reef was a must, of course. But apart from this internationally famous marine wonderland, I also saw the lesser known but beautiful Atherton Tablelands, the fertile hinterland of Cairns, with its banana plantations and crops of sugarcane, avocados, strawberries and macadamia nuts. And I took my time in the Daintree rainforest, which brought to mind the poet Andrew Marvell's description of the meditative state, 'annihilating all that's made to a green thought in a green shade'.

In Port Douglas, after I had seen the lovely little white-clapboard church of St. Mary's by the Sea, with its clear rather than stained-glass windows letting in views of tropical greenery, I found a hotel and settled down for a day or two to think about the direction of my life. An acquaintance in Alice had commented that I 'seemed a bit lost'. But you can't find yourself if you haven't first lost yourself.

To Vitaly, my erstwhile love in Moscow, I faxed a confessional, eight-page letter, trying to explain this insight; or was it casuistry? He was not thrilled by what he called the 'giant fax' but had the intelligence to write: 'You have uncorked your unconscious. Let things settle a while now.' And so we sort of got back together again.

I remained grateful to Adam for the lessons I'd learned with him and I know he too was thankful for the good things we'd shared. But it was with Vitaly that I had prospects of developing.

He and I used to joke that our sometimes difficult relationship was 'like a suitcase without a handle'. But it came to me then that at least it was a suitcase, with contents. Better a case without a handle than a handle without a case.

The Second Voyage
The Impossible Dream

When I returned to England, I went to stay with my parents until I found and bought a home of my own in Filey, on the Yorkshire Coast. Just south of Captain Cook's home port of Whitby, Filey was to become my anchorage; the haven where my ships were refitted between voyages to the Southern Hemisphere.

Number 8 Mariners Terrace was a three-storey fisherman's cottage, with an old kipper-smoking oven in the outhouse and a view of the sea from the top floor. The hospital-green carpet in the kitchen-diner and the ubiquitous marble-effect wallpaper were positively revolting but the house had potential. As soon as I had settled in, I invited Vitaly over from Moscow to take a look and we spent a very happy holiday together.

"You do know I'll have to go back to Australia, though," I said to him, for I was not done with Oz yet, not by any means. The conversations I'd had with journalist Dave Richards in the Date Palm Gardens in Alice Springs about better reflecting life in the desert had percolated in my mind and I'd applied for and got a business visa to return to Alice to set up an outback magazine. I didn't have a title for the magazine, however.

"Why don't you call it *BushMag*?" said my dad.

I liked the idea because the word *mag* in Russian means 'magician', as well as being short for magazine.

Vitaly quietly accepted that I would have to go and we agreed to wait for each other. Through the night before he took an early taxi to the airport for his flight back to Moscow, we meditated together.

I had another brief vision of the interconnectedness of everything, this time seeing life as a huge tapestry in which not a single thread was accidental. It was a mind-blowing picture, too overwhelming to see every day. But it was enough to have glimpsed it once to rest reassured that 'all shall be well, and all manner of things shall be well', to quote Julian of Norwich.

Now the time was coming for my own departure. I packed a large black suitcase. My white canvas sun hat was stained and battered but I knew I'd be able to pick up a new one in Sydney. I left on an autumn tide in Filey, heading for an Antipodean spring, although of course I wasn't sailing but flying from Heathrow, like all the other modern explorers and international commuters. I made a stopover in Bangkok again and this time visited the elegant wooden mansion of the late Jim Thompson, US intelligence officer and silk entrepreneur extraordinaire.

Once in Sydney, I didn't linger long in the big city but flew straight up to Alice Springs, where I had work to do. Luckily a unit was available in the place where I'd stayed before and I moved back into a beige bungalow at Sienna Apartments. Already, it was pretty hot in the desert.

Jet-lagged, I sat under the ceiling fan and asked myself: *Now what?* Every morning for a week, I woke up and asked myself what on earth I was doing back in Alice. I was supposed to create, edit and launch a magazine but, to be quite honest, I hadn't the faintest idea how to start.

Back in London, I'd been to see Andreas Whittam Smith, my former boss and one of three men who, in 1986, had mortgaged their own homes to found *The Independent*, free of influence from press barons such as Rupert Murdoch and Robert Maxwell. Andreas had been sympathetic and wished me luck.

Now in Alice, a coffee in the Date Palm Gardens with Dave Richards seemed like a plan.

"I've got an idea for a title," I said. "I think we should call the magazine *BushMag*. But we need content."

"Well, you can have an article from me about Olive Pink," he said, referring to the white anthropologist, botanist and Aboriginal rights activist who made waves in the desert in the earlier part of the 20th century and was famously feisty and eccentric. "And I reckon my friend the photographer Mike Gillam will give you a picture or two."

"That's certainly a start," I said.

I had in mind that *BushMag* was going to be as glossy and beautiful as *National Geographic*. Was I crazy?

I had some savings to live on, without earning a wage, but I couldn't afford to pay contributors until I had attracted advertising revenue. At least for the first edition, all the writers, artists and photographers would have to donate their work. That meant that although I had standards, I couldn't be too choosy about what went into the magazine, for you don't look a gift horse in the mouth.

I went back to my apartment, sat under the ceiling fan and quietly howled to myself, "Oh God, Oh God, Oh God..."

The phone rang. It was Meredith Campbell, the former ABC journalist and local politician with whom, on my first trip to the desert, I'd been camping at Rainbow Valley.

"What's up, doll?" she asked.

"I need a deputy editor, and a columnist," I said.

"OK," she replied. "Meanwhile, would you like to go out with me on a trip to Uluru?"

"Why not?" I said, sensing an opportunity to escape the scarily blank pages of *BushMag*.

On top of all her other activities, Meredith had become a marriage celebrant and she regularly drove out in a limousine to conduct magical dawn and sunset weddings at the Rock. The couple she was due to marry had no guests, so she needed me to go with her as a witness. Another guy would be there to take photographs, she said.

Gliding down the Stuart Highway in the car's leather front- passenger seat and listening to Mozart on the CD player, I had a first-class experience of desert travel to contrast with bumpier rides I'd known before. Overnight at Uluru, we roughed it in swags, though, waking very early the next morning to the virtuoso warbling of Australia's legendary magpies. (As well as being beautiful singers, they are known to swoop and peck passersby in the egg-hatching season.)

When the sun was up, we walked to a Rock viewing spot where Meredith was marrying the couple, who came from England. I had not been back to Uluru since the camping trip when I'd met Adam. Now, since we'd split up, I had rather mixed emotions about the place. I decided to be detached and observant, taking nothing from Uluru – no souvenir stone or flower – except what the Rock itself gave me, if anything.

The couple arrived for the ceremony. They were middle-aged; the woman had dyed black hair. I noticed she had accessorised her white dress with a purple handbag and shoes, the same combination of colours I'd chosen back in 1987 when I'd married my first Russian husband Costya at the Palace of Weddings in Moscow.

The ceremony was simple and informal. I did what was required of me as witness. After Meredith had pronounced the couple man and wife and a guy called Wayne had taken some photos, the bride surprised me by handing me her bouquet of white and purple flowers. So this was what the Rock had given me, then.

I found out sometime later that Costya had remarried in Moscow on the very same day I witnessed that desert wedding. In giving me back my old bridal bouquet, the Rock had restored my freedom. This is what I mean about the threads of the tapestry…

I was starting to pay more attention to life's apparent coincidences. I was learning to be more alert in the present moment, to take things step by step and to go with the flow. Strangely, the more I went with the flow, the faster the flow became, offering me more possibilities.

I did plan ahead, of course, but I was also open to the unexpected. This dual approach was working for me personally but I was soon to discover that it would also serve me in my professional capacity, where before I had tended to me more controlled.

What the flow brought next was an incredible offer from Wayne, this photographer bloke I'd only just met, to build a website for *BushMag*.

Bald and crazy-looking as a mad professor, Wayne Anthoney was a former government scientist turned professional actor and clown who, in his latest reincarnation, was helping to build a school called Nyangatjatjara College for the children of Aboriginal communities in the vicinity of the Rock. In what he called his Life B, he was living and working in a caravan in the shadow of Uluru. In Life A, he had a family and middle-class home down in Adelaide.

After the wedding, we repaired to Wayne's trailer and opened some tinnies of beer. Naturally, he wanted to know what a nice Pommie lass like me was doing in the desert and when I told him about the *BushMag* project, he offered to build the website.

"That'll be a bit costly, won't it?" I asked.

But Wayne offered to do it free, gratis and for nothing, saying that he liked messing around with websites in his free time in the caravan.

He was as good as his word and immediately set to work building a user-friendly website that would spare me the trouble and cost of producing dummy editions of *BushMag* on paper before the launch of the magazine itself.

The Independent had printed numerous dummy editions before it went public and I knew how much work was involved in that process. But to get an idea of what *BushMag* was going to look like, all I would have to do would be to slot articles and pictures onto Wayne's website, as they came in. The website, of course, would be kept under wraps until we were ready to launch our journal of the outback.

"What a great chap that friend of yours Wayne is," I said to Meredith, as we drove back up the Stuart Highway to Alice.

"Yeah, his blood should be bottled," she replied, using an Aussie expression of high regard for someone that I hadn't heard before.

"And you'll be *BushMag*'s deputy editor and write me a regular column?" I pressed Meredith, because she had a gift for wit and wordplay.

"Sure doll."

On the drive home, we tossed around ideas for a title for the column and came up with 'My Town of Alice', which had a faint echo of Nevil Shute's famous book *A Town Like Alice*. Two days later, Meredith delivered, and the first upload to Wayne's website was her amusing description of the annual exodus of Alice Springs's white population during the hot holiday season. Stress levels went through the roof as desert dwellers drove thousands of kilometres to make Christmas visits to relatives at the coast.

Meredith noted that Alice Springs song-writer and photographer Barry Skipsey had a song about this, called 'The Rellie Run'.

> *The tank is full, the Toyota's packed,*
> *We've got everything we could possibly need,*
> *Nappies and maps and screaming kids,*
> *We've got a glove box full of sedatives.*
> *It's that time of year when you disappear,*
> *Start climbing up the family tree,*
> *Uncles and aunts and long-lost cousins,*
> *There's just too many to see...*

Later, Meredith took me over to Giles Street to meet Barry. He was a roly-poly, bearded and jovial Territorian and I liked him straight away.

In those days, Barry made more of a living as a photographer than as a singer-songwriter – indeed he worked for *Australian Geographic* and was their Photographer of the Year in 1995. He showed me some of his pictures, which I instantly coveted for the centerfold of *BushMag*, although I wasn't so cheeky as to ask him to donate his valuable work at that first meeting.

Another very talented artist in Alice Springs did, however, give me some of his work without me having to ask, after I'd had nothing more than a coffee with him on Todd Mall. His name was Russell Guy and he was a writer, musician and broadcaster. He was perhaps best known in Australia for *What's Rangoon to You is Grafton to Me*, a radio play about a drug-fuelled trip from Brisbane to Sydney that became a cult classic in 1978.

Russell had some cartoons that he offered to let me publish in *BushMag*. They were off the wall in a gentle sort of way and I was thrilled to get my hands on them.

I would use the cartoons throughout the magazine but one in particular stood out for the inside front cover, the all-important first page the readers would see when they opened *BushMag*.

The cartoon strip showed a man in a magician's top hat and sparkly waistcoat sawing a piece of wood. 'One thing led to another...' said the first caption. The next picture showed the man wearing a pair of wooden wings he'd made from the plank. 'You know how it is...' said the caption.

Then the man was standing on a chair, wearing the wings and dreaming of flying. 'You dream the impossible...' said the caption. Next he was standing on a clifftop, wearing the wings and about to jump off. 'And when it happens...' said the caption.

In the last picture, which needed no words, the clifftop was bare and in the far distance, a little figure was flying in the sky.

It seemed incredible but my unlikely magazine *BushMag* was also starting to look as if it might take flight.

Concrete Help for *BushMag*

My second odyssey to Oz was all about creating *BushMag*, so I had no time for gallivanting around the continent as I had done on my first trip Down Under.

As the summer heat built up and the ceiling fan in my small unit whirred at increasing notches to less and less effect, I often felt like getting out of Alice Springs but I just couldn't. I was sweating at my desk, in regular contact with Wayne, sweating over the website he was building and maintaining in his caravan at Uluru. The most I could do for relief was to go out for a coffee in the shade of the Date Palm Gardens or walk up Anzac Hill for air and inspiration.

One day I was sitting on top of the hill, contemplating form and content, something that has interested me all my life. The two should go together like a horse and carriage. Form on its own may be beautiful but without content it is empty. Content on its own may be interesting but without form it can be difficult for the reader or viewer to digest. For every kind of content there is appropriate form and there is nothing more satisfying than seeing the two properly married. The modern world produces new media but the question remains: what do you want to say?

Up on the hill, looking out at the beauty of the MacDonnell Ranges, I asked myself what it was I wanted to communicate in creating *BushMag*. The answer came back: 'To celebrate the magic of the desert and the spirit of its resilient and creative people.'

We were a small team of Australians and Europeans, beaming out into a wide territory from Coober Pedy in the South to Tennant Creek in the North, from Broken Hill in the East to Kalgoorlie in the West. In a sense, it didn't matter whether the road signs said Northern Territory, South Australia or Western Australia. The Outback was One.

I was tapping into the philosophy of Rev. John Flynn, founder of the Royal Flying Doctor Service, whose priorities were the people of the vast interior rather than those who lived in comfort at the coast.

It was hot on the top of Anzac Hill but I had a hat on and a bottle of water by my side, so I continued sitting up there, thinking.

It was natural that when I'd first started creating *BushMag*, I had focused on its content. But now I had a small team assisting me and some material coming in, it was time to start raising money for the form side of things – design, layout and printing – none of which would be cheap. I needed advertising and I had no idea where to start.

I had another 'Oh God, Oh God, Oh God…' moment and, since the parched hill didn't look as if it was going to offer me any answers, I walked down to town and over to Bar Doppio for lunch. I hoped I might find my friend Dave Richards there and I was in luck. He had already chosen a quiche and a small flat white for himself and was sitting at an outside table, waiting for his order to be delivered.

"Sounds good; I'll have the same," I said and joined him.

"So how are things going with *BushMag*?" he asked.

"Quite well," I replied and updated him with the news that Meredith and Wayne had joined the team.

"So, we have your Olive Pink feature and Meredith's column…" I went on.

"But?" he asked.

"BUT I NEED CONCRETE HELP FOR *BUSHMAG*!" I said rather loudly, gesticulating so wildly that I knocked over a glass of water and half the café's customers turned round in their seats to stare at me.

"Sorry," I mouthed at them all.

A moment later, a very smart woman, wearing expensive sunglasses, walked over to our table and said in my ear: "Come and have dessert with me when you've finished with Dave."

So I did, and the woman turned out to be Roz Wade, co-owner of a ready-mixed concrete and building-supplies firm called North Concrete.

Roz had a very interesting background. She was born in Kenya of Polish and English parents. Her Polish mother had been taken by the Russians to a labour camp in Siberia. She escaped and, after World War Two, ended up in Africa, where she met her husband, an Englishman serving in the army.

The family lived in Tanganyika until it became independent Tanzania and they felt it better to leave. They didn't want to return to England, so migrated instead to Australia for its hot climate and wide, open spaces. I didn't know it then but was to discover that large numbers of both black and white people, forced to leave Africa for whatever reason, chose new lives in the Australian outback because it reminded them of the savannas of home.

In Alice, Roz met and married a South Australian called Clarry Wade. Having started their concrete business in 1989 with one small mobile batch plant and a ready-mix truck, they were now the royalty of the local building trade, providing concrete and other materials to the whole of Alice Springs and desert communities within a 600-km radius of the town.

"Wow!" I said, for Roz's story was proof that while the outback could easily defeat an entrepreneur, it could also provide fantastic opportunities. And I began to tell her about *BushMag*.

"I've got some articles already and a website is being built but we won't be able to afford to print a glossy magazine without financial backing from advertisers."

"Yes, and it does have to be glossy, doesn't it?" mused Roz. "A website is all very well but readers like to hold a magazine in their hands when they go to the hairdressers."

I could see I was getting through to this lady.

"How much do you want?" asked Roz.

That question threw me completely but I promised to go away and do the maths and come back to her with a schedule of prices for adverts.

"Go and see the *Centralian Advocate*," she advised, referring to the local Murdoch-owned newspaper. "Find out how much they charge for full-page, half-page and quarter-page ads and then offer your clients a small discount on that. In any case, Clarry and I will advertise with you."

And so, just when I needed concrete help for my fledgling magazine, I got the promise of an advert from North Concrete. In my excitement, I would have run all the way home to Sienna Apartments but it was a very hot day, so I took a taxi instead.

Back at the unit, I thought more about what Roz had told me of her family history. Australia was a migrant nation – everyone in Australia, except the Aboriginal people, had fairly recently come from somewhere else – so it stood to reason that all the business people in town, my potential advertisers, would have similarly interesting family stories to tell.

Although I'd avoided business for most of my life, thinking of myself as a 'creative person', I knew that those in trade and commerce were not rip-off merchants or number crunchers or sponsorship cows to be milked but human beings and members of the community.

I slept on the thought and woke the next morning with what seemed to me a brilliant concept for our advertising. In each ad, which I would personally write, I would tell the human story of the business promoting itself and in this way, not only raise money for the magazine but also reflect something of the economic life of the town and make heroes and heroines of the people who stood behind its shop counters.

"It's a winning formula," I said to myself, as I made my breakfast.

I was not ready for the bucket of cold water my journalist colleagues poured over the idea when we next met for a brainstorming session at the Date Palm Gardens.

"What's wrong with it?" I demanded.

"You're breaking a basic rule of journalism," someone said, "mixing editorial content with material that's been paid for."

They were right and I must admit I hadn't considered this but quick as a flash, I came up with an answer:

"No problem. We will make the distinction clear by printing the adverts in a different typeface from the articles and for those who are slow on the uptake, we can make it even clearer by writing 'Advertising Feature' at the top of each ad."

"Mmm, well that would work," said Dave.

"And I've already got the first ad from Roz Wade," I said, concluding the argument.

"Looks like you've created a new job for yourself then," laughed Dave, for I was the one who was now going to have to pound the pavements in search of other business people who were as imaginative and generous as Roz. (Everyone else on the *BushMag* team had full-time work and could only help me in their spare time.)

From sources at the *Centralian Advocate*, I had found out the going rates for advertising and decided that I would charge my clients 1,000 dollars for a full-page ad, 500 for half a page and 250 for a quarter-page. As it turned out, the Italian diaspora in Alice was very responsive to my appeal.

When I wasn't having coffee in the Date Palm Gardens, I used to go for my mid-morning latte to a little place in a shopping precinct off Todd Mall called Café La Piazza. The owner was a friendly man called Giuseppe Musolino. He liked the idea of advertising with *BushMag* because he said he wanted his grandchildren to know his story.

He'd called his café La Piazza because it reminded him of the *piazza* or town square in Careri in Reggio Calabria, southern Italy, where as a child he'd played football, whip-and-top and a game involving the throwing of hazelnuts.

"While we kids played, the grownups strolled or sat drinking wine and chatting in the wine bars. The *piazza* was the centre of the town's social life," he said.

Southern Italy was very poor back then and many people from the region were migrating to Australia. His father, Tomaso, set off to seek his fortune Down Under, leaving the family behind but promising to send for them when he could support them. He left in 1954 when Giuseppe was one year old. The family waited 11 years before he wrote, telling them to take a ship to Melbourne.

"Mindboggling," I said.

Giuseppe, nearly a teenager when he arrived in Oz, said he had found the country very strange at first. "At home, I had eaten healthy hunks of bread and cheese made by my grandfather. Now I was faced with funny little triangles of soft, white bread that left me hungry. My first job was in a Lyons teahouse in Adelaide. I was mixing jelly and custard for trifles. We Italians had another word for this dessert. We called it *zuppa Inglese* (English soup)."

After that, he'd started his own small business. Knowing how difficult that is and evidently sympathetic to me in a position he'd once been in, Giuseppe gave me 250 dollars for a quarter-page ad.

Sebastiano (Sam) and Carmela Giardina, the owners of the Casa Nostra Pizza and Spaghetti House, had a similar tale of early struggle in Australia that they were keen to share with *BushMag* and they matched Giuseppe's contribution with another quarter-page advert.

They too had come to Oz as teenagers.

"For me, it was a disaster," said Sam. "At first I thought I could run back home until I realised how far away Australia was. I cried every night for three months."

What upset him most was that, at the age of 13, he was put into the first class at school along with six-year-olds, because he couldn't speak English.

"I had a moustache growing and they put me in the class with the little kids. We had some big fights," he said.

Things got better when Sam left school and started work in a factory that made car seats.

He met Carmela in Melbourne, where the couple both worked in a shoe shop for a while. But then Papa Luigi, Carmela's uncle in Alice Springs, called them up to work in his restaurant. They married soon after and their wedding was the first to be held in Alice's newly built Catholic Church.

By the time I met them, Casa Nostra, which they'd set up 16 years earlier, was a very successful restaurant, attracting locals, tourists and visiting celebrities.

"I thought one customer looked familiar," said Carmela, "and I said to him, 'Aren't you that man off those animal programmes on the tele?' 'Yes, that's me,' he said, and it was David Attenborough."

I was laughing when I left Casa Nostra. I went to see Roz to report on the success of my advertising concept. She took out her fountain pen and cheque book and signed up for a half-page ad at 500 dollars.

Buoyed by the ease at which I was collecting money, I thought *what the hell* and dropped in to the offices of Zuellig Insurance Brokers. I boasted to the manager about my 'family history adverts' and told him that I already had three of them in the bag.

"Well, I'm not interested in family history ads," he said. "We have branches all over the Northern Territory." He gave me his card. 'John Sheridan, Manager, Southern Region,' it said.

There was an awkward silence. I waited.

"But I will take out a straightforward ad with our logo – *Zuellig Insurance Brokers – Serving the Territory, Covering your Needs*. Quarter-of-a-page, 250 dollars."

So that was that. It had been a rather dry conversation but I had another sponsor.

Chattier than Mr. Sheridan and happy to tell me her story was the co-owner of A Home Like Alice, a home accessories and gift shop in the Yeperenye Centre. Suzanne Bitar, originally from Canada, was married to a Lebanese Australian who traded in bathroom fittings and plumbing supplies.

"I realised that when clients had built their beautiful homes, they would want nice things to put in them, so I opened this shop, together with a friend," said Suzanne. "We go to trade fairs and people say, 'My goodness, do you eat off plates in Alice Springs?' They do not realise that there are some very fine houses here in Alice and sophisticated people with high disposable incomes wanting to decorate them elegantly."

It was an illuminating tale and another ad to add to my list.

But perhaps my favourite story came from Patsy Hayes, the owner of a chic dress shop called The Dressing Room. The daughter of cattle-station owners, Patsy came from the nearest the outback had to an old aristocracy. When she took out a full-page ad for 1,000 dollars, she became my biggest sponsor.

Her story was a delightful one. Because it was so dusty on the cattle station, Patsy's mother had sworn by bottle green as a 'good, serviceable colour'. She used to dye everything bottle green, even the children's shorts and singlets.

Patsy dreamed of pretty colours. In secret, she would look at the fashion pictures in the *Women's Weekly* and pore over the David Jones catalogue. But it was no good. When Patsy's aunt, who ran a boutique in Sydney, sent her niece dresses in pink and lemon, these had to be dyed bottle green too.

The only relief Patsy got was when she went to church in Alice Springs and saw women in the congregation wearing smart outfits and hats. When she grew up, of course, Patsy had to rebel by opening her own dress shop.

"My colours range from chic black and white to banana yellow, tangerine and emerald," she said. "I have pastel pinks, blues and mauves; a whole rainbow of colours, in fact. As for bottle green, you could get that colour in my shop, but you would probably have to order it specially!"

A Picture is Worth
a Thousand Words

There are times – for example when you want to put forward an argument, or when you want to stir the imagination – when well-chosen words do the job best of all. But more often than not, the news industry saying that 'a picture is worth a thousand words' is very true. Having got some editorial content for *BushMag* and adverts rolling in, I turned my mind to the images I wanted for the magazine.

Three fine photographers vied for ascendancy in Alice Springs. They were very different characters, with distinctive styles, and I believe there was a fair degree of competition among them. Like an avid butterfly collector, I wanted all three of them for *BushMag*.

Of the trio, Barry Skipsey, whom I'd met through Meredith Campbell, worked in what I felt was the most affectionate style. His desert landscapes were rarely empty but peopled with outback characters, such as the cattle-station worker riding home in an open truck with a dingo puppy at his side, or the lady from the camel farm taming one of her dromedaries.

Mike Gillam, whom I knew slightly through Dave Richards, took a less sentimental approach to the desert. A naturalist with more of an academic bent and a perfectionist's dedication to the tiniest detail, he achieved a jewel-like quality in exquisite pictures of local flora and fauna.

The third photographer, Steve Strike, had made his name at national level with a famous picture of Uluru, purple in a rare downpour of rain, and he had a gallery in a prestigious location, up an arcade off the main street.

I approached Barry first, for he was eminently approachable. In those days, he used to sell framed prints of his work from a stand inside the Yeperenye Shopping Centre but he was branching out and opening a proper gallery on Todd Mall to rival Steve Strike's business.

The new gallery was called Desert Express. Barry wrote:

Of life and love, I can write,
My words will convey the essence of a given moment.

I can speak. My voice will shape
that moment on a wave of
convincing breath.

But of this landscape before me,
this tapestry, this fanfare of glory
and colour; of its harmony,
light and shade and the pure
inspirational freedoms within...

I can only let the desert express.

I knew Barry needed somebody to sit in his gallery and watch the shop while he went out on errands, so a couple of times I did that small favour for him and our friendship deepened. I told him how *BushMag* was progressing and he was supportive to me in turn.

He let me have a number of his pictures for the magazine, including a shot of a cloud of green budgerigars flying across a blue desert sky and another of pelicans and people paddling in the Todd River after a burst of rain. Best of all, he gave me his 'tapestry' picture, layer upon layer of desert colour and texture, leading the eye up to purple ranges and a blue sky in the distance.

So now, thanks to Barry, I had the perfect centre spread for *BushMag*. This is what I mean about the threads of the tapestry...

Mike Gillam was also very kind when I visited him in his lair on Hele Crescent. He had a modest house but large patch of land that he was turning into an arid-zone garden and industrial sculpture park. He had plans to turn a 1961 silver bullet caravan into a café (the Silver Bullet Café didn't in the end do well as a venture but Mike later opened a successful art gallery on the site).

Mike greeted me in his usual garb of battered bush hat and khaki shirt and showed me round his grounds before taking me into his photo lab. "I've decided to give you my caterpillar and moth pictures," he said. "We'll need to choose the ones in sharpest focus."

Caterpillar awareness had surged in Alice Springs since the 2001 Yeperenye Festival. Locals and tourists alike knew that three different caterpillars (Yeperenye, Utnerrengatye and Ntyarlke) were sacred to the Arrernte people as the Dreamtime creator beings that had carved out the MacDonnell Ranges, fighting pitched battles with green stink beetles as they wriggled their way across the land.

The green, yellow and orange and black caterpillars exist in nature, of course, and Mike studied them. He called them 'living dot paintings'.

"Trouble is, they're so small and have to compete for market attention with koalas and kangaroos," he said. "That's why I want you to showcase them."

He also gave me a beautiful photo of the delicate brown and pink moths into which the caterpillars transform themselves and I realised it was a powerful symbol of emergence for the cover of *BushMag*.

Winning over Mike and Barry had proved relatively easy but now it was time to collect my third Alice Springs photographer, Steve Strike. I walked into his flash gallery, Outback Photographics, and introduced myself.

"You're a Pom, eh?" he said. "I hate Poms."

He was so rude that I wasn't even taken aback; I just laughed at him.

"I hate Poms," he said again, provoking another gale of laughter from me.

This might have seemed like an unpromising start but while Steve was testing to make sure I had a sense of humour, I detected that he had a twinkle in his eye. Eventually, we were to get on like a house on fire, which was a good thing, because we were going on a long road trip together.

Totally Eclipsed in Lyndhurst, SA

I heard it on the grapevine, as Marvin Gaye sang in '68. There was to be a New Age festival in the desert of South Australia, timed to coincide with a total eclipse of the sun. From all over the world, astronomers, lovers of trance music and hippies, young and old, were converging on the settlement of Lyndhurst for a huge party.

Being a bit of an old hippie myself, I was attracted to this event. I reckoned it would make both a good story for *BushMag* and an excuse for me to get out of town for a few days.

"Will you go with me?" I asked Steve.

I expected him to say 'no'. Poms were not his only pet hate, as I'd discovered. He also had contempt for aromatherapy and horoscopes – anything he viewed as flakey. But he surprised me.

"OK, let's do it," he said, and with no more ado, we threw our swags and eskies into the back of his landcruiser and set off down the Stuart Highway, marvelling at how green the landscape was after rain.

I'd made this trip south of Alice before but only as a passenger on a tour bus. Now I was travelling as a journalist, in tandem with a photographer, for me the most satisfying form of professional collaboration. I was excited.

In the heat of the day, an enormous, spinifex-coloured perentie (monitor lizard) waddled into the middle of the road and just stood there, ignoring the traffic. It moved to the verge when we got out of the car to peer at it but still showed no inclination to scuttle off into the scrub. It was obviously too old and worldly to panic at the sight of a few humans.

"It's humungous!" exclaimed a boy, leaping out of another vehicle that drew up for the spectacle.

"An auspicious sign for our trip?" I suggested.

"Nature," said Steve monosyllabically.

Just over the South Australia border, the police were waiting. Neither the highway nor landscape had changed in the slightest but suddenly there was a 110-kph speed limit and the cops had set up a trap to catch the road racers of the Northern Territory who failed to adapt in time. Knowing what to expect, Steve slowed down.

A little further along, there was a sign warning of roadworks and a detour. This turned out to lead straight past a police post, where a cop with a grin as broad as the brim of his hat was breathalysing all who passed by. Since Steve had not touched a drop, we had the luxury of laughing in the face of this uniformed trickster. In merry mood, we arrived in the late afternoon in Coober Pedy.

I wasn't sure that the opal-mining town, where everybody lived underground, would necessarily merit a second visit – for I'd already 'done it' on my first odyssey Down Under and found it a rough, if curious, sort of place. But with Steve as a guide, perhaps fresh insights awaited me.

"Let's go and see Crocodile Harry. He's a legend," said Steve, so I decided to give Coober Pedy another go. In any case, with night about to fall, and in the middle of the desert, there wasn't anywhere else to get accommodation.

Harry was an 'old Viking' of indeterminate Nordic background who in his youth had manhandled crocodiles in Australia's tropical Top End. Now he lived in what he called a 'crocodile nest' in one of the many disused mines hewn out of the rose-coloured rock. Industrial sculptures and cacti adorned his 'garden' and in the treeless landscape he had stuck up a drily humorous sign: 'Newly planted lawn. Please keep off.' Entrance to the crocodile nest came 'at your own risk' and cost two dollars.

Nervously, I entered the lair of the man proud to claim that he had screwed thousands of women. The dimly-lit cave was decorated with trophy bras and knickers while writhing female figures covered every inch of the walls. The radio was blasting out, so Harry was in there somewhere. "Hello?" I called out tentatively.

My heart pounded as I penetrated deeper into the nest. Was I about to be taken in a deadly crocodile roll? Then I saw the fragile body of the old man, curled up in the foetus position on his lonely double bed. He was fast asleep. I stood looking at him for a minute or two before retreating to the exit and writing in the visitors' book: 'God Bless you, Harry. Saw you asleep and didn't have the heart to wake you.'

When I emerged, I found Steve photographing the sunset over the opal mounds behind Harry's home. There was nothing there but 'potch', the worthless stuff that tantalises the opal hunters. I decided to tell Steve the old joke about the little hippopotamus that irritates a sleeping crocodile by running backwards and forwards, right past his snout: *chop, chop, chop, chop, chop.* 'Listen,' says the crocodile, 'if you do that once more, I'll turn you inside out.' The hippo ignores the warning and disturbs the croc again: *chop, chop, chop, chop, chop.* The crocodile goes *snap* and the hippo limps past: *poch, poch, poch, poch, poch.*

"I don't get it," said Steve.

"Well, *poch* is *chop* written backwards... oh, forget it."

It was getting late. On the way back to town, we gave a lift to a ragged man whose breath smelt strongly of liquor. He claimed to have been a millionaire three times over by striking it lucky in the opal fields but then he had lost it all again. Gambling and labouring down dusty holes; that had been his life.

Those who worked in the service industries were the ones who stacked up the quiet fortunes, I reckoned; people like Thelma and Jimmy at Traces Restaurant, where we went for dinner. They served us steak, chips and Greek salad, the staple they had cooked for their customers for 20 years, with scarcely a day off. Thelma shooed a pestering Serb from our table. He was trying to sell fake opal earrings for 10 dollars. He slunk off into a corner and lost himself in beer and television.

For the night, Steve and I had rooms in the underground Experience Motel. My room had lace curtains, although there was no window. I woke with a start in the pitch darkness and had no idea what time it was until, after fumbling, I managed to find the light switch.

Next morning, Steve fancied a round of golf at the Coober Pedy Golf Club where, instead of extensive grass with sand pits, you have extensive sand with grass patches.

"I'll go and have another look at the churches," I said and headed off in the direction of the Greek Orthodox Church, with its little wrought iron bell tower. It was closed but the Catholics were open for candle-lighting and at the Revival Church, I could have had a full baptismal bath and come out speaking in tongues.

I was happy enough when Steve said it was time to hit the road again and we set off down the barren Oodnadatta Track, destination Lyndhurst.

It was a dot in the desert, with a permanent population of only 30. But on December the 4th 2002, Lyndhurst would be overrun by thousands of party-goers, as it was in the direct path of an 'umbral shadow' (cast when the moon comes between the earth and the sun) and a rare 100 per cent solar eclipse was guaranteed. Rarer still, the eclipse would come at sunset and the colours in the sky were expected to be sensational.

At petrol stations along the way, we had already run into queues of young travellers, trying to buy special eclipse-viewing sunglasses. Stopping for a ginger beer at the William Creek pub, we got an update from the locals at the bar, who seemed less than fond of hippy types.

"We've seen quite a few tree-huggers coming through here," said one drinker.

"Out of their tree, more like. They'll be in for a rude shock when they get to Lyndhurst because it's a treeless waste, ha, ha!" said another. To the side of the bar, there was a notice that read: 'Fertilise the bush. Doze in a greenie. The only true wilderness is between a greenie's ears.'

"Typical," I said to Steve. "You know they hang feral cats here?"
"That's the outback for you," he grinned.

We continued our journey, past Curdimurka, where outback bachelors and spinsters come from miles around to attend a famous, annual 'B and S Ball'. Near Maree, which became a ghost-town when the Ghan railway stopped running there, some artists had made an attempt to cheer up the desert with giant sculptures – a Scottie dog made out of a railway container; a huge wind chime; an arch fashioned from old aeroplane wings and dedicated to 'the triumph of humanity over its own ignorance'. But nothing could dispel the sense of desolation in Maree.

A thatched mosque was testament to the passage of the Afghan cameleers through the town and there were white men's ruins, aplenty. Only the pub looked solid and seemed to do any business. The wind whistled down the abandoned railway platform. An Aboriginal boy rode a bike through the dusty streets. A mural on a community building used by the Aboriginal Arabana people had a sombre message:

> *If the transnationals and colonialist governments continue to defy the natural order in their quest for material wealth, Mother Earth will retaliate, the whole environment will retaliate, and the abusers will be eliminated. Things will come back full circle to where they started. This is the prophecy of all Indigenous peoples.*

We reached Lyndhurst as darkness was falling. The sight that met our eyes was like a scene out of a science fiction movie. Young people, some with dreadlocks down to their waists, others in black costumes created from netting, rubber and spikes, milled on the verandah of the Elsewhere Hotel, so named by its landlord, Rick Spaeth, because if you didn't like it, you could go elsewhere.

"Welcome to madness," shouted a man with a big beer belly.

A city had sprung up in the desert, peopled by exotic and, in some cases, scary-looking creatures in festive mood.

"We call them the soap evaders," joked Pat and Annette, who had come from the town of Whyalla to set up a catering tent offering hamburgers and chicken, only to find that most of the revellers were vegetarian.

"They do like their smoke, only not on their chicken," laughed the women. "But seriously, they're decent kids. We've been watching this camp grow for a few days. They've been arriving six or seven to a vehicle and literally falling out of their cars. But there's been no trouble and they've left no litter. There's a real feeling of fun and enjoyment in the atmosphere. It's party time. If our young people from Whyalla could see this, they would stand back and wonder. There's a lot of unemployment in our town and much more aggression and heavy drinking."

Up on the hill, the marathon rave party had already started. Seeking peace, Steve and I drove away from Lyndhurst and rolled out our swags as we liked them, sheltered from the wind in a dry creek bed and covered by the great dome of the starry sky. All night long, in our dreams, we could hear the trance music almost as clearly as if we had bought tickets to camp by the stage.

When the sun rose, we went to visit the festival site. Security was tight to prevent freeloaders from gatecrashing the music-and-light show but we assumed it would be OK to talk to the organisers and the young people who were breakfasting outside their tents. A friendly graduate of Cambridge University, who was checking that people were wearing their fluorescent green right-of-entry wrist bands, waved us straight in.

"It's been great," he said. "There are four stages, with different dance parties going on, and chill-out areas for those who want to unwind. There may be some drugs floating about here; it has been known. But people are looking after each other and everybody's being encouraged to drink plenty of water. It's been well organised."

Inside, we approached one group of twentysomethings, who were sitting under a camouflage awning like soldiers in a desert war, except that they were all warriors of peace and light. I plunged in and introduced myself. Steve hovered at the edge.

"Come and sit here next to me," said a young man called Stuart. "I'm a lesbian."

The group tittered.

Feeling awkward, like an aunt lost for words with her nephews and nieces, I asked them if they were students in their gap year

"Gap decade, more like," quipped another lad. "Next question."

A friendly guy called Hugh came to my rescue and started a proper conversation. He said he could only speak for himself, as thousands were gathered at the camp and they all had their individual stories.

"That's OK," I said.

He told me he'd had a good job in IT but felt the need to escape the angst and aggression of the city. He belonged to the 'free party movement' that organised non-commercial events where people could be 'creative in their own space'.

"Like the old hippies? Flower Power and all?" I asked.

"A progression of that. We have built on the experience of reggae and acid house."

When I raised the question of drugs, Hugh said they were 'incidental' to raves, as they were to society in general, but the watchwords of free partygoers were 'creativity' and 'compassion'.

"As it happens," he said, "I'm feeling a bit rough right now because someone spiked my drink last night. I ended up wandering off from the camp and getting lost. But I was rescued in the desert by complete strangers."

I also chatted with Madelaine, a politics student from Sydney, who said she was having a holiday from mainstream life. "It's fun in this tributary but I am afraid that I will have to return to the mainstream."

Stuart cracked his joke about being a lesbian again. It was even less funny the second time.

"Come on," said Steve, "let's go."

We left, in search of the organisers.

Security guards stopped us because we didn't have the green wrist bands and took us to their leader.

"We're just talking to people in the camp," I said.

"You have to pay 150 dollars to get in," said a man who gave his name as Zak.

"I realise you have to pay for the concerts but we're just doing a spot of journalism here. For *BushMag*. You know, the *Rolling Stone* of the outback?"

"Other media are paying," said Zak.

"Well, I don't pay for information," I said. "Can we get press passes please?"

"You should have told us in advance that you were coming."

"Sorry. We heard it on the grapevine. But since we're here, can we just do a few interviews?"

"Only if you pay. We don't need your publicity after the event."

"I believe that's what's known as a review, Zak. Would you mind giving me your full name?"

"Typical aggressive journalist," said a sidekick.

"Well then, I'll call you Zak in the Tropical Shirt."

"You do that," he said. "Let it be Zak in the Tropical Shirt."

They were little PR Nazis but it didn't matter. Steve and I got all we needed because the festival-goers were accessible as they walked into Lyndhurst for their cappuccinos and the music could be heard for miles around anyway.

So long was the queue for coffee in the Lyndhurst servo that we drove to the nearby village of Copley for kangaroo-and-claret pie and quandong (bush fruit) pudding in Tulloch's famous Bush Bakery. At the table opposite, a well-heeled, middle-aged couple were enjoying fresh sandwich rolls.

"Have you been to the rave?" I asked.

"Yes," they said. "Our son invited us. We had a great time, dancing until three in the morning."

They were from Melbourne, and a little conscious that in their smart clothes they must have looked like aliens, where feral was the norm.

"We saw the hippy revolution," said the mother. "Nothing much can shock us. I think it's a problem for the young these days. Their parents are so liberal that they have nothing to rebel against."

The magic hour of the eclipse was approaching but there was still time for Steve and me to visit Talc Alf, aka Cornelius Johan Alferink, a Dutch-born sculptor who had a workshop on the edge of Lyndhurst.

An Australian Union Jack-and-stars flag, incorporating the Aboriginal red, yellow and black tricolour, hung outside his studio as Alf was a firm believer that Australia should throw off the colonial yoke and become a republic. Above the door was a citation from Cicero: 'The Good of the People is the Chief Law'.

In the garden were Alf's energetic sculptures, carved out of soft, pearly-white talc stone. When we entered, the self-educated bush philosopher was standing at a blackboard, giving one of his lectures to a group of open-mouthed tourists.

"The boomerang was developed from the kangaroo leg," he boomed, holding up in one hand the traditional Aboriginal weapon and in the other, the bent leg of a long-dead roo. "When they threw the boomerang, the first people on earth reached for the stars."

Then he began to explain his personal alphabet and theory of the origin of words:

A is for Man, B is for Woman, C is for Child;
D is for Death, E is for Equal, F is for Forward;
G is for Give, H is for Height, I is for Individual;
J is for Judge, K is for Kill, L is for Low;
M is for Mountains; N is for Near, O is for Sun=Life;
P is for People, Q is for Question, R is for Roll;
S is for Swerve, T is for Top, U is for Under;
V is for Victory, W is for Water, + is for Christ;
Y is for Why and Z = the Beginning, not the End.

"Let's try to spell some words with this," he said. "'Australia' means 'Land of the Golden Sunrise'. Au=gold. S=sun. T=top. So the sun's rising. Ra is the Egyptian for sun. L=land. So we are going east towards the golden sun where the land is."

The audience looked bemused.

Alf tried another word, 'water'. "W=water, T=top, therefore 'water is dominant'," he said. "Or how about 'library', the place to 'liberate the soul with letters'?"

He was bonkers but harmless. In his system, 'God' meant 'good', 'Allah' stood for 'all' and 'Buddha' was 'brother'; he embraced everyone.

"What do you think of the festival?" I asked him.

"We can handle it," said Alf. "It's good for the economy. Lyndhurst has got a new airstrip out of this."

And indeed, as we spoke, chartered planes were landing, bringing professional astronomers to witness the eclipse that was fast approaching. One group, in matching yellow tee shirts, was from an observatory in Portugal. They were handing out British-safety-standard eclipse sunglasses and poo-pooing the 'excessive caution' of Australian opticians, who said there was no safe way to look directly at the sun.

Astronomers and ordinary spectators alike were starting to line up in the best spot, along the road running through the Farina cattle station. A high wind was whipping up the dust and the revellers coming from the party camp were wrapped in headscarves that made them look more like figures from the Palestinian *intifada* than witnesses to a celestial event.

Some were eclipse junkies, like Trevor, an English-born nurse from Adelaide, who said this was his third such experience.

"For me, an eclipse is always powerful. I saw one in Africa, among the wild animals. Even the one in Cornwall, when it poured with rain, was very moving."

Steve and I took our places in the viewing line. Our neighbour, a German-born statistician from Melbourne, had a huge telescope with which he pursued his hobby of gazing at the sky.

"I've got a filter on the lens," he said. "You can have a look. It's absolutely safe."

The time was 6.43 pm. The moon was just beginning to pass between the earth and the sun, making it appear that a small bite had been taken out of the world's source of heat, light and life. It would be nearly an hour before the sun was completely covered and became a black disc with just a 'corona' of light spilling out around the edges like a halo. I decided to go walkabout.

I was fascinated by my own shadow against the desert landscape. As more of the moon's shadow was cast upon the earth, the black shape of my body became tinged around the edges with a silvery light. It was as if I had a double shadow. I sat down on the sand.

It was growing darker and chillier. Little birds were flying low to the ground. I could well understand how ancient people had been terrified by eclipses and seen in them worrying omens. What if the light didn't return? I felt the need to huddle, to prostrate myself even. *I am dust, I am dust in the wind, I am the wind,* said an inner voice. The comments of the crowd seemed to come from very far away:

"I've got a photo of something."

"I'm excited, I'm excited!"

The moment of totality was very short, only 32 seconds. Then the sun began to reappear. What stronger symbol of resurrection? A new moon was also due; it would be a double resurrection. Before that, there was the rarest of sunsets, a still-partially eclipsed sun slipping beneath the horizon. The astronomers and photographers were in heaven.

When it was all over, Steve said to me:

"There's one of your mob over there. He's hitch-hiking. I've told him he can have a lift back to town. Have a chat with him while I pack up the gear."

By 'one of my mob', Steve meant a Pom. But having spent so much time in Moscow, I often think in Russian and for some reason addressed the stranger with a *zdravstvuyte*. He answered me in a Slav language and we chatted for quite a while before I realised he was indeed an Englishman, of Ukrainian parentage.

His name was Ivor and he was a gentle soul. With his long curls and neatly trimmed beard, he looked like Jesus. He said he went from place to place, doing voluntary work. At night, he rolled out his sleeping bag on a piece of cardboard. Far more than Steve and me in our Landcruiser, he was truly going with the flow.

He'd been drifting down the middle of the road when police picked him up for this eccentric behaviour and gave him a ride into Lyndhurst. He'd been walking towards the festival camp when a strong gust of wind blew in his face and he turned, allowing it to blow him to the viewing field instead. He was in awe of the eclipse he had just witnessed.

Steve and I invited Ivor to join us for an evening meal from the Chinese takeaway in Lyndhurst. "Perhaps you can have a lift with us when we leave tomorrow," I said.

"Yeah," said Steve, "but we're leaving early, so make sure you're on time."

At dawn, there was no sign of Ivor. We slung our swags and eskies into the car and left Lyndhurst without him. For the next 300 kilometres, I felt bad about it but I guess Ivor just went with another flow.

Steve was taking me home to Alice by a different route. We were on a mystery tour. We passed the derelict town of Farina, where 300 people had once lived and hoped to grow wheat on the arid land. On we went, past the white, salty expanses of Lake Eyre. If it had not been so hot, I could have thought myself in the Arctic. At Oodnadatta, we stopped at the famous Pink Roadhouse for tea.

The destination of the mystery tour turned out to be the fantastic Painted Desert and we arrived just in time to see the sun setting over the multicoloured Arckaringa Mountains.

Judging from the state of the road, no other car had passed that way since the rains several days earlier. There would be hordes of kangaroos the next morning to nibble at the sweet, new grass. We were completely alone in nature. In the palpable quiet, insect noises sounded as loud as drums and zithers. The new moon was a thin, silver smile in the indigo sky before the stars came out like diamonds.

Sunrise I watched from the comfort of my swag. All I had to do was turn my head on the pillow to see the morning light playing over the blood-reds, saffron-yellows and chalky-whites of the ochre cliffs. It was an artist's palette and the sight filled me with peace.

Back in Alice, Steve and I returned to work but it wasn't long before he was knocking on my door at Sienna Apartments.

"Here," he said and he spread out on my desk a fan of glorious photos – desert skies, arid landscapes and shots of quirky outback characters. "You can have them all for *BushMag*."

It was an incredibly generous contribution from a colleague who pretended to be gruff but really had a heart of gold.

All the Talent of the Town

Although I am not exactly gay myself, whenever I was in Alice Springs I found myself hanging out with the dykes of the desert. I was drawn to these strong, creative and supportive women, who invited me to their imaginative events and fabulous parties. It wasn't about sexuality as such; it was just that life with them was more fun. They embraced me as a sister and I was happy to be accepted as an honorary lesbian.

Over the years, I was to meet and come to love a number of women in Alice, which is rightly known as the 'lesbian capital of Australia'. Indeed, it would be no exaggeration to say that the little town is home to one of the biggest and most significant lesbian communities in the world. But there's no doubt that my platonic gay love affair began when I met Megg Kelham, a historian who taught me a great deal about Australia and the outback in particular.

Megg was outspoken, to put it mildly. There were those who thought she was argumentative to the point of being cranky. But she wasn't politically correct and often she made me rethink a complacent idea. And she had a heart the size of Africa. Indeed, some years after I first met her, when she was facing open heart surgery, which she knew would leave her with a scar on her chest, she threw a 'cleavage party' in celebration of the bosom. That was typical of her warmth and sense of humour.

Megg had worked as a teacher at Alice Springs jail, where a disproportionate number of the incarcerated were men of Aboriginal background, so she knew very well that not all indigenous people were angels, while also being fully aware of the cruelties and injustices they had suffered at various times since white settlement. Whenever I was baffled about Aboriginal issues, Megg was one of the people to whom I turned for a fair assessment.

Among the other things she and I discussed was the subject of journalists and historians and their relative roles. I didn't see a big difference; I used to tell my journalism students that they should be accurate today because they were writing tomorrow's history. But Megg said that journalists came under commercial pressures that made their work unreliable while historians were more scrupulous about sources and facts. It was an argument we never resolved.

When it came to *BushMag*, I was keen to answer the straightforward question: 'Why are there so many lesbians in Alice Springs?' I knew Megg was the person to enlighten the readers and asked her to write on the subject. In due course, she came up with a splendid memoir called 'Something of a Sisterhood', in which she recounted how free-thinking women had converged on Alice Springs in 1983 to protest at the gates of the joint US-Australian defence base at Pine Gap. This was Australia's Greenham Common. Megg wrote:

Which brings me to the disproportionately large size of the lesbian community in Alice. Of course there were a lot of lesbians at the Pine Gap protests because they were free to travel. Many of the women, straight and gay, who came up here were stunned by the beauty of Australia's desert heart. Many were also fearfully concerned at the plight of Indigenous Australians and chose to return to Alice as doctors, lawyers and teachers.

And so, by the early 1990s, the lesbian community had become numerically large enough to ensure continual regeneration. It's what the mathematicians call a 'critical mass'. As for it being visible to outsiders, personally I have never noticed it. Perhaps that is because it is harder to see a forest when you are one of the trees.

Megg's article was accompanied by one of Russell Guy's cartoons, showing a woman sitting by the side of a road, next to a bunch of bananas. The caption read: 'Picture of a woman contemplating leaving her man for a bunch of bananas'.

I was very happy with this contribution to *BushMag*. As I've said, the magazine celebrated every aspect of life of the outback. It wasn't an organ of positive propaganda that evaded confronting issues, if they arose, but neither did it set out to dig dirt gratuitously. It was an experiment in a fresher form of journalism.

Word was starting to get out that an exciting new publication was in the offing and locals wanted to be involved. Some of the writers were professionals but I was also keen to encourage amateurs who may never in their lives have put pen to paper, or tapped a computer keyboard, but who had interesting stories to tell.

In the car park at Sienna Apartments, I'd noticed a red camper van whose owners seemed to be staying longer than the average tourist in Alice Springs. They turned out to be a couple from Cairns called Sue and Richard Schulte. Sue was hairdresser and Richard a butcher and before they retired, they'd never left their native Queensland. Now they were doing the 'grey nomad' thing and travelling all around Australia, taking causal jobs to finance themselves along the way. They wrote a travel piece, datelined 'somewhere in Australia in a little red van', which had all the clear-sightedness of pathfinders seeing the world for the first time.

Another inspiring story came from the manageress of Sienna Apartments, Sue Nankivell, who revealed to me that she had gone into a downward spiral of various physical aches and pains because of stress and anxiety and only come up again because she had started to run.

"I had chronic fatigue/fibromyalgia," she said. "I felt so alone. It was hard to explain my suffering because on the outside, I looked perfectly healthy. It was clear there was no medical cure; it was up to me. So here's what I did – I dismissed the advice that rest was the best remedy and went out and bought a pair of running shoes. I started to run; to run for my life."

At first, Sue could only run for one minute at a time but she built up her stamina and joined the local running club. Eventually, she went on to win a silver medal in the Alice Springs Masters Games, running a half marathon in 44 degrees of heat, when four years earlier she'd been barely able to walk. I knew there should be a sports story in the magazine and this was it.

Other offerings I was pleased to receive included the story of how Ronn Slusser, the town's snake catcher, was forced to take his own advice – 'don't panic, don't panic' – when he got bitten by a western brown snake in his back garden; an account by Christian Joaquin Cruz, an American working at the Pine Gap base, of how he made jewellery from gem stones fossicked in the desert; and a piece by BBC journalist Sharon Mascall Dare about the contribution of pioneering Afghans to the opening up of the outback.

From Tarla Kramer, a professional nutritionist who advocated eating cholesterol-free kangaroo rather than beef, I had five recipes for cooking the marsupial, plus instructions on how to make a quandong (bush fruit) pie for dessert. And from a young indigenous woman called Yaritji Green I had a fantastic essay on how she went au-pairing and backpacking around Germany that smashed all the stereotypes about Aboriginal people.

I was still looking for more material, though; you'd be surprised how much you need to fill a whole magazine.

"Why don't you pay a visit to the Writers' Group?" someone suggested, so one evening I went out talent-spotting.

The budding writers were sitting around a table, reading out extracts of their work and commenting on each other's prose. There was Tarla again, a quiet young woman with long, straw-coloured hair and large glasses. Her natural and understated style of writing impressed me and I asked if she would contribute a piece.

She came up with 'A Season for Everything' in which she subtly wove the changing rhythms of the weather and her own emotions:

I had left a lover behind in La Paz, Bolivia. He was the father of my son. We were trying to get our act together as a couple but as week after scorching week went by, I heard nothing from him. Through January and February, the top temperatures stuck at around 40C (104F).

The heat continued relentlessly until the end of March, high thirties every day. I would find it strange to see fashion pages with winter clothing in the Woman's Day. Apparently it was autumn elsewhere, although there was no evidence of it here.

The locals commented that by now, Alice Springs was supposed to have experienced a few cooler days of around 30C (86F).

"Yeah, right," I thought.

Then one day it happened. I stepped outside in the morning to a breeze so cool it almost chilled and walked in the garden, letting it wrap around me. I found something warmer to put on and paced up and down some more.

I had not heard from my man for six months when, just like that first, cool wind, an unexpected envelope appeared in the letter box.

I felt Tarla had a future as a writer. More than that, I thought she could be sensitive when it came to handling other contributors' work. She became the Literary Editor of *BushMag* and, although the magazine ended up having more creative writing in it than I had perhaps intended, I didn't care. It was all coming together very nicely.

Christmas in the Desert

Christmas descended on the desert, as heavy and harsh as anything I'd ever experienced in the depths of the Russian winter. The heat was extraordinary and, as almost all of the white population had gone away to the coast for their summer holidays, there was very little to be achieved on the work front. I wandered aimlessly around the Alice Plaza shopping centre, where six white boomers pulled Santa's sleigh, a nod to the Rolf Harris song in the days before Harris was disgraced. In my small apartment, I pieced together a jigsaw of a Nordic snow scene. I found doing jigsaws helped me to gather my thoughts.

The phone rang. It was my old friend Ant, who had moved up to the gold-mining town of Tennant Creek to work at the hospital there.

"I have two days off for Christmas," he said. "Why don't you come up and visit me?"

So I caught the Greyhound bus to Tennant and went to stay with Ant in the nurses' quarters.

All along the road, the flame trees were in flower. Plastic Christmas trees dotted the central reservation and silver tinsel stockings and stars hung from the lampposts. Outside one house, decorated with Christmas lights, an Aboriginal boy sat on the parched lawn. To my English eyes, it all looked very incongruous.

Ant and I spent one of his free days at the nearly-deserted, open-air town swimming pool. Dark clouds massed in the sky and it looked as if we might have to dash for shelter but the rain fell elsewhere. On the other day, we made the best of a Christmas dinner at the local working men's club but I had a strong sense that I should really be somewhere else, with my family in the Northern Hemisphere.

After Christmas, another friend, Wayne Anthoney from Uluru, popped up to help relieve my boredom. Unlike other white fellas, Wayne was famous for doing gruelling January stints in the desert and he hadn't gone south with the holiday crowd.

"Hello Womers. I'm going out bush with Oakes," he said. "We're gonna check on the camel project. Wanna come with us? This could be your chance to visit an Aboriginal community but we'll have to speak to the boss first."

It all sounded very intriguing. Oakes was Wayne's colleague out at Uluru, a cheery Liverpudlian social worker whose first name was Dave. Wayne called him Desert Oakes because Wayne's favourite tree was the tender, swaying desert oak and Oakes did sway a little after a night at the pub. Together, they were working on a project to boost employment among Aboriginal youths by paying them to round up feral camels for live export to the halal meat markets of Malaysia and the Middle East.

Wayne and Oakes were planning to go out into the desert west of Uluru and see how the young men were getting on, building a stockade for the camels. The trip would also involve a visit to the Aboriginal community of Docker River, strictly closed to outsiders like me unless we could get the blessing of an Aboriginal elder called Charlie Walkabout.

Mr. Walkabout was a legendary figure whose word was law in a number of Aboriginal communities around Uluru. He liked to tell the story of how his ancestors had defeated the greedy and violent white explorer Harold Bell Lasseter by exploiting the moment when he was trousers down, taking a crap, to chase away his camels, thus leaving him in the desert without any transport. Mr. Walkabout, who like many Aboriginal people suffered from kidney disease caused by intolerance to the white man's diet, had also been in the news as one of the first patients to have dialysis in desert conditions.

He was frail and quite close to death when we went to visit him in

Mutitjulu community, by the Rock, to ask permission to travel to Docker River, three hours' drive away along the bumpy Tjukaruru Road. I let the men do the talking and after a while I saw Mr. Walkabout nod 'yes'. At long last, my dream of really seeing how Aboriginal people lived on their communities was going to come true.

The night before the trip, Wayne and Oakes and I went for a few beers and afterwards I slept on the deck outside Wayne's caravan. A faint drizzle was misting rather than falling over the Olgas as we set out the following morning but it promised to be another hot, dry desert day.

Up the red dirt road, at about elevenses time, we stopped for a short break in what to me looked like the middle of nowhere. "I always stop right here and eat a banana," said Oakes. "I call this place Bananarama." Frankly, I couldn't see how Bananarama was any different from hundreds of other patches of dry earth we could have chosen but I was starting to enjoy Oakes's humour.

As we left Bananarama, I noticed that the sky ahead had darkened considerably and three ducks were flying towards us, like the ducks-in-flight you used to see above mantelpieces in the homes of the tasteless.

"Mmmm," I said, "wonder what that means?"

"Ah, no worries," said Wayne.

We reached the half-built camel stockade. The young men, if they had been working at all that day, had all knocked off for lunch. Wayne and Oakes inspected some of the stakes in the ground before our thoughts also turned to our stomachs and we continued on to Docker River, or Kaltukatjara, to give it its Aboriginal name.

The landscape changed as we neared Docker, which is in the foothills of the Petermann Ranges. On the way, we had crossed, by my count, five dry rivers.

The community of around 350 people had an airstrip, a general store with a petrol pump, a school, a health centre and a home for the elderly, as well as an arts and crafts centre, a recreation hall, an oval for sports and two public telephones. There was also a Lutheran church.

We headed for the shop, where the food assortment was limited – mostly tins and very little in the way of fresh fruit or vegetables – and like all the other lunchtime customers, we ended up buying meat pies and packets of tomato ketchup. Camp dogs waited in the dirt outside, vying for any dropped crusts.

The community was undoubtedly scruffy – you would have to say Third World, really – except for the fact that through the Royal Flying Doctor Service and visiting nurses, the residents of Docker River had access to First World medicine. Thus, it is not quite accurate to compare the condition of Aboriginal people with that of the poorest in Africa.

The schoolchildren were bright-eyed and lively and their teacher, an indigenous man from the Torres Strait Islands, was very welcoming.

"Come out with us, we'll show you the rock art," they said, so we formed a convoy of three cars and set off for some nearby caves.

The cave art didn't make as big an impression on me as the joy of the kids, as we shared some oranges, sitting on the rocks outside. Rain started to come on and the schoolmaster said: "Better make a move."

The teacher and the children were in the two cars ahead of us, as we set off back to Docker River. The downpour and flash flood, of which the squadron of ducks had hinted, came so quickly and unexpectedly that Wayne, Oakes and I were left stranded in our car on the near side of a rushing river, while the others had made it over to the far side, with access to their homes. We could see some of the boys, prancing in the rapidly rising water and waving at us, whether sympathetically or derisively, I couldn't tell.

"Now what?" I said.

"Well, we could be stuck here for quite a long time," said Wayne.

"How long?"

"Days," mumbled Wayne.

"And we've just eaten all the oranges, as well as the hard-boiled eggs and the chocolate," I said.

"Yeah," said Wayne.

"Quite a challenge for our inner resources, then," I said.

"Yeah," said Wayne.

"We could tell jokes," I said. "I have a repertoire of 2,168 Russian jokes. Would you like to hear the first one?"

"Nah," said Wayne, who promptly fell asleep.

"He could sleep, pegged out on a washing line," said Oakes.

For Oakes's benefit, I told the first Russian joke:

"There was this Soviet worker, and he was so poor, he couldn't afford anything. He couldn't even afford to go to the factory canteen for his lunch. He used to take sardine sandwiches instead. One day, he opened his lunchbox and took out two small sandwiches with caviar. 'Hey,' said his mates, 'you're supposed to be poor. How come you have caviar sandwiches today?' 'Ah,' said the worker, 'that's not caviar. That's sardines' eyes.'"

"Very funny," said Oakes. "Maybe we'll skip the other 2,167?"

We fell silent, except for Wayne's snoring. I felt rather afraid. Mentally, I began calculating our supplies of drinking water. We could indeed have been stuck there for days. It happens all the time in the desert, when sudden rains cut people off.

But as luck would have it, the waters that had risen so dramatically, fell equally quickly and by late afternoon, we were able to cross the shallow river and get back to Docker River. Our hosts gave us nothing more than quick cups of tea, urging us to start out on the return journey to Uluru before we lost the last of the light. It was dark by the time we reached Wayne's caravan. In the clear night sky, a canopy of stars twinkled over the Rock.

"Great adventure, I'll never forget it," I said to Wayne and Oakes when I left them to return to Alice Springs the next day. We'd had so many laughs; I knew I was going to miss them.

As a parting gift, Oakes, who was a singer-songwriter in a modest sort of way, gave me the lyrics to his song, Beneath Uluru:

I look ahead to seeing you, you're just a week away,
And like so many times before
I'll want that time to stay for more
And yet before we know it, we'll be saying our goodbye.
Time will have come and gone,
To be seen through memory's eyes, on and on...

Time has no time, time's passing through,
No-one can hold it, it's always anew,
That was a time, a memory of you,
Under the starlight, beneath Uluru.

Back in Alice Springs, time started to tick again. The doldrums of the summer holidays were coming to an end. My birthday on 26th January coincided with Australia Day, after which the country would get back to school, college and work.

For the big day, I held a champagne party for my friends under the trees in the Date Palm Gardens.

"You're a real Aussie," they said, "having your birthday on the national day."

"You know I love this place," I told Mark Bunting, who with his wife Heather and assistant Kay ran the gardens and café.

"Why don't you hold the launch of your magazine with us?" Mark suggested.

It was a great idea, as all the brainstorming for *BushMag* had been done under the date palms.

"Thanks," I said, "I will. But first I have to find a layout artist and a printer."

Launch and Re-Entry

Glossy quality was what I wanted for *BushMag* and I knew I was going to have to pay for it. The contributors might have been volunteers but the layout and printing had to be done professionally. Fortunately, there was enough money from the advertisers to cover the costs.

The layout was done by a talented young Canberra-born artist called Nigel Campbell, who worked for a firm called Dunnart Design. The printer, a man called Max Kleiner, originally from Switzerland, brought a European flair to the job. I was thrilled when Max delivered the first issue of the magazine in a small print run of 2,000 copies. This was my baby and I felt proud. It was a shock, then, when the baby started to cry.

Packed in their boxes, the magazines filled my tiny apartment from floor to ceiling; I could barely move around them. Suddenly it dawned on me that I was going to have to sell them all and I had no marketing strategy whatsoever. In a panic, I went over the Date Palm Gardens.

"Give me a box," said Kay, who was selling scones in the café. "I'll flog them to our customers for you."

There wasn't even a price on the cover. "Let's make it 10 dollars," said Kay, "and see how they go."

So that was how the marketing started. I literally walked the streets, asking people if they wanted to buy a copy of the new magazine. I persuaded shopkeepers to sell them on my behalf. And I took them down to the Sunday market and hawked them there.

The launch party, which we held in the Date Palm Gardens at Easter, was really to honour the advertisers who had supported us. They were all invited to drink champagne and given complimentary copies.

"Good on yer," said Kay, as we were clearing up afterwards. "You're not a gunner."

"A gunner?"

"Yeah, someone who's gonna do this, and gonna do that. You could have given up and just left the magazine on the website but you went ahead and printed it. That means something."

As it turned out, *BushMag* sold quite well. The generous people of Alice Springs were always ready to back a creative community project. The journal might not have been exactly what I'd planned – something modelled on *National Geographic* – but rather, because it depended on donated work, it was a mixture of many strands. Each contributor brought something essential to the table and *BushMag* was precisely the magazine that was meant to be.

Thus, it was no accident that the last word went to Linda Wells, who contributed a prose poem called 'The Interconnectedness', written in the voice of the dry Todd River:

I am the river, the river that runs through the town. The desert river. The desert town. Significantly dry. There's nothing wrong with me, nothing, that is, that isn't wrong with the whole town. That isn't wrong with all the people here. I am in the people. The people are in me.

I'm messy. Sure. As are the people. I never was back then. Then, Those Who Knew Me Best held me sacred. They held everything sacred. Every little thing. Every big thing. They wouldn't have dreamed of messing me up, old Lhere Mparntwe. Not back then. No means.

Curious people advanced. On horseback. Heads held high, no invitations necessary. Invasion is like that. They brought things. New products. New packaging. Oppression. Concepts of superiority. Flavours and colours and ideas thus far unknown. To me. Spilling over from the township They were building. Spilling onto me...

The people on horseback shot Those Who Knew Me Best. "Put up or shut up," they barked before firing their carbines. That shut them up. No choice. Those Who Knew Me Best fought back with spears and the fury born of injustice. Both sides were maimed but spears and The Law can't match the firearms of the military. Blood spilt onto my sands.

Some people hate. They might go on hating forever. Others traced each other's profiles, moved forward, embracing. They nursed each other's infants, laughed at each other's jokes. Found the common love. Over tea or rum or biscuits or honey ants they rejoiced. Sometimes, with gay abandon, they threw away the packaging and sometimes it landed on my sand.

I am the river. What you do to each other you do to me. What you do to me you do to each other. Such is the interconnectedness. There's nothing wrong with me. Nothing that won't be righted when all the people remember that I and everything else in their world is sacred. Every little thing. Every big thing. When heaven returns to earth.

With the success of *BushMag* came a flurry of questions as to when the next edition was coming out. I felt dispirited because I was going to have to tell everyone that there wouldn't be a second edition. People had kindly given their articles and photos the first time but I couldn't expect them to do so again and neither could I go on working myself for nothing. The truth was I lacked the capital; for better or worse, I wasn't a Rupert Murdoch.

The conditions of my business visa were that sooner or later I had to start providing paid employment to Australians. I had failed, and so I would have to leave the country. I comforted myself with the thought that *BushMag* had been a rare flower, destined to bloom once in the desert (and indeed, years later, I was gratified to learn that quite a few people had kept their copies of the magazine, which had become a 'collector's item').

Friends in Alice released me kindly, saying I would always be welcome there. Alice was like that – a come-and-go town that you could keep leaving while knowing you would be embraced again, if you ever returned. And of course it stayed with me in my heart.

But now I needed a magic carpet to get back to Moscow, where Vitaly was waiting for me. I remembered the line from Homer's *Odyssey*: 'However far a man has travelled, a friendly god can always bring him home and that with ease.'

Out of the blue came an offer from *The Sydney Morning Herald* and *The Age of Melbourne*, who were looking for a journalist to string for them from Russia. For years, I'd written for the British press from Moscow. In 2003, I returned to Russia, wearing an Aussie hat.

Landing in bleak, autumnal Moscow felt as disconcerting as a cosmonaut's re-entry. Vitaly was oddly cool when he met me at the airport. It took a while for the story of what he'd been up to in my absence to emerge. It turned out that while I'd been living like a nun and sweating over the magazine, he'd had an affair with one of his colleagues. "Don't think I am some kind of Penelope, knitting while you are away," he said acidly.

I didn't know what to feel.

"Well, it's Liverpool 1, Arsenal 1," said my Yorkshire dad pithily.

He was right.

I went through the motions of being angry with Vitaly; I even hit him over the head with a breadboard. But he'd only done what I'd done. I realised everything he'd experienced, I'd experienced, everything he'd felt, I'd felt, and vice versa. We were one. It was an overwhelming thought. What if you applied that to every stranger you met on the bus or metro? *What if God was one of us?*

Vitaly and I got back together, although we didn't live together. I had a small flat near Moscow's Alley of Cosmonauts while he had a one-room box on the edge of the city. We commuted to see each other at weekends and he courted me all over again, regularly bringing bouquets of flowers.

The Third Voyage
Breakthrough Moment

Tourism Australia spent 180 million dollars in 2006 on a TV advertising campaign to attract visitors Down Under. The promo showed schooners of beer being poured in an outback pub, kangaroos bounding over a green landscape and some of Australia's pristine beaches before busty model Lara Bingle emerged from the waves to ask cheekily: 'Where the bloody hell are ya?' Britain's broadcasting authorities promptly banned the ad for the use of the word 'bloody'.

Of course, this only increased the hits on *YouTube* and I watched the video several times, drooling over the lovely, familiar scenes. But where the bloody hell was I? Back in the USSR, that's where.

After I'd returned to Moscow in 2003, I plunged into Russian reality and pretty well forgot about Australia, except that I was serving editors and readers who were in Oz. I was busy with the news – the Orange Revolution in Ukraine; the arrest of the dissident oil tycoon Mikhail Khodorkovsky that signalled the authoritarian way Vladimir Putin's regime was going to go.

Vitaly and I continued as a couple, living in separate flats joined by what we called 'the long corridor' between Metro Alexeevskaya and his place in far-flung Balashikha. It partly suited us to live apart during the week, as Vitaly, being a musician, needed to practise the piano while I needed peace and quiet to read and write. But property prices and wages being what they were, there was never any prospect that we might one day get a nice, large flat where we could be together. We were victims of the eternal Russian 'housing problem'.

We only managed to wake up and share breakfast every morning when we were on holiday. In the summer of 2007, we went to my house at Filey in Yorkshire, where it rained without let-up until the very last day of the trip. When the sky finally cleared and we were able to enjoy a sunset walk on the beach, Vitaly asked me to marry him and I said 'yes'.

I was immediately plagued with doubts that pursued me right to the morning of the ceremony in the Palace of Weddings in Moscow.

"Look," said Vitaly calmly, "we'll just do what suits us."

And when he said that, I felt ready to go ahead.

We both dressed in jeans for the simplest of ceremonies, without rings, or music, or guests, and afterwards wolfed down a plate of sausages at home before going to our respective jobs. That was on the 22nd of February 2008, a grey day, with slush on the pavements and spring still a distant dream.

I have often thought that Russia is really two countries; Russia in winter and Russia in summer are two entirely different worlds. In summer, I was always happy enough but during the long winters, I got depressed and then I would start fantasising again about Australia.

One day, I was at the Australian Embassy, asking about possible ways to get back to Oz. I didn't have much hope, as I was over the age – 45 – when I could be accepted for skilled migration and I had failed to meet the conditions of my business visa.

"You know, there is a way," said the consular official. "There's such a thing as a Distinguished Talent visa in cases where we feel the person has a special contribution to make to Australia."

"Oh," I said, "well my husband is a pianist. He's very talented. Maybe he could apply?"

"You have to show that you are internationally known," said the official. "I think you yourself might have a better chance."

I laughed at that, but applied anyway, and promptly forgot all about it. Summer was coming; Moscow life was getting good again.

The following winter, my depression returned. I lay on the divan and wallowed in self-pity. I tried to motivate myself with the old line that I had two arms and two legs for which to be grateful but it never really works, does it? Then I went out, fell on the ice and broke my shoulder, and my mood instantly soared. It was a breakthrough moment.

Actually, I was just a statistic in Moscow that year. We had an unseasonably warm January in 2009, with rain, followed by a plunge in temperature that led to the formation of sheets of black ice under the snow. Hospitals were groaning with fractured patients in the worst winter for fall cases in 30 years.

My own accident happened on a little incline outside my apartment block. The evening sky was purple with more snow to come. An inner voice said I should walk on the flat pavement but the hill offered a shortcut that of course I took. I was carrying a rucksack on my right shoulder, so when I slipped, I came crashing down on the left shoulder.

The immediate sensation was that my left arm no longer belonged to me; it was floating off somewhere in outer space. Then the pain kicked in, making me scream.

"Give me your good arm," said a passerby gruffly and dragged me to my feet. He walked off without any further inquiry into how badly I might be hurt. I stumbled to my doorway. A neighbour opened the metal door for me and carried my rucksack up the two flights of stairs to my flat, where she left me, again without asking how I was.

Once inside, I called my landlady, who happened to be head nurse of the local polyclinic. She arrived promptly with a driver. The question was where he should take me. I began ringing for help.

It was weird. Although only my arm was injured, I found I could not sit down. My whole body was betraying me. I made the phone calls, still standing up in my coat.

I was stupid enough to have gone for years without medical insurance, so I was going to have to pay cash for whatever treatment I needed. The switchboard woman at the American Medical Centre started listing prices before she asked what had happened to me. Even if I could have afforded the clinic, this attitude put me off.

Then I remembered that, 22 years ago, at my wedding to my first Russian husband, Costya, my mother had fallen on the ice and broken her wrist. She was well treated at the Botkin Hospital, which handled foreigners in those days.

"Will you take me to the Botkin please?" I asked the driver.

The Botkin is a city within a city. It took us ages to find the entrance to accident and emergency in the swirling snow.

The staff who registered me upon arrival said it was irregular that I had arrived by car, not by ambulance, and implied I was going to have problems because of this.

Nevertheless, I was sent for an X-ray. It showed that I had not just dislocated but actually broken my shoulder.

The doctor who then saw me was utterly indifferent, or perhaps dog tired. "We can't put a plaster cast on in that place," he said. "You need a cushion."

"Cushion, what cushion?"

He did a rough drawing and tossed it at me over the table, without further explanation.

"Do you want to make a complaint to the street-sweeping department of the city council?" he demanded.

"Hardly," I said, "the whole country's covered in snow."

He smiled at that and softened a little.

By this time, Vitaly had joined the scene and a good thing too. He had the presence of mind to ask if we could have my X-ray.

"Only if you apply for it in writing," said the doc.

Vitaly laid 2,000 roubles (then about 40 pounds, or 75 Australian dollars) on the table. The doc went and fetched the X-ray and gave it to us. Taking a bit more pity on me, he slung my arm up in a thin bandage. And he gave me a piece of paper. There was nothing more to do at that late hour than go home.

Later, I looked at the paper and saw it was to certify that I had refused to be hospitalised. Of course, I didn't want to be hospitalised but if they had ordered me to stay, I would not have refused. Now Vitaly and I were on our own, coping at home.

I passed a difficult night, waking up shuddering with shock. I think Vitaly suffered even more than I did. My groans terrified him.

The next morning, my landlady, the nurse, came back with a doctor from her polyclinic. He looked at the X-ray and declared my injury complicated because the bone had shattered, not broken cleanly. He tied me up in a stronger bandage, told me to take calcium tablets and aspirin against possible thrombosis and left without charging a kopeck. (Two days later, I was sorry to learn that this good doctor had himself ended up in plaster, having been hit by a car that skidded on the ice.)

I was learning what I could and could not do with one hand. Fortunately, after the initial shock, I could sit and stand, which meant that I could go to the toilet unaided. I could sponge-bath myself. I could type with my right hand. I could heat up pre-prepared food. I could stroke my cat. But I couldn't put my socks on.

I was now confined within four walls but I wasn't bored; rather I was exploring my new situation.

The evening before my accident, I'd had dinner with the travel writer Jeffrey Tayler, who was just about to publish his new book about the back roads between Moscow and Beijing. We had talked about the ultimate task for any author – writing about the inner journey. Now, with Jeff's book to keep me entertained in my armchair, I was going to have to practice what I preached about sitting still and travelling in inner space.

Meanwhile, Vitaly was investigating the matter of cushions. He found a specialised chemist's shop that sold walking sticks, support stockings, toe separators and other orthopaedic aids. What I needed, it turned out, was a special medical cushion that would hang round my neck, keep the shoulder in fixed position and allow me to rest my lower arm. It would be a bulky thing to wear but at least I would not be itching under a plaster cast.

"Oh, what a pity you won't have a pot," said Costya, with whom I'd remained friends despite our divorce. "We won't have anything to sign."

In a taxi, Vitaly took me to the chemist's to be fitted with the cushion.

"Who is the doctor treating you?" asked the man at the counter, a kindly Central Asian, I guessed probably Tajik.

"I don't have a doctor," I said.

So he took responsibility on himself and fitted the cushion for me. It turned out he was a qualified doctor, who happened to be working as a dispensing chemist. His name was Rustam Hailobekov. He took me into his underground clinic for guest workers and others who found themselves outside the official system.

His touch was gentle, he worked for an hour fitting the cushion expertly and he refused to take one kopeck more than the cost of the aid itself. He told me I had a 50-50 chance that my bones would reassemble and grow back naturally. Otherwise, I would need an operation to put a metal pin in the joint.

"You will need another set of X-rays to check that I have positioned the arm properly," he said.

Back at home, the phone was ringing off the hook with big-hearted Russian friends offering all manner of practical help and advice. My 53rd birthday was a magical day when I was showered with love and counted my blessings. Vitaly gave me blue hyacinths that filled the flat with their perfume.

One Russian Orthodox friend came round to offer sympathy and counsel. She said broken bones never happened just like that but were always a sign from God that somehow or other you were on the wrong track and needed to rethink your life. That upset me a bit until my Yorkshire father said: "Don't be daft. God's not sitting up on a cloud, thinking 'today I'll strike Helen'." Another Russian friend suggested the universe was telling me to get out of a country with too much 'snow, ice and crap'.

In my pain, I was of course taking stock of my life but the conclusion I came to was that I knew myself well enough and should just go on doing all the things I had been doing, but with renewed vigour and no more depression. I vowed to further consolidate my home life, travel more and seize every opportunity that came my way.

'Cushion' was not perhaps the right word to describe the object hanging round my neck and depriving me of a decent night's sleep. It was more like a piece of luggage that I could not put down or a minstrel's drum. Fortunately it was black, as was the tee shirt I had been wearing when it was fitted and could not now remove for at least a month.

This gave me an idea. For years in Moscow, music had been a serious hobby. Before my fall, I'd been due to sing in a concert with a string quartet. I suddenly saw no reason to cancel it. My arm might be immobilised but I could stand up straight and breathe and I was in good voice, with a black costume ready-made. I decided I would go ahead and try to perform.

I was singing the role of Cornelia from Handel's *Guilio Cesare in Egitto*. Cornelia, the widow of Pompey, is presented with the head of her murdered husband on a plate. Her son Sesto is taken away by the army. In an aria of total despair, she sings that she is deprived of all comfort and cannot even commit suicide.

Before my accident, I couldn't get into the role without making it sound like Monty Python. But now I felt vulnerable enough to become Cornelia; I knew what injury felt like.

My vocal coach and singing partner, the Dutch soprano Henriette Schenk, came round to work with me. The string quartet also gathered in my small flat for a rehearsal and I took revenge on neighbours who'd disturbed me with their drunken fights and karaoke sessions. The rehearsal went well and we decided I would take part in the concert.

But first I had to go back for more X-rays and a check-up with Rustam.

Vitaly was busy, so Costya took his turn taking me to hospital. The

X-rays showed that Rustam had done his job brilliantly and that my shoulder was healing naturally.

"Can I take the cushion off now?" I asked.

"Oh no, not yet," said Rustam, refitting and tightening it. While he did this, his nine-year-old son made a pencil drawing of me, very life-like, with a determined if not grim expression on my face.

"Cheer up," said Costya and invited me to spend a couple of weeks with him on holiday in Goa when I got better. Vitaly said of course I should go. You see what I mean about my blessings?

The day of the concert arrived. The sky was bright blue, which meant the frost was hard and conditions underfoot would be slippery. Friends drove me to the 18th century estate where the event was taking place. I was wrapped in a blanket because I couldn't get my arm into my coat sleeve. I was an odd-looking diva, to say the least.

Frankly, the concert did not go well. Henriette and I sang a good duet and received bouquets and shouts of 'bravo'. But when it came to my aria, the string quartet and I parted company and the result was rather cacophonous. The audience was forgiving.

I should have felt terrible but in fact I didn't. I knew there had been nothing wrong with my vocal technique. It was just that we hadn't rehearsed enough. I fell off the horse and got straight back on. I resumed practising the aria and fixed new rehearsals with the quartet for as soon as I was well again.

And then came the real breakthrough that my broken shoulder had evidently been heralding all along.

A couple of days after the less-than-fabulous concert, I opened my emails to find a letter from the Australian immigration service. I'd forgotten all about my application for a Distinguished Talent visa but here they were, telling me that I'd been awarded one. The great thing was that it applied to my spouse as well, meaning that Vitaly and I had the green light to go Down Under together and try to make a new life for ourselves.

A is for Adelaide

Vitaly and I were under no illusion about our special gifts, or so we honestly believed. We did know we were lucky; that to receive permission to migrate to Oz in middle age was like winning the lottery. I assumed the reason an exception had been made for us was that I'd shown something of a commitment to remote Australia. But I couldn't hope to drag my piano-playing husband to the outback; he needed a city.

Where were we to go? We both reckoned that Sydney, while very attractive of course, would probably be too expensive for us. The rents in smaller cities might be more reachable while we both looked for work.

"What about Adelaide?" I said.

"Yes, it begins with the letter A," said Vitaly.

So, daft as it sounds, we chose Adelaide because it began with the first letter of the alphabet. We read up on it and learnt that it had a Mediterranean climate and wineries. It seemed we'd made a good choice.

As soon as I had recovered sufficiently from my shoulder injury to travel, I flew to Budapest to consult a vet about my cat, Jack Pantera, going into EU quarantine prior to being transported to Australia. Blackjack would have to be caged and carried as cargo on the long-haul flight. He wasn't going to like the journey, that was for sure.

In Budapest, I swam at the thermal spas, which did wonders for my shoulder. The vet also gave me some horse gel to rub into the arm muscle, which had a fantastic effect. That was the extent of my physiotherapy. I'd been treated by a Tajik doctor, using the most old-fashioned methods, and a Hungarian vet, and I was as good as new.

In Moscow, all that remained was to hold a farewell concert and a round or two of leaving parties and to pack my suitcase, a new grey one on wheels. As it was June, and I would be heading into the Australian winter, I threw a couple of jumpers and a raincoat into the case. I was going ahead of Vitaly, who would stay a while longer at his job in Moscow, to find work and a place for us to live in Adelaide.

I flew via Bangkok and Sydney. On arrival in Adelaide, I was met at the airport by my friend Wayne Anthoney, who immediately took me to lunch at his old boys' club. The food was excellent, although I felt a little out of place among the retired accountants and lawyers, all men.

Wayne himself was little changed, except that he'd swapped his bush hat and khaki for a suit and tie. He'd moved from his caravan at Uluru to resume his family life in South Australia. As he was living with his wife Meredith in the coastal town of Willunga, his flat in the city was free and he said I was welcome to borrow it until I could find work and a home of my own. Such is the generosity of the Aussies.

Wayne's apartment, in a colourful 'eco village' right in the middle of town, was very pleasant but I knew I should not make myself too comfortable there. I immediately started looking for a job and within a few days, though my friend Sharon Mascall Dare, managed to get the promise of some casual work, teaching journalism at one of the local universities when the new semester started in July.

The money wasn't great but I'd taken on board my father's advice that I should be 'willing to start at the bottom', so I happily accepted the deal. The environment sounded very nice and I looked forward to teaching students outdoors on a campus where koalas regularly came down to the lawns.

The next thing was to find a house, with enough space so that Vitaly could make music, I could have peace and quiet and the landlord would accept a cat. I began surfing the net and on an estate agent's site soon found a two-storey townhouse, which fitted the bill and was surprisingly cheap. It would be affordable, provided Vitaly also got a job and we had two incomes coming in. Meanwhile, I had savings to cover a deposit and rent for a few months.

I phoned the mobile number given and was answered at the other end by a man claiming to be in London. He spoke English very poorly, with an African accent. He said I could see the house only after I had transferred money to his bank. The suspiciously low price should have alerted me. Of course, this was a scam.

The conman had downloaded real pictures of a real house from a real and reputable Adelaide estate agent's website but altered the price to lure the naïve. I phoned the realtors to tell them their property had been misappropriated and the manager asked me to come in and see him.

"We're very grateful to you for tipping us off about this," he said. "How can we help you?"

I explained our needs and also that our budget was limited.

"I see," he said. "Well, our own managing director has a house that he is looking to rent out. It's in the suburb of Marryatville. I think he would be glad to have such decent tenants."

I knew Marryatville was salubrious, up market and expensive; way out of our league, surely? But the rent offered was hardly more than the townhouse would have cost.

"There is just one other consideration," I said.

"Yes?" said the manager.

"We would need permission to keep a cat."

"I think we can allow that."

"Great. When can I see it?

"Now," said the manager, and he drove me out to number 11B Clapton Road, a semi-detached house behind high, cream-painted gates.

Inside, the house was spacious and light. True, the atmosphere was a little like that of a hotel but if we put away all the artificial flowers and filled it with our own things, it would soon start to feel like home. There was also a garden with outdoor table and chairs and fuchsias that spilled over onto the path.

"Thank you very much," I said. "We'll be very grateful to have this." I informed Vitaly, who started to make his plans to join me. He found a cheap flight via China and we began counting the weeks until we saw each other again.

Meanwhile – and with the necessary groundwork done in Adelaide – I saw no reason why I shouldn't escape to my beloved Alice Springs. By happy coincidence, the BBC expressed interest in a story for radio about Aboriginal art. There was something of a scandal, as an Aboriginal politician had said that some Aboriginal art should not be shown to the public. They wanted me to go up and investigate.

How wonderful it would be to return to the mesmerising, vibrating, Red Centre. It was six years since I'd last seen my friends in Alice and I was keen to catch up with them again. I was also curious to see what, if anything, had changed in society since two important political developments had taken place.

One was the official apology to indigenous people for the abuses they'd suffered since white settlement, made in parliament by then Prime Minister Kevin Rudd in 2008, which in theory should have eased any racial tensions. The other was the government's decision in 2007 to intervene in supposedly dysfunctional Aboriginal communities not only with an army of social workers but with the army itself, which had led to howls of protest.

In Adelaide, before I set off, I watched Warwick Thornton's beautiful but grim new film, *Samson and Delilah*, which opened with shots of an Aboriginal teenager playing in a wheelchair and ended with him sitting it in for real, permanently handicapped because of the brain damage done by glue sniffing.

Mixing Up the Colours

My first port of call whenever I went to Alice Springs was always the Daily Grind café, where I was sure to meet my friend and fellow journalist Dave Richards. Along with an injection of caffeine, I got a succinct update on all that had been happening in my absence and was soon back in the loop. To my delight, I learnt that Dave had carried the *BushMag* idea forward and was successfully running his own news website, called *AliceOnline*.

"And what are you up to?" he asked me.

"I'm doing a report on Aboriginal art for the BBC," I said. "Not sure where to start."

"Why don't you go and see the Emily Kngwarreye?" he suggested. "It's just sold for a million dollars."

So I walked over to the Mbantua Gallery, where the painting, entitled *Earth's Creation*, was on display.

I was a bit disappointed to see that the gallery, having spent a record amount to acquire the work, was showing it to poor advantage. The picture was roped off in a small room and thus managed to be both inaccessible and too in-your-face at the same time. It needed the space of a larger hall so it could be viewed from a distance. But despite this, the painting itself glowed, buzzed and danced with life.

I got talking with a student, who was working at the gallery. "When you look at the painting," she said, "and you see Emily's use of white on green, with the red and brown next to it, you can really see the famous white gums and the brown dirt, and the spinifex and all the blue skies that never end. I think it's a great interpretation of our landscape."

It was, and I went away feeling cheered that positive things were happening on the Aboriginal scene.

Everywhere I looked, there seemed to be Aboriginal galleries, a real explosion of indigenous art. A lot of it was tacky stuff for the tourists but the dot-painting movement had developed to produce some world-class contemporary paintings and the galleries were promoting them.

Some art shops were privately owned while others were cooperatives belonging to the painters themselves. The gallery owners tended to be secretive while the artists, many of whom lived on remote communities and didn't necessarily speak English, were hard to interview.

"You won't get people to talk easily," one gallery owner told me. "Good artists are like prima donnas and the galleries are very protective of them."

Stuck, I went back and drank some more coffee with Dave.

"Go and see the people at Many Hands," he advised.

It was a good move to visit the Ngurratjuta Iltja Ntjarra (Many Hands) Art Centre, where both the white administrators and Aboriginal artists were open and friendly. The centre was financed from royalties paid to Aboriginal people in compensation for oil and gas extraction on their traditional lands. The artists were bussed into the centre for their day's painting and provided with lunch. To some extent, I understood, the centre fulfilled a social as well as a creative function.

The manager, Anna McKenzie, showed me a small gallery hung with luminous watercolours by descendants of the great Aboriginal watercolourist, Albert Namatjira. Other painters at the centre worked in naïve, dot and contemporary styles and their canvasses were sold not only to tourists in Alice Springs but also to galleries all over Australia.

"The artists are encouraged to do those paintings that buyers want," she said, "to keep the quality there, not just to do them quickly, for money. It can be a slow process but a rewarding one in the end."

Contemporary works were the most sought after but even there, Anna said, if you looked carefully, you could always see the traditional symbols and references to Dreamtime stories among the abstract patterns. Some artists and buyers still preferred the old ochre colours but the use of non-traditional blues, greens and purples was becoming widespread and accepted.

"When you've got lovely colours available to you, why not use them?" said Anna, who was herself an artist.

Anna took me to meet one of the Aboriginal artists and I sat down on the ground with Pansy Napamari as she showed me her red and white, and white and brown dot paintings.

"My Uncle Johnny, he learn me painting," she said. "I was watching my uncle, 'Uncle, learn me, can I do a painting?'

"'Yeah, yeah, you, you,' he said. I was drawing. Brush. After that I started painting. After drawing I learn about doing the dot.

"This is my country, my mother's and my uncle's Dreaming. That's why I do sometimes double colours, white first and after that red."

"Is it daytime or night?" I asked.

"Teatime!" said Pansy. "Gotta put a red and a white. That's why I do it my way. And a white and a black, white and brown."

Pansy said she liked traditional Aboriginal colours but would also use other tints and shades. "Anything I can do, yep, when I see colour, mix it up!"

Then Pansy began to whisper, telling me that some subjects she would never paint because they were too private. Pansy came from the settlement of Papunya, west of Alice Springs, and was related to some of the male artists from that community who'd been there at the very start of the dot-painting movement.

I realised we were getting close to the subject of forbidden art, which was what the BBC was really interested in. How come Northern Territory Indigenous Affairs Minister Alison Anderson had said that some paintings, kept in the vaults of a museum up in Darwin, should not be exhibited to the general public?

I needed a real expert and luckily the historian Dick Kimber agreed to see me. He was a kind old gentleman, who lived in a bungalow up an

Alice Springs backstreet. Over tea, he told me the extraordinary history of Papunya art.

Aboriginal people, as I was well aware, had painted and drawn for many thousands of years but their rock art had been vulnerable to the elements. It was not until a white school teacher called Geoffrey Bardon arrived in Papunya in the 1970s, bringing with him stacks of masonite boards, that the tribesmen were able to record symbols they'd previously only drawn in the sand or painted on their own bodies. The patterns and images thus became permanent and possibly saleable for the first time.

Painting for Bardon in the absence of their womenfolk and with no idea that the images might reach a wider audience, the men gave away male ceremonial secrets so powerful that in the past, women could have been killed for seeing them. These earliest icons, the original Papunya boards, were now held in the Museum and Art Gallery of the Northern Territory and the discussion as to whether or not they should be exhibited was understandable, Mr. Kimber said.

Later, of course, Aboriginal artists began to omit things they didn't want outsiders to see – not only sexual secrets but also geographical details they might not have wanted other Aboriginal tribes to know. I was fascinated to learn that one reason why dots and bright splashes of colour were often used was to cover up secrets hidden underneath.

I noticed that Mr. Kimber had two early Papunya paintings on his walls, although not the controversial ones. I imagined they were priceless.

"There's a universal view," he said, "that old paintings are worth a lot more than new ones but when I bought these, I didn't have the intent of making a fortune.

"This one here cost me 400 dollars. It's a very plain black background, with a goanna painted in a stylised form. Its tongue is extended right out and follows round the edges of the painting. In the middle, there's a circle with two little boys in it. And it was painted with deliberate intent that there would be public viewing. Geoff Bardon had said 'we want children's stories that can be shown to anyone'."

I could have sat for hours, listening to this kindly and expert man. He talked a little about the subsequent development of Aboriginal art. Sadly, he said, it was now more often Aboriginal women than men who painted for the simple reason that male life expectancy in the desert was lower than women's because of alcohol abuse and dangerous driving.

And although they painted on paper and canvas, Aboriginal people still drew in the sand, like their ancestors.

"Both men and women do a great deal of drawing on the sand," he said. "It's a desert thing to do – sit opposite one another and sketch, particularly words and meanings. They're often tapping with a little stick and they draw with their fingers in the soft sand. They're constantly drawing and then they sweep it away. So you're telling a story. You don't have to be speaking; you're just drawing all the time.

"The men do that, but I don't think nearly as much as the women do. The men can do all that because they grew up as children with their mothers and aunties looking after them. But the women seem to develop it much more. They can do it rapidly and wonderfully well, these images. It's just like writing but it disappears instantly, and there's no sense of permanence to this world."

The Big Jump

From Alice Springs, I went to Sydney to meet Vitaly, who was making what he called his 'big jump' from Moscow. I had a day or two in hand and managed a trip to the Blue Mountains, which were beautiful but cold in July, before Vitaly landed at Kingsford Smith Airport.

Waiting in arrivals, I wore a pink cowboy hat as a disguise. "Unrecognisable," said Vitaly drily, spotting me instantly in the crowd. We hugged. He'd come on a punishing flight, with a nine-hour stopover in Beijing, and a change in Shanghai, but he looked as fresh as a daisy.

"I slept in Beijing," he said. "So, what are our plans?"

We went into the city on a double-decker metro train, posed by the Opera House and got a bite to eat. Vitaly was ecstatic as we strolled round the sunlit harbour and peeked into the botanical gardens. "It's fabulous," he said. "I never want to go back to Russia."

That same evening, we had to be at the domestic terminal for the flight to Adelaide, and still he said he wasn't tired.

Of course he slept long and deeply when we finally got home. When he woke the next morning, he seemed happy with the new house.

"Two toilets?" he said. "And all these rooms for the same price you'd pay for a one-room flat in Moscow."

"Check out the garden," I said. "We can have our coffee outside. It's not that cold."

Actually, it was nearly as cold inside the house as it was outside. It can come as a shock to Russians, used to the suffocating central heating that offsets their sub-zero winters, when they find themselves having to wear jumpers indoors. Vitaly tried not to complain.

We spent the first few days after his arrival just wandering around the neighbourhood, looking into people's gardens. I'd become somewhat accustomed to Oz but now I was seeing it through Vitaly's fresh eyes. We stared at the parrots on the flowering eucalyptus and marvelled at how daffodils and lemon trees, roses and lavender, all bloomed and fruited at the same time. "I don't understand the seasons here at all," he said.

Vitaly was nervous of spiders and indeed, on one of these early walks, he did get bitten by something that fell on him from a tree and made his arm tingle. "Probably an ant," I said. "Don't worry about it. You're more likely to fall under a bus than die from a creepy crawly."

"But what about sharks?" he said. "And crocodiles?"

The new university term started and I began dressing in a suit three times a week and walking up the hill to tutor students. I fell into the habit of having a flat white and an apricot biscuit in the café before classes. One day, on a notice board, I saw an advert for an artist's studio in a warehouse in Port Adelaide that was being offered for the ridiculous rent of 35 dollars a month. I decided to take it, as I thought I might be glad of solitude from time to time and the chance to do a bit of painting.

Home alone, while I was out at work, Vitaly was settling in, making pans of borscht (Russian beetroot soup). He discovered Woolworths down the road and shopped for lamb and avocadoes and camembert. He liked cooking and for a while seemed satisfied to mess about in the kitchen. But we both knew his holiday couldn't last.

It was Wayne Anthoney and his wife Meredith who helped Vitaly to get a start with work in Adelaide. Rather mysteriously, they invited us to spend the weekend with them at their house in Willunga. Unsure what to expect, we took a bus out there on the Friday night.

The next day, we ate oysters at the local market and walked on the beach; in the distance we even saw some whales. We admired Meredith's achievements in the garden. It seemed like a social visit.

But Meredith was putting a lot of effort into making an orange and almond cake and on the Sunday, we found out why. She and Wayne had invited an influential man to come and hear Vitaly play the piano.

"Oh no, it feels like an exam," he whispered to me in the bedroom. "Get out there and do your worst."

Of course, he passed the test easily.

Nothing came of it immediately but a few days later, Vitaly got a call from the Elder Conservatorium of Music, asking if he would accompany a New Zealand tenor in a master class he was giving. Now Vitaly had a foot in the door at 'The Con', which was notoriously difficult to infiltrate.

"It's only a one-off job," said Vitaly, worried that he had no contract, unlike me with my slightly firmer arrangement at the university.

"Never mind," I said, "it might lead to something."

Working with singers was what Vitaly did best, as he'd specialised in accompanying vocalists back in Moscow. The tenor, a former star called Patrick Power, who in his day had sung in European opera houses and shared a stage with Dame Kiri Te Kanawa, liked Vitaly and introduced him to other teachers at The Con. It looked as if things were going to work out magically for us.

We celebrated with a visit to Penfolds Winery, which was in convenient walking distance from our house.

It was a cool winter day. I dressed in my South American 'multi-coloured dream coat', something I wouldn't have been seen dead in in Europe but that seemed fitting in Oz, and Vitaly put a padded shirt over his jumper for the walk up the hill. We nipped the lavender bushes as we went and noticed that birch trees grew among the oranges and lemons.

Once inside the winery, we were shown the cellars, with noble old barrels, stained pink with years of use. Vitaly's face glowed as he inspected row upon row of sleeping bottles. We learnt about Penfolds' pride and joy, a wine called Grange Hermitage, created by vinter Max Edmund Schubert. A Barossa Valley German, he went to France in the

1950s and brought back to Australia the secrets of aging wine that he learnt in the Bordeaux region.

Prices for Grange ranged from 600 to 1,500 dollars and were beyond our meagre budget but we bought two bottles of Tawny, a delicious sweet port that we took home in triumph.

"To you!"

"To you!" we clinked glasses, and planned some more excursions.

Adelaide nestled, or rather sprawled, between hills and sea. From the shore you could see the hills and from the hills you could see the sea.

Meredith had recommended a place called Largs, so we went out there for a day and walked on the rather bleak, windswept beach. The café where we had fish and chips sticks in my memory for the honesty of its owners and customers. I forgot my umbrella there – an expensive one that belonged to our landlord – and when we went back, it was still propped by the door, waiting for me.

"No one nicked it?" said Vitaly.

On another sunnier day, we went up into the Adelaide Hills. Vitaly had already walked through housing estates to the foothills and suspected there was a path that led up to the heights. That day we found it and climbed through fields of delicate orange flowers that locals identified as the weed sparaxis. From the top, we could see the whole city laid out before us and beyond that, the sparkling sea.

We'd made it into Cleland National Park, where we had a good chance of seeing koalas. Vitaly was the first to spot one. "Up there," he whispered.

Sure enough, there was one of the lazy, loveable creatures, its fat bum lodged in the fork of a gum tree.

"How do they manage not to fall?"

"He looks well wedged in, if you ask me."

We stared up at it for ages. It was one thing to see these animals in zoos but quite another to find them in the wild.

Inspired, I dashed off one of my naïve paintings, entitled *Communing with a Koala*, and showed it to Vitaly when I took him to see my art studio out in Port Adelaide. The sun was so strong that day that we had to wrap our jumpers round our heads and as we walked through the glare, we looked like Tuareg tribesmen, lost in an industrial zone.

Separately from Vitaly, and on another occasion, I went to a rehearsal of a local choir, where I met a woman called Rachel Evans. She was married to a man called Michael and had a brother called Mike.

Rachel and Michael lent me a bike but I felt uncertain in the Adelaide traffic and returned it. Then Mike lent us a car but we couldn't afford the insurance, so it sat on the drive, unused. Rachel also came round to our house with a second-hand keyboard for Vitaly.

"It's no good," he said. "It's a child's keyboard. There aren't enough notes on it for me to play Rachmaninov. We'll have to give it back."

Vitaly was initially suspicious of Rachel, Michael and Mike but I understood they were being genuinely kind. They were sketching in the kind of life we could have in Australia. It was up to us to achieve it.

It All Goes Pear-Shaped

From childhood, Vitaly had been crazy about trams. He'd had an aunt who was a tram driver and allowed him to 'drive' hers when he was a little boy. This experience had led to a lifelong passion. So naturally he was delighted to learn that Adelaide had trams.

One day, we saw an advert in *The Adelaide Advertiser*. The tram company was looking for trainee tram drivers.

"Actually, driving a tram was the only other thing I could ever see myself doing, apart from playing the piano," he said.

"Well, apply for the job then," I said, jokingly.

I didn't expect him to fill in the application but he did.

"State your experience of driving heavy vehicles," the form said.

"Grand piano," he wrote.

He put the application in the post. I realised part of him seriously hoped to get the job because it would mean a good salary.

While we waited for an answer from the tram company, we went riding on the city's trams, whenever possible sitting up at the front to get a driver's-eye view.

"What is it exactly that so attracts you to trams?" I asked.

"It's hard to explain. It's the smooth movement on the line, like legato in music, I guess."

For me, trams suggested something else. Even when they went round a bend, so the way ahead was hidden, they never deviated from the line. Like fate; horribly final.

Vitaly didn't get the job at the tram company. Instead, the conservatorium kept ringing him up with small jobs. Students found out he was available and started phoning as well. Soon his diary was filling up with appointments but all of it was freelance work; 100 dollars here, 50 dollars there. What he really wanted was the security of a contract.

One evening, he came home in a very black mood, having accompanied a wretched performer in a run-down club. Another time, he was sunk in despair because a student hadn't paid him and he felt it was beneath his dignity to have to chase her for the money. All his life in the Soviet Union and Russia, he'd been used to a wage that might have been low but at least was regular.

"And what we will do through the long summer holidays, when the semester ends?" he asked. I had no answer to that.

We had a couple of stupid rows, bizarrely one over which language we should speak. In Moscow, we had always spoken a mixture of Russian and English and this bi-lingual life made us multi-faceted. Now Vitaly, desperate to succeed in his new world, wanted to speak English, only English.

This upset me to an irrational degree. It wasn't just that I feared losing my Russian through lack of practice, although that was a concern. More, it was that Vitaly was subtly different when he spoke Russian and I feared losing that part of him. When he spoke English, it was as if he was wearing a suit; when he spoke Russian, he was in his raggy home clothes. I experienced a loss of intimacy and couldn't understand why he wanted to cut off one of his arms – one of my arms – when we had two.

Worrying news came in from Moscow. The people with whom I had left my cat Jack – because I wasn't going to put him through quarantine in Budapest until I was absolutely sure there was a stable place for him in Australia – rang to say that he was behaving badly and they couldn't cope with him anymore.

In desperation, I emailed friends in Moscow to see if anyone else might be willing to take Jack. It seemed hopeless but eventually one loyal soul did come to the rescue.

Almost simultaneously, Megg Kelham in Alice Springs emailed to say she had a friend who was looking for a cat sitter so she could go away for the summer. Reckoning that one good deed deserved another, I put my hand up for that job. The person in need was a woman called Maya Cifali and her cat was called Momo.

"At least our problem with the summer holidays is sorted," I said to Vitaly. "We can go up to Alice Springs and house-sit with a cat until the next semester starts in Adelaide." He didn't seem very keen on that idea.

"We've got to stay positive," I said.

"Let's have a party then," said Vitaly.

So we invited Patrick Power and his wife and children and Sharon Mascall Dare and her husband and kids to thank them for giving us a leg up on the work ladder in Adelaide. The menu was shepherd's pie – and we made far too much, so that we ended up eating shepherd's pie for a week afterwards – but the company was good and we had a jolly time.

"How's it going at the uni?" Sharon asked me.

It was going OK, I suppose.

The students were pleasant and responsive. Some of them were more promising than others but all were keen to be journalists and obviously frustrated at having to sit in the classroom, talking about the profession instead of practising it.

I suspected the school system hadn't served them well. They were shocked when I failed them in some tests but came to learn that my distinctions meant something. Word got round that 'Helen actually reads our homework'. Staffroom feedback was that I could be 'too harsh'.

One young man in particular astonished me. He was writing his CV. Like many of the others, he'd put down that he followed sports, especially Australian rules football.

"Can you think of anything else?" I asked.

"Well, I do speak Japanese," he said.

"Well, for heaven's sake, put that down too."

It seemed he was afraid of looking like a tall poppy but after I encouraged him, he went on to write a very fine project about China.

No, there was nothing wrong with the students. Rather, it was the culture of mediocrity that worried me. Or perhaps I just wasn't enough of an academic to teach journalism. I guess I too still wanted to go out and do it, not talk about it.

To my further chagrin, I discovered that while my hourly rate for teaching looked generous, I was expected to do a massive amount of unpaid marking. Staff and casuals lived on different planets. Despite Australia's promise of a 'fair go', I sensed the best jobs were reserved for long-standing locals, which was understandable, if disheartening for a newcomer. Still, I hadn't totally lost hope and was hanging in at the uni.

What I hadn't told anybody, even Vitaly, was that out in my art studio in Port Adelaide, I was comforting myself by hanging up old pictures I'd painted back in Moscow. I was suffering from what I thought was light nostalgia, which was why I was totally unprepared for the tsunami of homesickness that suddenly hit me.

Vitaly was out. He'd gone to see Patrick at the conservatorium. I was sitting at my desk at home, writing an exercise for the students. It was a 'breaking news' story about how a plane had gone missing from radar; how it had been found crashed in India; how it had emerged that a Bollywood star was on board; how it had further emerged that the Australian cricket team was on board; how in the end it turned out that one Indian child had survived.

It was an exercise in updating news and finding the right priorities for the relevant readerships. Of course in Oz, the fate of the cricket team would trump the miracle of the Indian child's survival. I finished this work of genius and broke down in floods of tears.

Like a vision, I saw all that I was missing in Russia – dear friends; my beloved cat; meaningful work in the field, not the classroom; golden-domed churches; the birch woods in May; old architecture; galleries and concerts; the handle on the door to my singing teacher's house. Yes, it sounds ridiculous, but I saw this ornate, carved door handle, hanging in the air like some Dickensian ghost.

For relief, I ran out of the house. The last thing I expected was to bump into Vitaly, who was walking up the street with a grin on his face, having just enjoyed lunch at the con with Patrick and some other colleagues. He was horrified when he saw me.

"What on earth is the matter?" he asked. "Has someone died?"

"I want to go home," I wailed.

"Where's home?"

"Moscow."

Vitaly was derailed by my outburst, although later he admitted I'd only expressed what he too had been feeling behind a fixed smile. We didn't give up immediately but since we'd allowed the poison of doubt to enter our minds, we started seeing reasons to leave Adelaide.

At the uni, I made half-hearted inquiries about the possibility of going back for a second semester. Vitaly saw a senior woman at the con, who told him he could be the 'King of Adelaide' if he freelanced for five years but there wasn't going to be a permanent contract for him.

I came into the kitchen one morning to find Vitaly on the phone, speaking in Russian. He was checking that his staff job at the state concert agency Mosconcert was still open for him. He hadn't, in fact, resigned from this old job and could return to it, providing he made it back to Moscow by the 8th of December.

We went out and booked an air ticket for him to Russia. He'd made his big leap but as it turned out, it was a bungee jump, with a thick rubber band pulling him in.

We'd made the mistake of Orpheus, given the chance to recover Euridice from the Underworld providing he didn't look back. We had turned for that fatal glance backwards.

Making the Most of It

We felt very ashamed when we told the Australian friends who'd supported us of our decision to go home. We were afraid they thought us ungrateful; not distinguished talents at all but just a pair of prissy whingers, snootily up themselves. We had fallen at the first hurdle.

Vitaly was going back. I had less reason to return immediately – I'd given up my flat and work in Moscow and made a promise to look after a cat in Alice Springs over the summer holidays – but eventually I too would be heading to Russia. Meanwhile, I thought, we should have fun.

"Look," I said, "I'm going to spend the summer in Alice. Why don't you come with me to see the red desert before you go back to Moscow? We have a whole week between the end of the semester and your flight from Sydney. You could see Uluru. It's a once-in-a-lifetime chance."

As soon as we'd made all these plans, life started to look up. With clarity about the path forward, we were able to make the most of the time left to us in Adelaide and appreciate the beauty of the place. We even started to enjoy our jobs better.

Vitaly, in particular, got a good opportunity at the con. He'd been interviewed some weeks earlier by the strings tutor, who'd glanced at his CV and said: "Well, you look great on paper but let's see how you play." Vitaly must have played well enough because now this man was asking him to accompany his most promising violin student in a fiendishly difficult sonata by Richard Strauss. It was an experience that stretched both the student and Vitaly himself.

Vitaly benefited from something else at the con, too. He saw that the demanding Soviet approach in teaching, where you basically only praise anyone after they're dead, was not always as effective as the

Western way of telling a student: 'Well, that was very nice but…' This knowledge he was to carry back to Russia and use to great effect with a new generation of students there.

Meanwhile in Adelaide, the weather was warming up, enabling us to dine out in our backyard.

"Hey look, there's a possum on the fence," I said.

There was, and we called him Petya, and fed him slices of apple when he came to visit us on repeated, balmy evenings when we sat out and drank wine in the yard.

Swimming was also on the agenda. For the locals, it was still too cold but we were happy to swim lengths in the empty, open-air, Olympic-sized Burnside Pool; delirious pleasure.

"I want to swim in the sea," said Vitaly.

So we took the tram down to Glenelg but that didn't quite satisfy him. The beach was too crowded; there were too many people eating ice creams and queuing for the Rodney Fox Shark Experience.

"I'm dreaming of a wild beach," he said, "we where can go nude."

"Not sure where we can find that," I said.

Instead, we walked along the banks of the Torrens River, admiring the black swans, their ruffled feathers like the petals of black tulips. And we went up again into the hills.

In the gum groves, we heard the most terrible sound, like a motorbike engine revving up. It was the mating cry of the koala and we saw quite a few of them, high in the trees. Heavy rain had filled the gullies, creating waterfalls, and everywhere were clumps of white calla lilies. To top it all, Vitaly saw his first kangaroo, a huge grey male that just stood on the path in front of us and watched us for ages. Only when a party of noisy schoolchildren came along did it hop off into the undergrowth.

Back in town, the city was starting to look its best, as the jacaranda trees came out in purple flower. We could have filled a whole photo album with all the pictures we took of the jacaranda in bloom around the conservatory. The con looked refined as an Oxford college, although one stormy day it reminded me more of a Scottish castle, with flags flying against a dramatic sky.

And still Vitaly wanted to find a nudist beach. It was Rachel Evans's brother Mike, the bloke who'd lent us a car, who helped us. Since we were not driving the car ourselves, he kindly offered to drive us out to a place called Maslin Beach, where nude bathing was allowed.

Mike was a quiet chap, a farmer who was struggling with various problems to keep his farm going. He seemed to enjoy the madness of our company. He took us over an idyllic landscape of fields and valleys to reach Maslin, where a turquoise sea lapped against ochre-coloured cliffs.

We stripped off and cavorted in the water while Mike sat fully dressed in the shade, not, I think, from prudishness but rather from a healthy respect for the Australian sun at midday. There were no sharks in the shallows, although there could have been. Mike pointed out a snake slithering near the cliffs, where we laid out our towels afterwards and shared a picnic.

Once Mike had shown us the road to Maslin, we were keen to return there under our own steam. We found we could take a train as far as Noarlunga, and then a bus, and then walk the rest of the way. We had a splendid day, just the two of us, swimming, sunbathing and photographing each other in front of a sign at the end of the nudist section of the beach that said: 'Clothes must be worn beyond this point.'

We had such a blast that we left it rather late to start our return to Adelaide. We found ourselves standing by the roadside in the dark, praying that a bus would come. Luckily, one did.

Thus, when it came to planning Vitaly's 50th birthday, which we intended to celebrate on Maslin Beach, we decided not to be dependent on the evening bus timetable. We'd go out there in the afternoon, watch the sun set and the stars come out, spend the night on the beach and wake up to another day of pleasure in the sun. What could go wrong?

We took our towels, two thin bed sheets and a watermelon. What we hadn't reckoned on was the bitterly cold Antarctic wind that blew off the sea during the night, which we spent huddled together, shivering, our teeth chattering.

As soon as the sun came up, it was baking hot again. Vitaly went off down the beach, looking for rock pools. He found his own private pool and stretched out in it for most of the morning. When he returned at lunchtime, he was as red as the lobster we were having in our sandwiches.

"Have you seen yourself?" I said. "The reflection from the pool must have intensified the sunburn."

I slathered him in UV protection cream but it was a bit late for 'slip, slop, slap' (slip on a shirt, slop on the sunscreen and slap on a hat, as Sid the Seagull advised in a famous skin-cancer prevention campaign).

Red and sore though he was, Vitaly went home happy. He'd experienced the full force of the wind, sea and sun and reckoned he couldn't have had a better gift for his jubilee. Indeed, once his sunburn eased, he would have been up for another trip to Maslin, except that our time in Adelaide was running out.

The academic and musical season was over. We were packing our suitcases for our trip to the Red Centre before Vitaly returned to Moscow. As a special treat for Vitaly, who loved trains as well as trams, I'd booked us tickets on the legendary Ghan.

On the last morning, we tidied up the house at 11B Clapton Road and swept the backyard. Vitaly was cleaning the outdoor table, where we'd sat for many a meal and glass of wine. Suddenly he went very quiet.

"Come over here," he hissed. "Look, a redback."

Sure enough, hanging on a thread under the table, was one of the deadly spiders he'd read about in his encyclopedia.

"And we were sitting here all the time," he said.

"Yeah, but it didn't bite us though, did it?" I said. "Come on, let's finish packing. The taxi will be here soon. You're going to love the red hot desert."

Red Hot Disaster

The journey on the Ghan did not turn out to be the wonderful, romantic experience I had planned. Short of money, we couldn't afford the expensive sleeper berths, so we sat up all night in cattle class. Vitaly was happy enough for the first couple of hours, watching the flat yellow fields outside Adelaide gradually rise to become the tawny Flinders Ranges. But then numb bum syndrome set in.

The seats really were incredibly uncomfortable, as if they'd been designed for people who were dwarves from the waist down and giants from the waist up. Our heads didn't reach the headrests while our legs were impossibly cramped.

"We're not going to get much sleep tonight," Vitaly grumbled.

"Never mind," I said with irritating cheer, "let's get some coffee from the buffet car and watch the sunset."

The sunset was beautiful but the coffee was probably a mistake.

Through the night, we tossed and turned, swapping seats to see if that would make any difference, but sleep evaded us. It was as bad as a long-haul flight.

Restless, I realised Vitaly would have a better chance of dropping off with his head on his folded arms if I got up and left him, so I went to the buffet car. The light was on there, enabling me to read. Unfortunately, the air conditioning was also on at full blast, so I sat up and read in a refrigerator.

At about four in the morning, a colourful character, wearing an orange tee shirt and rainbow headband, stumbled into the freezing dining car, holding his head in agony.

"Can't get to sleep?" I asked.

"It's horrendous," he said.

"Come and sit with me. It's better if you just stop trying to sleep altogether. Let's have a chat instead."

He introduced himself as Dave, a British tourist. We passed the next hour or so in pleasant conversation until dawn began to glimmer over the desert and, from the smells coming from the kitchen, it seemed as if cooked breakfast might also be on the horizon.

Zombie-like, Vitaly stumbled into the diner and joined us. We had a jolly breakfast together before going back to our seats and trying to get a bit more sleep.

When the sun was fully up, we looked out at the desert.

"It really is red, isn't it?" said Vitaly.

"It's hot too, and I promise you're going to love it."

On arrival in Alice Springs, we decided to be gentle to ourselves and booked into a motel to recover from the journey and acclimatise to the scorching heat. Vitaly was relieved to be able to loll around naked in the room but disturbed when there came a soft knocking on our door in the middle of the night.

"Who could that be?"

"Probably Aboriginal people, wanting beer," I said. "Nothing to worry about. Go back to sleep."

The next day, we went out and hired a car. With the money we'd earned in Adelaide, we had just enough for a small green bug with two doors, which we christened 'Gertie'. Vitaly's spirits lifted. He hadn't driven for a long time and missed having a car, which he said made him feel 'free and whole'.

It was madness but we were going camping. Who goes camping in the red desert in the middle of December? My friend Meredith Campbell raised an eyebrow but nevertheless lent us her pink swag, as well as an eskie to keep our food cool.

Vitaly had become addicted to camembert in Adelaide – he would eat whole camemberts for lunch and then wonder why his waistline was expanding.

"Better put something simpler in the eskie, don't you think?" said Meredith.

We took tins of tuna and trail bars, not forgetting ample supplies of water.

Out on the empty desert roads, at the wheel of Gertie, Vitaly was getting some satisfaction at last. We saw white brumbies (wild horses) running against the backdrop of the rugged MacDonnell Ranges. Making a stop at Standley Chasm, we spotted delicate green lizards sunning themselves on the red boulders.

I suggested we headed for Glen Helen, where we could relax at the waterhole and spend the night. "In fact," I said, "if you like it, we could stay the whole time there and do nothing but swim. We don't have to do the tourist thing and go rushing off to Uluru, just because it's there."

What was not to like about Glen Helen, a pretty little freshwater lake, hidden between great red cliffs? Nearby was a campground, with civilised facilities.

We went to the reception desk to check in and pay a small fee for the use of the showers and kitchen.

"But we want to camp in wild nature," I told the desk clerk. "Where can we throw our swag?"

"Out there, on the edge of the camp, where the tall grass is growing," she said.

We went to the very edge of the camp and rolled out our bed. In the campground, we'd noticed the ashes from lots of small fires, so we assumed there would be no problem if we lit a fire too. We made a careful circle of stones to contain the flames, gathered some brushwood and struck a match. There was a full moon that night, so for a magical few minutes we sat in moon and firelight.

Suddenly, pounding through the grass, came a ranger, flashing a torch.

"Put out that fire immediately," he shouted.

"But others in the campground have had fires," I said.

"You're not in the campground. You're just over the boundary, in the national park."

"How were we to know? There are no signs."

"Well, since you've rolled out your swag, you can stay here tonight but you must put out the fire," he said.

Our idyllic evening spoilt, we went early to bed.

Vitaly's snores suggested he was getting some sleep. I had another sleepless night but it didn't matter, as I lay gazing up at the stars.

At first light, I saw a black dingo walk right past the swag. Was I dreaming? The wild dogs of the desert are usually sandy coloured. Later, I asked the ranger, who was having his breakfast at the campground reception, if there were any black dingoes.

"Yes," he said, "it's rare but occasionally you do see a black dingo."

He seemed to have forgiven us for the fire incident but Vitaly was no longer comfortable at Glen Helen and wanted to move on.

"Are you sure you want to go to Uluru?" I asked. "It's quite a long drive from here and it's just a big, red rock, swarming with tourists."

But Vitaly did want to make the pilgrimage. Coming all this way and not seeing the Rock would be like going to Moscow and not seeing Red Square, he said.

So we packed up our gear and set off on the five-hour drive to Uluru. I made a point of stopping at Stuarts Well roadhouse, thinking Vitaly would be amused by the pet dingo there that had been trained to sing. Vitaly played an opera aria and the dingo obliged, as best it could.

"Pathetic," said Vitaly. "Let's get out of here."

We drove on and by late afternoon, saw a huge red rock on the horizon.

"Is that Uluru?" asked Vitaly.

"No, that's another rock called Mount Conner," I said. "It cons everyone." We laughed and agreed how silly it was that one rock was famous and another wasn't.

To local Aboriginal people, all rocks and trees are sacred but Uluru is their cathedral. Vitaly and I were not planning to show disrespect by climbing it. In any case, it was far too hot. We contented ourselves with a walk around the circumference. Vitaly touched the Rock; he rested his back against it and felt its warmth.

"That's it then," he said, "I can say I've done it now."

The sun was setting, so we headed to the designated 'sunset viewing grounds', where tourists are herded behind a fence to see the Rock's colours change from red to pink as the sun goes down; as if the sun can't set without official permission.

We opened a couple of tins of tuna for our evening picnic. With one hand, Vitaly ate the tuna while with the other, he waved away the flies. In a small protest against authority, he littered the 'sunset viewing grounds' by leaving his empty tin on the top of the fence. "Naughty," I teased him; we'd been in a happy and peaceful mood for most of the day.

But as darkness fell, Vitaly became agitated.

"Where are we going to sleep?" he asked.

I took him to the lookout above the campgrounds, where I knew from experience no-one would disturb us. Because in the morning, as soon as the sun was up, all the tourists would be off in their buses to see dawn over the Rock, not climbing this modest little hill.

From the top of the slope, we could see the great red Rock, now black in the moonlight.

"But where will I get my coffee in the morning?" moaned Vitaly.

We settled down for the night. Vitaly said he felt sick. He didn't get much sleep but I slept soundly in the swag.

"Get up, get up," he whispered when dawn broke. "People could be coming soon and they'll find us here."

"Give me another half hour," I said and rolled over.

"I told you, I told you," he hissed, "there's someone here and he's looking at us."

I sat up in the swag and who should be there, looking benevolently at us, but Dave, the guy we'd met on the train?

"Hello darlings," he said. "I didn't want to go with my tour group to see the Rock up close at dawn. You can see it better from here."

I was pleased to see our morning visitor; Vitaly less so.

"Anyone for coffee?" Dave asked. "While my group's away, I can use our camp kitchen and brew up some instant. There's a drop of milk too."

So that was the coffee problem sorted. Things were looking up.

On the way back to Alice, I wanted to show Vitaly Rainbow Valley, a place I'd found extraordinarily beautiful and that meant a lot to me. But going to the valley would have involved driving off road into the desert and we were already tired by the trip to the Rock, so it seemed to make better sense to have a hot meal in a café in town and then find another waterhole in the nearby ranges.

I was at the wheel now, aiming for Ellery Creek Big Hole, closer to Alice than Glen Helen but with rocks and a lake no less spectacular. We were running low on petrol. Unfortunately, at Ellery Creek there was no petrol pump, so we ended up going all the way back to Glen Helen, where we had spent our first night.

Anxious not to get into trouble with the ranger again, we asked at reception where exactly we could lay out our swag.

"If you put it in the dry river bed," the young woman said, "you'll be outside the campground, getting the wild experience you want, but not trespassing in the national park, so you shouldn't have any worries."

While it was still daylight, we laid the swag out on the sand of the river bed. I noticed some cow pats, evidence that cattle sometimes wandered here, but decided not to worry Vitaly with this information. We went to the campground kitchen to make supper.

"What have we got?" asked Vitaly.

"It's trail bars and tuna again."

"Let's finish off this wine," he said, offering the dregs of a bottle we'd opened two days ago. It had gone a bit fizzy, not to say sour.

"I'm not a traveller," said Vitaly gloomily. "I'm a stay-at-home sort of type, you know."

"Bedtime, then," I said. We walked in the dark to the dry river bed. The moon wasn't up yet but the sky was a jewelled net of stars.

"There's someone here," muttered Vitaly when we reached the swag. True enough, in the distance was a camp fire; perhaps some Aboriginal people were camping nearby.

"They won't hurt us."

"I don't like it; I don't feel safe."

"Well, let's move to the campground then."

"Oh God, oh God, I can't stand it," he shouted. "I haven't had a crap for four days."

"Right, we're going to stay here and try to relax," I said.

Neither tribesmen nor cattle disturbed us but we woke the next morning far from refreshed. We filled up with petrol and drove in a hard silence back towards Alice.

"If it's easier for you to be without me than with me, just release me," I said.

He didn't answer.

Gradually, the mood lightened. We reached Ellery Creek, our campsite for the last night out bush. Here were simple facilities, with clear instructions on what to do and what not to do. We went swimming, ate a meal and had a peaceful night in the swag, sometimes sleeping, sometimes looking up at the stars. It was all I'd wanted from the start of the trip.

In the cool of the morning, we went swimming again. Nobody else was up and we had the waterhole to ourselves. We swam to the far bank, where squadrons of desert finches swooped through the air.

With the sun still low in the sky, the sand wasn't yet baking and we were able to walk barefoot into the desert. After a while, I sat down on a rock and let Vitaly go ahead by himself.

I don't know what he saw or experienced out there but when he returned, he said: "I found my own Rainbow Valley."

"What did you call it?" I asked.

"No Name Valley."

After that, we returned happily to Alice and had a companionable last evening, watching the kangaroos at the Telegraph Station. The next day, Vitaly was flying to Sydney, en route back to Russia.

I accompanied him to the airport. "You'll need this," I said, giving him a wooly beanie that would come in handy in Moscow in December.

It turned out he needed the wooly hat a bit sooner than that for, although he could have stayed with friends in Sydney, he insisted on going straight to Kingsford Smith Airport, only to find it closed overnight. Thus he spent his last night on Australian soil sleeping like a tramp on a bench, with his coat collar up and the hat pulled down over his eyes.

The Alice Embrace

To be honest, I felt a measure of relief after Vitaly left, as I no longer had to worry about his needs but was free to concentrate on my own and to enjoy the aspects of Australia I loved. Adelaide had been a compromise but Alice was IT for me – the arid, red landscape; the rainbow community that time and again welcomed me home.

My house and cat-sitting job at Maya Cifali's wasn't due to start until New Year but Megg Kelham offered me a room at her place for a week and another friend, Ann Davis, said I could stay at her house over Christmas if I looked after the family dog Trevor, so accommodation wasn't a problem.

I checked out of the motel and into Megg's welcoming spare bedroom, hung with beads and crystals. In her garden, I was fascinated to watch the resident bower bird that collects stones and shiny objects to make an alluring nest for his mate.

I was back in the Alice embrace and it was party time. A friend called Liz Archer, whose piano playing I admired, was turning 50. The sisters sometimes splashed around together in a synchronised swimming team called the Pumpakinas and especially for Liz, they were planning to hire a pool and put on a display. I leapt at the invitation to take part.

We had one rehearsal and it was not as easy as it looked to perform the movements of the water ballet. I was handicapped by my recent shoulder injury and unable to do a proper backstroke.

"Don't worry," said Megg. "You can be the clown and get everything deliberately wrong."

Kate Lawrence, my doppelgaenger, had designed the costumes. We would be wearing black bathing suits, with fishnet stockings and flashy headbands, and over the top, brightly coloured gowns to keep us warm.

On the night of the party, the guests took their seats at one end of the pool, with Liz in pride of place. We pranced on in our gowns and did a striptease to raunchy music before diving into the water.

"Wait for me!" screamed Megg, who had been fiddling with the sound system. So Megg turned out to be the clown. The crowd roared with laughter as we swam in and out, opening and closing like water lilies, and I got most of it wrong.

Liz was delighted with her aquatic birthday tribute, after which we had supper and danced in the starlight. I met a number of other sisters that night, including a vibrant woman in a peacock-blue waistcoat, whose name was Joy Taylor. She was Joy by name and Joy by nature and over time became one of my dearest Alice friends.

I also met an Italian woman called Mary Menotti and we exchanged the stories of our lives, her telling me about roots in Sicily and me telling her about Russia, of course.

"Wow," she said, "after the life you've had, how can you be ordinary?"

It was the most pertinent question anyone asked me in Australia.

Like everyone else, I really just needed to earn a living and I certainly wasn't work-shy. When my colleague Dave Richards asked if I would like to stand in for him for a month at the local newspaper, *The Centralian Advocate*, while he took a break from routine to do other projects, I was glad of the humble sub-editing job.

The fiddling with text, the dreaming-up of snappy headlines, the tea and pie breaks, the camaraderie of the other hacks – it all took me back to the early days of my career on a British provincial paper and I was perfectly happy. I wasn't teaching journalism; I was doing it. And there on the desk was Erin, one of my former students from Adelaide, who was also now practising the trade, not learning about it in theory. We went for coffee like mates, not student and teacher.

There was a good story in town that December, one that was big enough for me to offer to the national and even international papers.

Five young white men had been arrested over the death of an Aboriginal ranger and Alice's reputation for racial tolerance was taking a battering. Everyone knew this was a test case for Australia in which justice not only had to be done but had to be seen to be done.

The story was indeed tragic – a lose-lose situation for everyone. Donny Ryder, referred to as Kwementyaye Ryder under the Aboriginal rule of not speaking the name of the dead, was 33 when he was found with a fatal head wound in the dry Todd River. His mother Therese, an artist from the Catholic community of Santa Teresa, said he'd never been in trouble and was doing well as a trainee ranger.

The five white men, aged 19 to 24, and all from respectable Alice Springs families, were committed for trial after it emerged they had gone on a drunken joy ride in their Toyota ute through the Aboriginal camps in the river bed and got into a fight with Mr. Ryder after he objected to their behavior.

I didn't cover the trial itself but investigated disturbing reports that the white wooden cross erected in Mr. Ryder's memory had been burnt. Journalists took off with the racist angle and stories flashed round the world that Alice Springs had its own version of the Ku Klux Klan.

There was some racism in Alice, of course; where is there not? Aboriginal teenagers complained that they couldn't walk into shops without being accused of stealing and blacks said they found it harder than whites to get accommodation. There was reverse racism too and whites could be the victims of black prejudice.

But Ku Klux Klan in Alice? Surely not.

The police said Aboriginal mourners had themselves burnt the Ryder cross but could that be true?

Eventually, I found some relatives of the dead man, who quietly confirmed that they'd had a rather embarrassing mishap when they placed candles on the dry ground, among the inflammable plastic wreaths. The cross had been charred from the base but the wild headlines about a flaming cross had been inaccurate.

The truth made a less dramatic story but it was important to nail the lie. Alice was no more the 'racist capital of Australia' than any other town or city; rather less racist than other places, I suspected. Indeed, both Aboriginal and non-Aboriginal workers came together to make a new cross for the Ryder family. It was made of steel, not because they feared another fire, but because the men worked for a firm of boilermakers.

As for the five white men on trial, they received jail sentences varying from six to four years for manslaughter. The court heard that Mr. Ryder had had a pre-existing aneurism that might have contributed to his death but the judge said racial antagonism had played its part in the tragedy.

What with the Ryder trial, and the heat, and being far away from home, I was not much in the Christmas spirit but the festive season was fast approaching.

My new friend Joy Taylor and her partner Kalika invited me to a party to celebrate the solstice, the shortest day in the Northern Hemisphere but the longest Down Under. Their house and garden were like a holiday resort, complete with palm-fringed swimming pool. The guests were invited to dip ripe cherries in a bowl of melted chocolate and bless each other in their new beginnings.

I also went to the Christmas market. On the town lawns, the good citizens of Alice had put up a fir tree and Todd Mall was decorated end to end with fairy lights. I wandered among the stalls that were selling handicrafts and snacks. A brass band played, followed by the local rock talent.

I was surprised when, walking towards me, I saw Dave, my friend from the train and the Uluru campground. He was resplendent in a white trilby hat and wore a diamond earring.

"I thought you'd gone back to England."

"I'm off next week but I wouldn't have missed this for the world."

Both hungry, we repaired to the fish and chip shop and ordered large portions of shark and chips.

Meanwhile back at Megg's house, I'd become friendly with a young woman who was renting the granny flat in the back garden. Her name was Farida Khawaja and she was working as a doctor at Alice Springs Hospital. Farida, who was of German-Pakistani background, made some wicked curries and we had some excellent conversations. I was rather sorry that I was leaving Megg's but was invited to return for a party that Megg and Farida would be holding on New Year's Eve.

Over Christmas itself, I stayed in the home of the Davis family, who were off on holiday. My job was to 'keep the living alive', in other words to water the garden and look after the dog, Trevor.

Being more of a cat person, I wasn't sure how I would cope with Trevor but he turned out to be the easiest and most grateful of creatures. He even took himself for a walk and all I had to do was put biscuits in his bowl and make sure he had enough to drink.

In the comfort of the Davis home, I went down with flu. Shivering and poorly, I curled up on the thickly padded sofa. The living room was luxurious, rich in paintings, furniture, fabrics and rugs. The colours were as vibrant as the red earth, blue sky and green parrots outside.

I can't explain it but I had a sudden longing for subtler, more northern shades – fawn, cream, grey and even black. From the sofa, I caught sight of my South American multi-coloured dream coat, hanging from the back of a chair. An urge came over me to turn the coat inside out, so that the black lining was on the outside and the colours inside.

Hugging myself in this now outwardly drab garment, I put the kettle on and made tea. Eventually my temperature came down and I started to sweat.

I recovered in time for the New Year party, which was another splendid bash in the hospitable Alice Springs style. Farida was leaving Alice, it turned out, and heading to Tasmania to continue her medical training. We had known each other for only a short time and yet we both felt a strong connection. On parting, we hugged silently and

Farida gave me a little metal dragonfly.

The beginning of January saw me moving again to house sit and look after Momo the cat, as I'd promised to do so that the owner, Maya Cifali, could take a holiday at the coast. Before I came to Australia, I'd never really heard of house sitting but I came to discover it was a fairly common win-win arrangement between those who needed to go away and those looking for somewhere to stay. Little was I to know that 13 Jarvis Street would become my home from home whenever I was in Oz.

On that first occasion, I barely had time to get to know Maya. She showed me the garden, which I had to water, and the spa pool, which I had to keep clean, and gave me instructions on how to care for Momo. I was allowed to borrow the car, in which I drove her to the airport and waved her off for a month.

Returning to the house, I realised to my dismay that the key Maya had given me didn't fit the lock. In a panic, I phoned my old friend Barry Skipsey, who helped me to break into the house I was supposed to be guarding. We explained to the neighbours why I was crawling in through a window and they supplied a key to the back door.

It was weird but Maya's house was extraordinarily similar to my old flat back in Moscow. Maya, born in Egypt to French and Italian parents, was cultured and well-travelled and her home was full of objects from all over the world.

There was a Russian samovar and a red and black Afghan carpet, just like one I had. There was an upright piano. And of course there was a cat, only unlike my Blackjack, Momo was grey and white, with green eyes. It wasn't long before he sat on my lap and joined me in bed.

Three days a week, I went to work at the paper. I came home, fed Momo and read a book or watched TV. I ate on the verandah, strolled in the garden and chilled out in the pool.

I could get to like this, I thought, until it dawned on me that I was living in someone else's house, doing someone else's job and stroking someone else's cat.

While I stayed at Maya's I made the most of her extensive library. I found a copy of *Le Petit Prince* by Antoine de Saint-Exupéry and decided to re-read it to brush up my French. I rediscovered the message of the desert fox, speaking to the Little Prince, who has fallen to earth, leaving behind the flower he once cultivated on his distant planet.

The flower is capricious – a thorn in the side, a pain in the arse – but she belongs to the prince. There may be millions of other flowers but this one is special because the prince has watered her. 'Don't forget,' says the fox, 'you are responsible for those you have tamed.'

I realised I had to get back to Vitaly and Jack in Moscow but I wasn't sure how, as I had given up my flat and work there. The obvious was staring me in the face. All I needed to do was reconnect with editors in Sydney, who would be glad to take my foreign reports again. Getting a new Russian visa and accreditation would be a longer process but I set the wheels in motion. Once I knew I was headed back to Moscow, I was free to enjoy what remained of my time in the Southern Hemisphere.

It's always the same, isn't it? Just when you're about to depart, you meet interesting new people. Just as I was about to leave Alice, Dave Richards introduced me to Noel Ferry, a New Zealander who taught at the Steiner School. (He was a gifted artist and illustrated his lessons with fantastic chalk drawings on the blackboard.)

It had been raining hard. The Todd River was a rushing red torrent and the waterholes had expanded to the size of lakes. Dave suggested an early morning drive out into the desert to see how the landscape had been transformed.

We went in Noel's car, an old banger he'd painted all over with frogs and called his 'frogmobile'. While Dave waded into the water to photograph reflections of gum trees, Noel and I got on a roll of uncontrollable laughter. You'd have thought we'd been smoking marijuana but we hadn't; we just hit it off with each other. The funniest thing was we shared a birthday, which was also Australia Day, so of course we had to organise a joint party.

I reckoned Maya wouldn't mind if I held it on her verandah; it was just a pity she wasn't there to join us. I made a mountain of food and a good thing too, as first invited guests and then friends of friends started to arrive until it seemed the whole town had come to celebrate with us. The washing up afterwards was monstrous but I was glad to have been able to return just a little of the hospitality I had received in Alice.

New Zealand Detour

Sitting on Maya's soothing verandah, with its lush plants and green Buddha statue, I considered what I would do when the owner herself returned home and I had to give back the key to Alice's best oasis.

I was aware, having read the Australian writer Robert Dessaix on the subject of Homer's *Odyssey*, that if you failed to keep Ithaca in mind, you were 'not travelling but merely drifting'. On the other hand, on Maya's marvellous bookshelves, I'd found the work of a Dutch travel writer called Cees Nooteboom, who relieved me of the guilt I sometimes felt for my insatiable need to roam.

'Anyone who is constantly travelling,' wrote Nooteboom, 'is always somewhere else and therefore always absent. But there is always one place where you are constantly, all the time, namely with yourself. It began to dawn on me that I was the one who was always at home, namely with myself.'

There was no competition between the travellers and the home bodies, he went on. 'It's not about which of us is the hero here, but about which of us is doing his soul's bidding.'

YES! I thought and immediately went out and booked myself a short trip to New Zealand.

My parents had recommended it but New Zealand had been low on my wish-list of places to visit. As a journalist, I went where the action took me. Later, as a travel writer, I sought out the rugged, the arid and the crocodile-infested. New Zealand was green and sleepy; so boring, I thought, there was a good reason it was at the end of the earth.

But now it occurred to me I might not have another chance to visit the Southern Hemisphere and would I be happy to die, not having seen New Zealand? I had 10 days, enough time to drive a camper van around the North Island.

In Auckland, I rented a Jucy Crib – the latest in small camper vans; a car really, with a backseat bed big enough for one or a couple very much in love. It took me a good two hours to find my way out of Auckland's tangled streets but eventually I was on the highway to Paihia.

The countryside was a pastoral symphony. The further north I drove, the more tropical it became and my sense grew that this was a Pacific island. I found a quiet spot of coast and settled for the night. In the campground, I was a lone bird – neither bungee-jumping backpacker nor quite yet grey nomad.

The next day, I went out into the Bay of Islands on a cruise that promised we would swim with dolphins. Rainbows played in the spray from our boat as we buffeted over the turquoise waves. Not far out, we found the dolphins, sporting for our entertainment. But the sea was too rough for us to join them safely, the captain said. We would have to make do with watching. To my surprise, none of the passengers groaned with disappointment or demanded their money back. Perhaps, like me, they were stunned by the wonder of simply seeing the wild dolphins. I gazed out at the archipelago, drinking in the beauty for myself, seeing it on behalf of absent loved ones.

Hired vehicles are not insured to drive on the treacherous sands of Ninety Mile Beach, so to make that trip I had to go in a tour bus. Nothing could have been more frustrating than to look out of the window at the expanse of beach; to set foot on it for five minutes in the company of 30 other people. But it gave me ideas for other wild beaches I would find myself. And at Cape Reinga, where the turquoise waters of the Tasman Sea meet the visibly bluer waters of the Pacific Ocean, I was moved to hear of the passing of the Maori spirits. After death, they are said to travel up the country, bidding farewell to their loved ones, before entering the waters at land's end and returning to Polynesia, whence they came.

"Are you a lady travelling on her own?" said a man at the campsite that evening.

"Yep."

This was encouragement enough for Grant to get out his map and suggest where I might like to go next.

I was planning to drive south, via the Waipoua Forest, where the 2,000-year-old Kauri tree, Tane Mahuta, grows, as old as Christianity. Then I intended to visit Hamilton on my way to Rotorua.

"Don't go to Hamilton," said Grant. "Avoid Hamilton. It's boring."

He suggested a more picturesque route via the Coromandel Peninsula. For a traveler like me, with limited time, the peninsula would be a microcosm of the country.

"Thanks," I said, "that's good advice. Now could this lady travelling on her own trouble you for one more service? Where's the lever to open the petrol cap on this van?"

Grant showed me and then left me in peace. He was the perfect Kiwi gentleman.

The Coromandel Peninsula was a revelation, beauty upon beauty at every turn of the serpentine road. Leaving the town of Thames, with its wooden 'gothic' cathedral, the road first hugged the coast, offering misty vistas of distant hills. From rocks, trees bent to the water as in Japanese pen drawings. Then the road swerved up, through yellow, sheep-dotted fields, to alpine slopes, with glorious views out to sea.

Keen to catch every landscape, each lovelier than the next, I swiveled my neck like an owl and drove at a snail's pace. Snaking tails of local vehicles, including timber lorries, built up behind me, honking impatiently until I let them pass.

In places, road crews were laying fresh bitumen. I noticed the highway workers were often Maori. Apart from appearing in cultural shows for the tourists and cleaning hotels and campsites, this was the sphere of employment where they were immediately visible to an outsider's eye.

At the top of the peninsula, the town of Coromandel was a good place to stop for a seafood lunch. Then it was back down the other side, the wilder, Pacific Coast, boasting the famous Hot Water Beach.

Here, crowds of tourists were digging in the sand for the boiling water that bubbles up from underground and wallowing in the hot pools they had created for themselves. It was a circus but I only had to go a mile or two away to find wild, isolated beaches for myself. The sands were pristine, the surf strong.

On the horizon, the blue of the sea was barely distinguishable from the blue of the sky. Sea and sky merge in my native Yorkshire, too, but the difference was that here the air and water were blessedly warm.

New Zealand was one of the purest environments I had ever seen; the place where my inner dreams of bliss were almost matched by outside reality. Could it be the nearest thing to paradise on earth?

Certainly the homemade blackberry ice cream in the next town was heavenly. I realised that all these years I had been missing something. New Zealand was a well-kept secret, one that I had kept from myself. It was a subtle country and only now was I mature enough to appreciate it.

On the way back to Thames, on the sweeping road that cuts through the high Coromandel Range, the music of Mahler filled my mind – *Das Lied von der Erde*, his love song to the earth that one day we must all leave.

I stayed that night in the Miranda holiday park and enjoyed the thermal pool, a foretaste of the pampering I was planning for myself in Rotorua. And indeed the spas of Rotorua, with mud and mineral baths, and spouting sulphurous geysers, did not disappoint.

On the day I had to return the camper van in Auckland, I decided to take rural roads, anything to avoid the boring town of Hamilton, of which I had been warned.

The back roads from Rotorua were less spectacular than the Coromandel Peninsula but the kiwi plantations and late summer meadows were nevertheless pleasant. Again Mahler came into my mind, that old 'Song of the Earth' – '*ewig, ewig*, always, always'.

I came to a crossroads; left was Hamilton, right some village, where the road surface quickly deteriorated. I knew I had to get the camper van back by late afternoon. Was I perhaps making a mistake by turning my back on Hamilton and the smooth motorway?

Pausing to have a think, I found myself at the gates of the Hamilton cemetery and crematorium. No, I decided, I would NOT go to Hamilton but continue on the rural road, which would surely take me to Auckland by tea time.

The road became a dirt track. At the next crossroads, I was again faced with a choice between the main road to Hamilton and a picturesque but uncertain country road. It was weird but at this crossroads there was a graveyard too.

Reluctantly, I decided to play safe and surrendered to the road more travelled. Let it be Hamilton after all.

Grant had not been wrong about this town, a wasteland of bungalows with an ugly concrete centre. I parked at the bus station and went in search of a public lavatory.

Coming out of the toilet, I looked across the car park and saw a white building decorated with black staves and notes, a giant musical score. This I had to investigate.

It turned out to be one of the biggest music shops in New Zealand, packed with instruments, scores and recordings for all tastes and abilities.

"Do you have *Das Lied von der Erde*?" I tested the man behind the counter.

"No, but I can order it for you," he said.

It didn't matter because I had the score and recording at home.

"Never mind. Thanks all the same," I said, glancing up above the counter.

Portraits of composers hung on the wall and there in the middle was Gustav Mahler. I could swear he winked at me.

Back in Auckland, on my last day in New Zealand, I sat in a park and admired the golden rod, glimmering in the early autumn light. The words of another German, Rainer Maria Rilke, came to mind:

Lord, it is time. The summer was huge.
Lay your shadow on the sundials
And loose your winds upon the fields.

Bid the last fruits to fullness,
Give them a couple more sunny days,
Bring them to ripeness and
Press the last sweetness into wine.

Whoever has no home now will build none,
Whoever is alone now will so remain,
Will stay up, read and write long letters and
Wander the leaf-blown avenues, up and down.

It was time to get back to Moscow and to Vitaly, for whom the beneficial effects of Australian fresh air had already worn off and who was struggling alone through another Russian winter, coughing with bronchitis.

The Fourth and Fifth Voyages
The Long Commute

Returning to Moscow in 2010, I was reminded of all the hardships that had prompted Vitaly and me to migrate to Oz in the first place, chief among them Russia's unending problem of cramped housing. I stayed with Vitaly in his one-room flat and slept on the floors of friends for several months until I was able to rent a tiny apartment of my own, a bus ride away from my husband's place. This was the only way we could realistically arrange our lives there; as good as it got in Moscow.

At the same time, when popular protests started against the falsification of elections and Vladimir Putin was 'elected' to a third term as president, I realised I still had a mission in Moscow to cover the struggle for democratic rights. And I would not have completed my book about Russia, *The Ice Walk*, had I not returned to the land of snow, discomfort, miracle and revelation. As always, all was for the best.

I didn't entirely give up on Australia, however, as I'd made a surprising discovery about the nature of the Aussie visa system. In Russia, the visa that allowed me, a British citizen, to live and work in Moscow was given so that I could be on Russian territory for a certain time; when it expired, I was expected to go. But the Australian migrant visa was given so that Vitaly and I could cross the border. Once in Oz, we could stay as long as we liked; forever if we wanted.

Or to put it another way, having left, we could go back, as long as the five-year permission to cross the border remained valid, and stay as long as we wanted each time. There were innumerable chances to settle in Oz and not just the one chance that we thought we had blown.

This struck me as extraordinary. Russia, which needed migrants no less than Australia, treated newcomers as temporary guests while Australia, a true melting pot society, encouraged its migrants to stay, or come again if they failed the first time. And it was enough for me to put in time in Australia to keep the door open for my spouse as well.

All in all, I had to clock up two years out of the five-year life of the visa in order to be considered resident and eligible for an extension when it ran out. So while Vitaly stayed at his staff job in Moscow and looked after Jack Pantera, which I think suited both these creatures of stable routine, I started commuting back and forth between Russia and Australia in order to keep open our options Down Under. It was a hell of a long commute between hemispheres and in 2011 I managed the dubious achievement of doing double winter, rather than double summer, which was the aim of cleverer migrating birds.

I went to Australia in 2011 to work as a census officer in that year's national population count. I'd seen an advert for the temporary job on a government website and thought it might suit me, as information gathering was a basic journalistic skill and I reckoned I could learn a lot about Australian society in the process of door-stepping citizens. As an Aussie permanent resident, I was eligible to apply, which I did, from Moscow, but heard nothing.

An Aboriginal gentleman intervened to help me get the job. On my last visit to Australia, I'd been up to the gold-mining town of Tennant Creek to give a talk to the local Rotary club about the surprising similarities between Russia and Australia. (The two countries have very different climates but both share a convict and pioneering history and both live by the extraction of natural resources from remote areas. Both have indigenous populations, too.)

To be honest, at the time, I hadn't been particularly keen to make the tedious bus journey all the way from Alice Springs to Tennant Creek to give this talk to a small group of people, for which my only payment would be a roast dinner and pudding with custard. But I'd done it, nevertheless, and when I met the Rotarians, of course, I was glad I'd made the effort.

It's funny but you never know where things will lead. I'd completely forgotten about the talk but one of the people in the audience still remembered it and here he was now, recommending that the Australian Bureau of Statistics (ABS) hire me as one of its team of census collectors. The job was casual and low paid but the money would be enough to finance me on my latest expedition to Oz.

I was interviewed for the post on Skype from Moscow by the man who would be my boss, a New Zealander called Neil Broad. He was genial and seemed to like me and we agreed that I would join the census team, arriving in Alice to start work in July.

Vitaly, never one to restrict my freedom or stop me seizing opportunities, made no objections to me taking off on another adventure. Others didn't believe we were a 'proper couple' but we were.

Heading into the Southern Hemisphere winter, I packed a red suitcase with cool weather clothes and booked a flight to Oz, this time arranging a stopover in the Middle East rather than the Far East. I loved the old Sufi saying that a person should have 'roots and wings', the roots of home and wings to see the roots of others. In Abu Dhabi, I fancied I would see old Arab souks, with carpets, hookah pipes and exotic perfumes.

The Grand Mosque of Sheikh Zayed was certainly a pearl, or rather collection of pearls, with its shining white domes and marble courtyards. But as for the souks, they were modern-day malls, where women draped in black burqas shopped for scarlet lace underwear, smart phones and delicacies with a Harrods or Fortnum and Mason label.

The rich Emiratis made up only a fraction of the population while all the work was done by labourers, salesgirls and taxi drivers from the Indian subcontinent, the Philippines, Ukraine and other poor countries. I quickly saw this was a society built on the virtual slave labour of people who could never hope to become citizens. Australia looked shabby compared with the UAE but immediately upon arrival in Oz, I could smell freedom and equality in the air.

I landed at Yulara on this occasion, the flight from Sydney to the Rock being cheaper than the one direct to Alice Springs. From Uluru, I would take the Emu Run tourist bus to Alice but before that I had another opportunity to see the big, red rock of which I had dreamt.

On all my previous visits to the Rock, I'd been distracted by other people – Adam, the wedding couple and Vitaly. Finally, I had a chance to be one on one with the Rock and contemplate its meaning for me.

It was bitterly cold when I rose before dawn and dressed in all the clothes I had with me, adding the brown motel room blanket as a cape on top. I sat in the scrub, watching the sky lighten from indigo to oyster until the sun came up and hit me in the eye, a glorious splash of yellow over the monolith.

"Rock, big red rock, you are indeed as I dreamt you," I said and let go of my obsession with it. I'd seen it, I'd always remember its power and beauty but it no longer exerted such a pull on me. I could let it be.

Once in Alice, I attended the introductory briefing for the collectors of the 2011 census. The boss, Mr. Broad, turned out to be a fascinating character who, when he was not busy collecting census data, was translating the Bible into Arrernte, the language spoken by Aboriginal people in the Alice Springs area. One of the other census collectors was a Balinese man called Gede (pronounced g'day). He joked that when Aussies greeted him, it sounded like 'G'day G'day'. I was going to have fun with these guys.

It comes as a surprise to some foreigners to learn that taking part in the census, as well as voting in elections, is a legal obligation in Australia and unless you have a good excuse for being absent, you can be fined for not doing your civic duty. Our job as census officers was to go door to door, taking forms to every householder, and then to return to receive them. If people had problems with literacy, we were allowed to help them fill in the forms.

As my beat, I was given the Gillen area of Alice, which had a mixture of fine mansions and poorer public housing. Issued with a large yellow satchel to carry the forms and a big book to record deliveries and returns, I felt myself a face of the Australian government, with a responsibility to be courteous, discreet and helpful.

"You're going to be cold in that little coat though," said my old friend Meredith Campbell, herself a resident of Gillen and one of my 'customers'. The government had rightly chosen the winter season for pounding the pavements, which would have been impossible to do in the summer heat. But I was thinly dressed in the crocus-coloured coat I wore in spring back in Europe.

Meredith took me to Vinnies (the St. Vincent de Paul charity shop), where I picked up a very fine black leather jacket, second-hand, for only 40 dollars.

"You'll need a hat as well, doll," she said. "Don't forget the sun is strong, even in winter." And she gave me one from her own collection, a straw trilby, decorated with blue flowers.

So I went out onto the streets of Gillen, dressed in black leather and straw, with a fluorescent yellow bag. You couldn't really miss me.

Looking at my map, I realised what a big job it was going to be to visit every single household in one district of Alice, let alone the whole town. Houses were one thing but there were warrens of flats, hidden granny flats and caravans that all had to be included. Even homeless people on park benches had to be counted. I began to understand why the ABS needed an army of temporary staff to cover the country.

I did a few streets each day and clocked off in time for tea. In the evenings, I went to choir practice, for I had joined an 'African choir' called Asante Sana. On some days, if I was too footsore to go out, I gave myself a break and sat in the Daily Grind café, going through old press clippings for the book I had started to write about Russia.

Yes, strange as it may sound, I wrote a good part of *The Ice Walk* in Australia, just as I have written most of this memoir about Oz in Moscow. You need distance to write with love and longing for a place that you take for granted when you are there.

The Census and the
Crime Statistics

The target for delivering the census forms was fairly easy to meet. If householders were out, I could slip the envelopes through letter boxes, pugnacious dogs permitting. Catching citizens at home in order to take the forms back was trickier, like herding cats. God bless the progressive few who filed their submissions electronically.

Most people who answered my knock or ring were understanding and friendly; quite often they would invite me in and offer me a glass of water or lemonade. Some were difficult, like the depressed woman who wouldn't open her door, or the shift worker who slept during the day.

One white guy was particularly obstructive and I couldn't understand why until I spotted some Chinese youths living in two caravans in his back garden, perhaps not entirely legally. But I was only a census officer, not a police officer, and there were limits to how far I could exert my authority. In the end, it was his problem, not mine, if he failed to declare how many souls he had under his roof.

What was most surprising was the attitude of Aboriginal people towards the census. I had imagined that they might see it as another example of white bureaucracy or interference in their affairs but I could not have been more wrong.

If, for most whites, the census was at best a necessary piece of research for future social investment and at worst a chore, for Aboriginal people it was an honour to take part. I should have realised this, of course, for until 1967, when whites voted in a referendum on giving citizenship to the Aboriginals, indigenous people had been classed as the 'flora and fauna' of their own country.

An elderly Aboriginal couple spotted me walking down the street with my distinctive yellow bag. They crossed the road to come and speak to me.

"You that census lady?" the man said. "When you coming to our place?"

I assured them that they were on my list and would definitely be getting a call in due course.

In one home in a run-down block of flats, I visited an Aboriginal man who needed help in filling out the form, as he could barely write more than his name. We finished it, and he signed it, and I smiled and got up to go.

"Wait minute," he said. "Brother."

The door opened and another man came in from the corridor outside. We added this brother to the census declaration.

"Wait minute," he said. "'Nother brother."

And this went on until I had added about a dozen relatives to the original census declaration. I was struck by a number points here – the size of the family, the cramped conditions in which they lived, their urban, rather than desert, lifestyle, and the fact that every last one of them wanted to be recorded. It was a humbling experience.

I was loving the job, and having a very happy time, until one day I became a crime statistic.

Tired after work, I returned to the place where I was renting a room to find that all my valuables had been stolen from under the bed where, not very imaginatively, I had hidden them. In other rooms of the house, clothes had been thrown around but nothing was missing. In my room, there had been a surgical operation to take my computer bag, containing laptop computer, camera, I-pod and worst of all, my British passport.

Not realising I was the main victim of the burglary, the owner of the house had already reported the break-in to the police. I went separately to the Alice Springs police station to make my own statement.

The police officer looked wearily at me and asked whether, if the culprits were caught, I wanted the case to come to court.

"Surely, it's not a matter of what I may or may not want but of the law?" I said.

"No, you have a say in it," he replied.

We agreed that the offenders were likely to be Aboriginal youths. Indeed, we had a pretty good idea which particular Aboriginal youths, as the owners of the house worked with troubled teenagers.

I was not vindictive and had no desire to see the Australian prison population, already disproportionately black, swollen with more indigenous kids in custody. On the other hand, I didn't want anybody else to suffer the shock and trauma of burglary. And I did believe that bending over backwards and making allowances for Aboriginal people was, in its way, a kind of racism. I judged each individual, black or white, on their merits. For me, it was a simple as that.

"Yes, I would want it to come to court," I said, "and let the judge decide."

The loss of my gear was regrettable but the loss of the passport was a real blow, as it was stamped with my Russian visa and work permit, documents not easy to replace. And the silly thing was that these were of absolutely no use to the thieves.

In desperation, I put an ad in the *Advocate*, asking for the return of the passport, no questions asked. I hoped that the culprits might just drop the passport somewhere and it would be handed in. If they did that much, they were welcome to keep the other stuff, I reckoned.

But they didn't. I was forced to apply for new documents, which meant a delay in my return to Russia and loss of income as a result. As far as I know, the offenders were never caught.

You have to build a bridge and get over these things. I quickly forgave the robbers for, in the words of the Bible, they knew not what they did. But that didn't stop me from feeling shaky; I wished Vitaly was with me.

The night after the burglary, I was alone in the house. I thought I was OK and went to bed at about midnight. But at two in the morning, I woke up, trembling violently. Despite the late hour, I phoned Cathy Skipsey, the wife of my friend the photographer, Barry Skipsey.

"Sorry to disturb you but I am feeling rather afraid," I said and explained the situation.

"Oh, for heaven's sake," she said, "I'm coming straight over to get you. You can stay with us."

Cathy and Barry put me up in their house for the first night and after that, let me move into the granny flat in their back garden. "You can stay as long as you like," they said.

On the terrace of the granny flat, I took out my big census book and started to make my final tally of deliveries and receipts. It was quite a complicated task, involving cross-referencing, a bit like cashing up at a bank, I suppose. Every household had to be accounted for.

The ticked boxes (or more alarmingly, absence of ticks where I thought they were supposed to be) swam before my eyes. I was nearly in tears when Mr. Broad arrived and calmly took over.

"It's fine," he said. "You've got it all right. You've done a good job."

I wandered aimlessly into the garden and picked up some of the oranges that had fallen from the citrus tree.

Only months later, when all the census data was published, did I grasp the enormity of the operation in which I had played a small role. I had taken part in a huge sociological survey, one that showed, among other things, that Aboriginal people were a tiny minority in their own country while white people of British and Irish descent were still the majority. But increasingly, Australia was a multicultural country, with migrants from all over the world.

As a nice finishing touch, the Australian Bureau of Statistics sent me a certificate, thanking me for my contribution to the community.

Musical Life

The choir saved me that difficult winter in Alice Springs. 'Asante Sana', which means 'thank you' in Swahili, was an 'African choir' in the sense that we sang African repertoire, including liberation songs from apartheid-era South Africa. The conductor, a pastor called Morris Stuart, came originally from British Guyana but had strong connections to Africa. The rest of us were white Australians but we looked quite African in our black and orange kaftans, and we made a convincing African sound when we sang the Zulu spiritual 'Vuma'.

A few months earlier, the famous Soweto Gospel Choir had visited Alice Springs and sung with Asante Sana. I was sorry to have missed that but keen to take part in two concerts the Alice choir was planning for the coming season, one in the Araluen Arts Centre and the other outdoors, in the spectacular setting of Ormiston Gorge.

When I arrived in Alice in July, the choir had already started rehearsing and I'd missed a couple of practice nights. I managed to persuade Morris to let me in by showing that I'd had some classical training in Moscow and by swearing that I wouldn't miss a single rehearsal from then on.

That was an easy promise to keep as the evenings we spent rehearsing in the Uniting Church were the highlight of my social life and I looked forward to them very much. I sang with the altos and stood at the back, where from time to time, with no disrespect to Morris, we ladies of deep voice had a bit of a giggle.

I was delighted to discover that one of my fellow altos was Maya Cifali, in whose house I'd stayed during my last visit to Oz. Now I had a chance to get to know her properly. We went out for a bush picnic together and had billy tea and muffins one chilly desert afternoon.

Another choir member was Denise Grieshaber, who'd also previously given me a few days' accommodation in her home. I deepened my friendship with her and we became 'cinema buddies', going together to all the films at the town movie house. Denise wasn't averse to an ice cream afterwards, a valuable quality in a mate.

A third choir friend was Jane Coleman, an English woman who'd played the violin in top orchestras in Europe and now taught violin privately in Alice Springs.

Jane and I exchanged glances when Maurice gave us the text of a new song we were to learn:

Welcome where grass is green
As green as it can be
Where rainforest greenery
Is beautiful to see

I was used to singing Bach arias and to be honest, I was a bit sniffy about this ditty.

"Don't worry," said Jane, "we could do some more serious music together, if you're interested."

Jane and I started meeting outside the context of the choir. She introduced me to Ashley Sparrow, an earth scientist who was also a fine pianist. At home he had a Bosendorfer grand piano, which he'd had shipped from America when he'd relocated to work in Alice.

The three of us started working on Bach's 'Erbarme Dich', Peter's cry of anguish when he realises he has betrayed Christ. It's a fiendishly difficult piece because the top notes are a tad high for a true alto like me while the low notes are too low for a mezzo soprano. The English opera singer Rosalind Plowright, who once gave me a lesson, said I should sing 'Erbarme Dich' but I never thought I would be able to do it.

We practised in the Uniting Church, which had a stand-up piano.
"Am I getting those top notes?" I asked Jane.
"Yes, no problem."
"But am I in tune?"
"You're doing fine, honestly," said Ashley.

I was able to relax and think about the meaning of the aria. When Jane suggested I should sing it in the church at the Sunday morning service, I felt confident enough to agree.

The congregation was mostly made up of old ladies, wearing hats. I didn't feel the nerves that would have crippled me in front of strict Russian singing teachers. For the first time in my life, I didn't really care if it was a 'good' performance or a 'bad' one.

The woman minister preached a sermon about Christ seeking out ordinary fishermen to follow him. A German marine biologist, who for some reason was working in the desert, gave a reading from the Bible in heavily accented English. I sang the Bach aria in heavily accented German. At the end of the service, a young man came up and said: "Thank you. I have never heard such music before."

Jane presented me with a pair of sparkly earrings that had belonged to her mother. We became firm friends after that. Of an evening, I would go round to her place, where she and her housemate Penelope Bergen sat in their pyjamas, eating burnt fig ice cream and watching endless episodes of *Grand Designs*. Penelope was in the process of building her own tiny, Norwegian-style house in the middle of the desert and was glued to the British series on designing your own home. Jane had other plans. She wanted to travel and had applied to join a Canberra-based group of musicians and singers called The Wayfarers, who were gearing up for a world tour.

"We'll be going to Moscow," said Jane.
"Well you must come and see me when you're there," I said.

Meanwhile, the rehearsals continued for Asante Sana's upcoming concerts. 'Vuma, vuma, vuma, vuma…'

The African performances were part of the Alice Springs Festival that September. Lots of other interesting events were scheduled in the programme.

My Italian friend Mary Menotti gave me a free ticket to Wearable Arts, an annual show of recyclable fashion which she supported and in which she once 'flew', attached to wires, of course. I was both amused and amazed to see the weird and wonderful outfits on the catwalk – dresses made from plastic bottles and string, feathers and velvet, bicycle wheels and leather, you name it. It was very colourful and creative.

Mary and I also took blankets and thermos flasks and went to hear the Darwin Symphony Orchestra perform a concert under the stars. I had high hopes for this event but was disappointed. It wasn't that the orchestra played Borodin to a lower standard than I was used to hearing in Russia; they were only semi-professionals and amateurs, after all. Rather, it was that after playing two or three classical pieces, they devoted the rest of their programme to accompanying an Aboriginal guitarist. Don't misunderstand me. I have nothing against Aboriginal guitarists in the right context but Mary and I had set out our stall to hear an orchestral concert. We left at half-time, feeling a bit cheated.

Asante Sana's first concert was approaching and our choir gathered for a dress rehearsal at the Araluen Arts Centre. To my surprise, we were joined on stage by a women's choir from the remote Aboriginal community of Areyonga. I hadn't realised but in parallel with us, Morris Stuart had also been coaching the Areyonga ladies. We stood to perform together what I'd dismissively thought of as the 'green ditty'.

Welcome where grass is green
As green as it can be
Where rainforest greenery
Is beautiful to see

Welcome to all people
From your beautiful lands
To this land of ochre
And the coloured sands

Welcome where desert lands
Are also people's homes
Where kangaroos and emus
And other natives roam

Welcome to all people
From your beautiful lands
To this land of ochre
And the coloured sands

The song was written by Ruby Hunter as an Aboriginal welcome to Oz for people from all over the world. Performed by the Areyonga ladies, it gave me goose bumps and when the women started singing the national anthem 'Advance Australia Fair' in Pitjantjatjara, I was in tears.

The second Asante Sana concert in Ormiston Gorge would be the icing on the cake for me before I left Oz and returned to my other life in Moscow. The night before the concert, Cathy and Barry Skipsey took me camping at Glen Helen, which was a special treat because they knew how to camp properly, with steaks and wine and comfortable swags.

The day of the concert was crisp and sunny. The choir took their places on a rock on one side of the canyon while the audience gathered on the sand on the opposite bank. Nature provided the acoustics and our voices carried across the river, resounding round the gorge:

Vuma wena vuma vuma vuma
Vum' usindiswe

Ekhaya eZulwini
Kunezithembiso

Vuma, vuma, vuma
Vum' usindiswe

(Believe in the Lord
And you will be saved
There's hope and promise in heaven
Just believe and you'll be saved)

Women with Attitude

Saying goodbye to Australia was hard in some ways but it was Russia, with its gross injustices and grand idiocies, which still provided the best nourishment for me as a journalist. The medieval inquisition that was the Pussy Riot trial was the perfect example of Russian cruelty, insanity and courageous dissidence. It beggared belief in the West that two young feminists could be sent to labour camps for making a harmless, if perhaps tactless, political protest in a church. In 2012, I was busy covering their court appearances in Moscow and had no time for a trip to Oz.

If I couldn't go to Australia, though, Australia could come to me. As part of their world tour, the musicians from the Wayfarers group had been in Taiwan and China and were now heading for Moscow on the Trans-Siberian Railway. I went to the Yaroslavsky station, traditionally the place where Russians met political prisoners returning from the gulags, in high excitement at the prospect of meeting my Alice friend Jane Coleman off the train.

The laid-back Aussies, with their easy jollity, were very obvious among the former subjects of the Soviet empire, sweating as they dragged their cases along the platform. The Aussies were further identifiable from the musical instruments they were carrying and a vague whiff of Vegemite that clung to them after their long, sandwich-munching journey.

But to my huge disappointment, Jane was not among them. "She couldn't come on the tour. Her dog got sick," someone said.

So instead, I got to know and look after twenty strangers from towns all over Oz except Alice Springs. We were not strangers for long.

The leader of the group was a Canberra-based composer and conductor called Judith Clingan. Her assistant was a pianist called Renate Turrini. Judy had studied in Budapest and Renate in Warsaw, so we had a shared interest in Eastern Europe. We enjoyed each other's company so much that I ended up staying in their room at their hostel after a long day during which I'd shown them the sights of Moscow, including the famous Tchaikovsky Conservatory.

The Wayfarers were due to give a concert at St. Andrew's Anglican Church, which had only recently been given back to the English community, having been used as the studio of the state recording company Melodia in Soviet times. Keen to include me, even though I hadn't rehearsed with them, Judy let me sing one piece with the group, which was a joyful experience.

"If you come back to Australia, we might do a concert together," said Judy, who as a soprano was interested in me as a possible partner for duets. And Renate would be the ideal accompanist.

"I'd be up for that," I said, and we left it at that.

I was sorry to see them go, these bright spirits who brought a little bit of Australia to me in Moscow that summer.

By autumn, however, an opportunity for me to make another foray Down Under did present itself. Joy Taylor wrote to say that 8CCC, the community radio station in Alice Springs for which she volunteered, had won a grant to make a series of programmes about outback life. The series was to be called *Centralian Yarns* and Joy reckoned I could be useful to the team in gathering some of the stories of the desert's heroes and heroines.

I loved the idea. The SBS channel, best in Australia for world news, might pride itself on the fact that it covered 'six billion stories and counting' but we would do 40 yarns with Alice characters that would be an achievement for local broadcasting. Historian Megg Kelham would search the archives for tales of old timers while Joy and I would try to reflect the modern life of the town.

The same red suitcase I'd used last time was still on its wheels and I flew via Dubai, taking in the Burj Khalifa, the world's tallest tower, to be in Alice in time for the start of the project in November 2012.

Over Christmas, I'd be house-sitting for Cathy and Barry Skipsey and at New Year, I'd have my favourite job of looking after Momo at 13 Jarvis Street, but in the meanwhile, Joy and her partner Kalika gave me a room in their lovely home on Coolibah Crescent.

Joy and I did a bit of desultory work on the yarns. Although we'd had the intention of exchanging skills, it proved quicker if I did what I was best at, namely interviewing, while Joy played to her strengths as an audio editor. Making 30-minute radio programmes was more time-consuming than either of us had realised. In just under a month, we finished one show, so we only had another 39 to go.

But it was getting hot, Joy's ukulele-playing niece was staying at the house and Christmas parties were already on the horizon. We were not very productive in what remained of November.

The house on Coolibah Crescent was a cross between a holiday resort and an Indian ashram. Kalika was a swami and yoga and meditation teacher. Of an afternoon, we would stretch out on the floor and do 'yoga nidras', which usually resulted in me just dropping off and snoring on the carpet. It was very relaxing.

I roused myself and went to talk to the students of U3A (University of the Third Age, education for retirees), who were reading *War and Peace* and were interested in comparisons between Tolstoy's Russia and the modern state under Vladimir Putin.

But with each small rise of the mercury – the temperature was creeping up into the high 30s Celsius – it became harder and harder to concentrate on anything serious. You can't really work in the height of an Alice Springs summer; only have a good time.

So we got together in a girl band.

Liz Archer, classically trained as a pianist, brought a keyboard round to the house and another friend, Metta Young, got out her electric guitar. Joy, with her fabulous voice, ranging from the heights to the depths, was lead vocalist, while Kate Lawrence, Kalika and I sang 'shawap, shawap, oooh, oooh,' in the background.

Since we were mature and had some dignity as well as passion, we called ourselves Women with Altitude. We rehearsed by the swimming pool and drank plenty of lemonade.

The band had been Metta's idea. Before I arrived, the girls had played together to honour a friend who had died. After I left, they went on to become Northern Territory winners in an ABC competition for middle-aged rockers who didn't make it first time round called 'Exhumed – The Bands You've Never Heard Of'. In between the first concert and the dizzy heights of competition victory, I played a minor part in the group but rocking with them that summer was an unforgettable blast.

We got a gig in a small art gallery. For this, we put together a programme of songs that sounded pretty good, but something was missing. Madonna and other rock artists were speaking out in support of Pussy Riot.

"We should do the same," I said.

So Kate – of course it had to be creative Kate – came up with the costumes and props. For the concert, we all wore flaming orange and at the end of the final number, we turned up the heat by unfurling banners and placards that read:

'FREE PUSSY RIOT!'

Nadezhda Tolokonnikova and Maria Alyokhina, serving their sentences in icy labour camps in Russia, were the women with attitude. We were an older generation of feminists, from the fiery antipodes, Women with Altitude.

Star Lady

The phone rang. It was Mary Menotti, inviting to me a show. "Another of your mad fashion events?" I asked.

"Not exactly. It's the launch for a film, about a hairdresser... Look, hard to explain. Just come to the Olive Pink Gardens tonight."

So I went, and watched an amazing performance by a transgender hairdresser called Star Lady, who was making a huge difference to the lives of troubled young Aboriginal people by teaching them to dye their hair and look fabulous.

I caught her backstage afterwards and got an interview, which I reckoned I would be able to pitch to a magazine. "But I'll only let you say I am making a difference to indigenous people if you also write that they have made a difference to me," insisted Star Lady. So that was the deal, and she told me her story.

Growing up as a gay boy in rural Victoria, Star, who wouldn't reveal her real name, suffered homophobic abuse. "When I was 16, it was an incredibly violent time. I had death threats and hate calls and was beaten up and spat on. I didn't know there was a world out there where I would be accepted."

Since then, she had seen a 180-degree turn in her fortunes. Star had become the star of a documentary called *Queen of the Desert*, which showed how in Aboriginal communities she had found love and tolerance because she gave warmth and care to people as socially marginalised as she herself had once been.

"We've struggled and suffered persecution and prejudice," she said. "It's unspoken but this common experience brings us together."

From the mainstream white perspective, Australia's Aboriginal communities are often seen as dysfunctional, squalid and violent. The government throws money at the problem and from time to time intervenes.

In one unpopular move, the government dictated how Aboriginal people could spend their welfare benefits in an attempt to stop family budgets going on booze. Sober families felt it was unfair, as everyone was tarred with the same brush.

By contrast, with a bit of hair dye, glitter and theatrical panache, Star Lady seemed to have achieved more than a whole conference hall-full of bureaucrats and do-gooders. For example, because in her desert salons she had taught kids to wash their hair before applying outrageous shades of red, orange and blue, the incidence of head lice had dropped.

"Until you solve the problem of overcrowding, you won't get rid of lice and scabies entirely," she said. "You see kids with major sores on their heads from infection. Obviously you can't dye their hair; you have to get them to go to the clinic first. I had one kid, he said: 'Look, no sores, now hair dye.' That kid had taken responsibility for his own health."

The film about the outback salons was having its premier in Alice Springs, prior to being shown nationally on the ABC. For the launch, Star Lady had brought children from Areyonga community to strut their stuff down a pink catwalk.

Glamorous in purple capes and silver pants, with hair colour ranging from red to turquoise, the kids were a match for the town's flamboyant dressmakers, one of whom attended the party in a loud skirt hemmed with the ring of a child's plastic paddling pool.

Star Lady's mother, introduced to the crowd as Star Mum, hovered in the wings. She was dolled up in a royal-blue evening gown with diamonds, presumably fake. She said her real name was Wendy Sanders and she and her builder husband Bob, a Vietnam War veteran, came from Wangaratta in Victoria.

"Star was a real pain the arse from the time he was born," she said as her famous son/daughter enjoyed the limelight. "He wasn't interested in sport. He was always a performer and practical joker."

Wendy and Bob had no trouble accepting Star's homosexuality but he did give his parents a hard time when he went through a period of heavy drinking and drug abuse.

Star Lady confirmed that as a young man he had used drink and drugs as an escape from a hostile world.

The rebellious young Star took part in demonstrations against uranium mining and the detention of illegal migrants. Obsessed with superheroes, Star changed his name by deed poll three times from Star Power to Supreme Commander Star Power to Strike Commander, Starlight Laser Force, Saviour of the Universe, Doer of the Impossible. He was arrested and subsequently given a token fine for carrying a toy gun.

But since finding a new life in the Aboriginal communities, the only gun Star had carried was a well-aimed hair dryer.

"I suppose you were inspired by the film *Priscilla Queen of the Desert*," I said.

"Of course."

So, like the three Sydney gays from the 1994 movie, dressing up and discovering the outback, Star had taken a bottle of bleach and a pair of clippers and gone initially to the remote community of Kintore. His impromptu hair salon made a big impact on indigenous people, who had traditionally decorated their hair with flowers, emu fat, ochre and charcoal.

Star then went back to Melbourne to study hairdressing properly before returning to Alice Springs with a few hundred dollars and a dream of opening a network of salons in Aboriginal communities across the desert.

It was in the desert that Star Lady decided her gender was really female, although she hadn't had a sex-change operation. Aboriginal people, with their traditional concept of 'men's business' and 'women's business', had no problem with this.

"An Aboriginal lady said to me, 'you jungari-nungari' (man-woman)," said Star Lady. The elders didn't put any pressure on her but eventually she felt more comfortable being Star Lady Nungari and spending most of her time with the women, rather than the men.

"It's mindblowing," said Star Lady, "considering what these people have been through, that they can be so open and accepting. Government policy is still horrifically paternalistic and achieves little. Those who are bossy and racist get nowhere. The Aboriginal people say, 'they don't live here; we will just wait until they have gone.' You have to sit down with Aboriginal people, in the dirt, by the fires, and talk to them."

Star Lady was having particular success in relating to Aboriginal teenagers with drug problems. Marijuana was rife, she said, but the dangerous habit of petrol-sniffing was a greater concern.

"I know what it is like to lose hope completely; not to want to live in the world. I've been at rock bottom and personally created my own pathway out."

Robyn's Story

Christmas came and went, and there were New Year parties too, but finally, in around mid-January, we got back to working on the series of *Centralian Yarns* we were making for 8CCC radio. Megg had made considerable progress with her historical programmes but Joy and I, having been lazy at the outset, had some catching up to do.

"Have you got any ideas for interviews?" Joy asked.

"Well, have you seen that long room at Metta and Robyn's place?" I said. "They've got a huge rowing boat hanging from the ceiling. I think we should investigate."

"The breezeway," you mean, said Joy, giving the correct Aussie term for the corridor-like space running through the middle of the house, letting in air from the front to the back door.

"OK, but what's with the boat? We're in the desert here."

"Robyn was in the Olympic rowing team," said Joy matter-of-factly.

"There's a story there then, I reckon."

And we got cracking on a programme called *The Boat in the Breezeway*.

Robyn Grey-Gardner, to give our mate her full name, worked in the desert as a water consultant to remote Aboriginal communities but in her youth she'd had very different water connections, having been the youngest member of the first Australian women's rowing team to win an Olympic medal. She'd been a member of the coxed-fours crew to be precise, back in 1984, at the Los Angeles Olympics.

Robyn's old school, Unley High in Adelaide, had presented her with a five-metre, wooden King boat and named it after her in recognition of her Olympic achievement and this was the craft adorning the breezeway.

"We transported it up to Alice Springs in a truck," grinned Robyn. "We stored it for a while until a local architect worked out how to hang it from the beams. Then we hoisted it up and had a party."

Joy was busy finding '80s music to please Robyn, who was rather like a guest on *Desert Island Discs*. She picked Cyndi Lauper's 'Girls Just Want to Have Fun'. I was interested in how Robyn went from school rowing to making the Olympic team.

"I just loved it; I loved it like no other sport," she said. "I worked up through the state ranks until I reached Olympic level. You see people rowing hard and earnestly at the gym but it's actually more about how you connect with water. Rowers have an innate feel for this, like swimmers."

Of course, it was also a great team effort. When the girls of '84 knew they had been selected for the Olympics, they gave up their jobs and dedicated themselves to full-time training for four months. "We did weight sessions and sand-hill running. It wasn't glamorous but bare bones," said Robyn.

During training, accommodation was provided in Adelaide but there was little other state funding for athletes in those days, so Robyn and her crew members went on the dole. They had to sign on and show their availability for work, although the unemployment-benefit staff, knowing they were gearing up for Los Angeles, never forced them to take waitressing or cleaning jobs.

The neighbours on the street where Robyn grew up, Ashbourne Avenue, also pitched in to sponsor their star sportswoman. They held a street party and an auction to raise money for Robyn's expenses. After that, the crew was off to the US to acclimatise for six weeks.

In California, the head Aussie coach was very strict. Men and women were allocated separate lodgings and training at the shared boating sheds was staggered so the women rowers never got a chance to see their boyfriends on the men's teams.

"Our group was isolated outside Los Angeles, in a town called

Solvang," said Robyn. "It was all drug stores, or should I say chemists, and fudge shops. They called the town 'the little Denmark in the heart of California'. People were wandering round in Danish costumes. It was a bit weird."

More unnerving was the tense political atmosphere surrounding the Los Angeles Games. The Soviet Union and its Warsaw Pact allies were boycotting the gathering in retaliation for the West's boycott of the Moscow Olympics in 1980 because of the Soviet invasion of Afghanistan.

"It was disappointing for us," said Robyn, "but we decided to meet the competition that was there on the day, and to do our best."

Terrorism had also been perceived to be a threat at Olympic events since the Munich massacre of 1972, when eleven Israeli athletes and a German policeman were killed in a hostage-taking assault by the Palestinian Black September group.

The American authorities feared convoys of athletes' busses going from the official accommodation to the sporting venues could be a target and so, because of this, Robyn and her team were housed simply in someone's house.

"We were on stretcher beds in someone's lounge room," she said. "Because I was the youngest, I got put on the plastic mattress. We weren't allowed to go to the opening ceremony on the Sunday because our race was on Monday morning. We watched the opening on TV. It seemed unreal that we were going to head out next morning and compete."

On the big day, the young women were up at 4.30 for a race starting at 7.30.

"We sat in the kitchen, trying to eat. We didn't even think we might take home a medal. We just focussed on what we had to do. Of course, we were over the moon when we won the medal."

They lined up for the race, all ready to go.

"In a situation like that," said Robyn, "you can be like a rabbit in the headlights, overcome by pressure. I knew I had to think slow and controlled."

Half way through the 1,000-metre race, the Aussie girls were in sixth place.

"Then the cox said, 'you're second, go harder'. Towards the end, the pain was excruciating. It was a photo finish. Afterwards, we paddled around. An official in a speed boat roared up and said Australia was fifth. We shouted at the cox, 'what, you said we were coming second!'

"We had to do a lap of honour, lining up in the lane corresponding to our position. Fifth was not what we'd wanted but we had all done our best. We were back at the start, lining up in lane five, when the corrected results came through. 'Australia, lane three,' they said, and so we won the bronze medal by a small margin."

After this victory, Robyn was in big demand to work as a coach, which she did for many years. But in the end, she decided to make a clean break from rowing and the best way to do that was to disappear up into the desert. She did a degree in environmental sciences and started to work in water management.

She does miss larger bodies of water, though, and also the physical satisfaction of rowing

"These days, I go to the gym for a workout. And when I hop on the rowing machine, my body feels this is right."

Maya's Story

Like sand in an hourglass, my time in the desert was once more running out. Joy and Megg were to do the bulk of the work on *Centralian Yarns* – and reach the Community Broadcasting Association's national finals for 'best new radio talks' – while I made only a modest contribution to the project. But while I was still in Alice, I was keen to get one particular story on record, that of Maya Cifali, whose house at 13 Jarvis Street and whose cat Momo I had looked after on a number of happy occasions.

We talked on Maya's verandah, admiring the back wall of the house she'd just had painted blue to remind her of the dwellings in Egypt, where she'd spent her childhood. Maya, half-French and half-Italian, had grown up in cosmopolitan Alexandria, familiar with the sounds of the mosque and the bazaar. When she was exiled from this legendary city, she'd felt lost for a long time before she found a new home in Alice.

As a little girl in Alexandria, Maya had lived in a third-floor apartment, with a balcony shaded by three eucalyptus gum trees. "My eyes, as a child, were at the level of those gums," she said. "When the wind blew, the gum trees swayed over the balcony and I could hold their leaves and smell them. When I came to Alice and saw the gums, I was really taken by them, and knew I had to stay here."

Back in Alexandria, Maya's French mother chose for her a French convent education. There were many other communities living closely together in the city – Greeks, Russians, Jews, Lebanese and Syrians – and they all maintained and shared their cultures. This cosmopolitan world was different from multicultural Australia, Maya said.

"Multiculturalism doesn't work here; the communities in Australia do not feed each other. We welcome new arrivals from other cultures because we need a workforce but we don't welcome their culture."

This was a subject that exercised Maya considerably. She warmed to her theme.

"Take the asylum seekers coming on the boats now. The minister for immigration wants to give them a bridging visa for five years, with no access to work, or study, nothing, just a bit of money thrown at them like lettuce leaves to pigs. And then they want them to integrate!

"People are frightened of the foreigner in this country. They don't assimilate them. There is no symbiosis. We need people and we decide who we want and who we don't want. You might have a PhD in neurosurgery but you can be the cleaner at the Sheraton Hotel."

Maya hastened to add that Australia had been good to her since she arrived in 1966 and took citizenship in 1973. "I experienced generosity; individually, there is generosity but politically, there is not."

Had she been an Egyptian citizen, back in Alexandria?

"No, we were French and Italian. It was an exciting time. We did not know it was exciting then, but I find it exciting now, 60 years later, looking back."

The urban, bourgeois foreigners in Egypt had little to do with the local fellahs (peasant farmers) but Greek friends of Maya's parents had land and a house in the Nile Delta, where Maya spent holidays. "I would walk down to the fields and ask for a donkey and ride all day. I observed how they lived, growing cotton, tomatoes and zucchini."

In 1954, after finishing the French baccalaureate, Maya went away to university in Paris. Little did she know the day was fast approaching when she would not be able to return home to Alexandria.

Revolution was sweeping Egypt, and King Farouk I, the last of an Albanian royal lineage, had been forced into exile. The army wanted 'Egypt for the Egyptians'.

"Our cosmopolitan life began to feel uneasy," said Maya. "For the first time in four centuries, my father and uncles were required to have work permits. They didn't like it."

At first, Maya came back from university for holidays.

"Summer holidays in Egypt, happy, happy, but things were more tense than usual. In 1956, President Gamal Abdel Nasser nationalised the Suez Canal. People these days know about this in a vague way. The canal was a free trade route between Europe, the Far East and South Africa. It was run by the French while the military zone was protected by the British.

"My friend Nasser – I say 'friend' because he was mad but he had vision – decided he was not going to give money to the French and British when the canal was Egyptian.

"There was a short war. The Europeans in Egypt were unhappy. 'This doesn't look good,' said my father and put me on the first boat back to Paris. *OK*, I thought, *next year I will come home again and see my teddy bears, and my friends, and the beaches.* But it turned out that after Suez, all the foreigners were expelled in the shirts they were wearing, so to speak. I left in July 1956 and it was not until May 1990 that I saw Egypt again."

Maya said she understood why the Egyptians had to take power in their own country.

"It was right. The older generation of Europeans kept repeating, 'at home in Egypt this, at home in Egypt that', but I thought, *it was not your home. You were only there because it was beneficial to you.* At last Egypt was for the Egyptians."

But of course Maya was very homesick for Alexandria.

"I wasn't able to say goodbye properly. And I missed the air, the smell; my friends."

Her Alexandria friends were scattered all over the world, going to live in France, Italy, Sweden, Germany, Brazil and Argentina.

Maya married and migrated with her husband to Australia, settling in Canberra. They spent time working in Iran but got thrown out of there too when the shah was overthrown in 1979. Back in Canberra,

Maya didn't really feel at home but something stirred in her and life changed for the better when she came to the Red Centre.

"For me, to have lived in Alice Springs has felt like the closest thing to being in Egypt. The fact that there are indigenous people all around, and people of mixed colour, makes me feel comfortable. And I like the gums, the dry air, the oranges, the jasmine, the pomegranates and the palms."

Maya worked for years, helping indigenous people with such things as literacy and numeracy. After the handover of Ayers Rock to its traditional owners in 1985, three Aboriginal women adopted her as their sister.

"To be a sister means to have a relationship of duties and reciprocal benefits from others in the community," said Maya. "It is a two-way exchange that has enriched my life tremendously and I am very grateful to be accepted."

Indeed, so much a part of Maya is now in the desert that she has decided to die and be buried in Alice Springs.

"After a recent operation, I realised I could die and I told my daughters, who live down South, that I wanted to be buried here. I went to the town council and bought my little plot in the town cemetery and I will be buried here.

"Home is where you die, not where you live. There is a row, marked HBCD whatever, and number 24–26, like at the theatre. And I know I will be sitting there for the rest of eternity."

Baroque in a Banana Plantation

Strains of sweet music drew me over the mountains into New South Wales for the last few weeks of my fifth journey to Oz. If I hadn't had a commitment to take part in a concert there, I would probably just have stayed in the desert instead of crossing the Great Dividing Range to find a lush green world, quite different from the red, arid country that had held me for so long.

For this discovery, I was grateful to composer Judy Clingan and pianist Renate Turrini from the Wayfarers touring musical group. When we'd met in Moscow, we'd talked about doing a concert of baroque airs and duets together and now it was going to happen.

The concert was set for the 2nd of February in the regional art gallery in Coffs Harbour, a coastal town halfway between Brisbane and Sydney that was mainly famous for being the site of a giant sculpture called the *Big Banana*. I had seen a little bit of this Pacific world when I'd briefly visited Brisbane on a previous trip and found it full of beauty and light.

For the concert, Judy had brought in a former cellist from the Sydney Symphony Orchestra called Trish O'Brien, a second pianist called Alice Jamison, baritone Mark Williamson and a number of recorder players. They were all top-class musicians and somehow I was going to have to match them.

In Alice Springs, I'd been warbling away on my own, no doubt driving Joy and Kalika mad, practising my parts while staying at their house. Now I was joining the team for the final rehearsals in Coffs Harbour and I wasn't sure what to expect, except of course the glorious unexpected.

The first delight was that I was put up in the welcoming home of Leigh Summers, the director of the art gallery and an expert on Victorian women's underwear. Her bookshelves were a joy to browse, I can tell you. The next thrill was that our practice sessions were held at Alice Jamison's parents' place, so there we were, rehearsing Monteverdi in a banana plantation. Coffs Harbour was nothing if not surreal.

Judy was, quite rightly, a slave driver but the concert preparations seemed to be going quite well and the Australia Day public holiday was approaching, so she said we could have some time off to go to the beach. I think if she hadn't, I would have run away anyway because I had already seen those golden sands, that crystal surf.

Both Leigh and Renate were strong swimmers, born mermaids of the Pacific Ocean. As a daughter of the North Sea, I thought I was their equal but they warned me to be careful. It wasn't so much the sharks I should worry about, they said, as the powerful rip currents. Unsuspecting European tourists had been known to drown on their first days in Australia, diving ecstatically into waters they didn't understand.

I took their advice and spent my birthday, 26th January, very quietly, swimming in a safe creek and paddling in the shallows at the shore. The girls had invited me to go up into the mountains with them to listen to some opera at a festival but I wanted to be totally alone. 'Two paradises 'twere in one to live in paradise alone', as the poet Andrew Marvell so rightly put it.

A couple of days later, Renate herself took me swimming at Moonee Beach, so I was pretty sure I would be safe there. Moonee is known as a place where kangaroos come down to the sea and I really hoped to see Skippy ride the waves.

We undressed and entered the waters of the creek. Creeks are fine, as long as the tide is coming in, but dangerous if the tide is going out because then you can get sucked out to sea. I'm not quite sure how this happened, given Renate's experience, but we were swimming in a creek, with the tide going out. Afterwards, Renate was to say, "I should have paid attention to those bubbles on the water."

Oblivious to the risk, I swam gaily ahead of Renate. Suddenly, I felt myself pulled by an assertive current. Within seconds, I was helpless. It was as if I was being flushed down an enormous lavatory. I'm afraid I cried out in real fear.

"Don't panic, whatever you do don't panic," shouted Renate.

Renate's voice recalled me to my senses. Fortunately, I noticed a rock protruding nearby. I managed to hurl myself at it and cling to it.

"Stay there," shouted Renate, and she started to swim out to me. I was still whimpering but not quite so terrified.

A bloke in the water shouted out: "You guys OK?"

We'd been seen; extra help was available just in case.

Watched over by this man, Renate eventually reached me and pulled me off the rock. She guided me to calmer water and we both made it back to shore. Perhaps I exaggerate a little and I would have managed on my own, if I'd had no choice but to pull myself together, but I'm not sure about that. I think Renate probably saved my life.

I stood on the sands, trembling. I was so shocked that it was a minute or two before I noticed that my body was streaming with rivulets of blood from dozens of tiny cuts caused by razor shells on the rock.

Judy was due to pick us up in her car to take us to our next rehearsal, in a local church. She was not very pleased when she saw her alto soloist, looking like something out of a horror movie. "We'll just have to hope you don't get an infection," she said tartly.

Luckily I didn't and I was able to continue working towards the concert. I was just a bit subdued for a day or two after this drama, which had reminded me of the colossal force of nature.

The day of the concert arrived. Renate gave me a Chinese silk jacket, red on the outside and lined with gold, which made me feel glamorous when I went out on stage. The hall was packed; standing room only. Apparently, there was appetite for culture in Coffs Harbour.

Inevitably, I stuffed up a few notes but I don't think the audience noticed. We all gave of our best and the performance went well. After the applause died down, one man came up and said: "What a lovely programme. We don't often get to hear such music in our small town." Back at her house, Leigh laid on a party, with champagne and canapés, to celebrate our success.

The next day, I said a reluctant farewell to Coffs Harbour and took the train down to Sydney, where I was meeting two of my best friends for a girls' good time on the town. Mary Menotti was flying in from Alice Springs and Farida Khawaja was coming over from Tasmania and we were going to stay in a boutique hotel and have nice meals and pamper ourselves, all of which we did.

In Moscow, I'd had two women friends for periodic cocktails and cake consumption and we'd called ourselves the Three Witches. In Sydney, Mary, Farida and I were the Three Graces. Mary was Beauty because she was a sensuous person, who loved the arts. Farida was Goodness because of all the care she gave, working as a doctor. And I was Truth, the one who told it how it was, at the risk of causing offence. We had a lot of laughs and fattening desserts.

Creamy puddings aside, I noticed that Sydney was an exceptionally fine city and started to ask myself why I had not spent more time there. But it was too late now; I was within hours of catching a plane back to Moscow. And then a very odd thing happened.

My mobile rang and it was Farida, by this point back in Tasmania, asking if I would have time to see a friend of hers called John Vallentine. He was a doctor she'd met, working in the outback, but he lived in Sydney and his passion was sailing.

He was preparing to take his yacht Tainui through the inland waterways of Russia and she wondered whether I might be able to give him any tips before he set off on this adventure. Well, and yes, strangely enough I could. Because I'd had an Irish friend who'd made that same journey through Russia in the early 1990s, when the authorities had opened up the system of canals built by prisoners under Stalin and for years kept out of bounds to foreign sailors.

John and I caught each other for literally half-an-hour in a café in Cronulla and I filled him in, as best I could, on the route from the Barents Sea to Astrakhan. John had done his research and knew more about it than I did, really, but I was able to put him in touch with the family of the Irish sailor.

"Thanks, that great," he said. "If you ever come to Sydney again…"

"Yeah, I do hope to, one day…"

And at that, I grabbed a taxi and rushed to the airport.

Indian Digression

Australia receded into the distance again, as it inevitably did every time I returned to the Northern Hemisphere, but until I get could get back to Oz I did at least have a chance to be with Aussie friends when I went on a bus trip with them through India. It was weird. We were in an Australian bubble, looking out of the window at child beggars and the Taj Mahal. I was both in India and Australia at the same time.

The trip had been organised by my Alice friend Kalika, who not only taught yoga and meditation but was also a proper, ordained swami. The other group leader was Kalika's teacher, Swami Muktibodhananda, or simply Mukti, who came from Brisbane.

Both were white Australian women but they followed the teachings of the late Swami Satyananda, who'd founded a global yoga movement, based in Northern India. There were two Australian ashrams, one at Mangrove in NSW and one at Rocklyn in Victoria, that were affiliated to the main ashram at Rikhiapeeth in Jharkhand state.

Our group of yoga enthusiasts, some very experienced and some, like me, complete beginners, were going to have plenty of fun in India, including elephant rides and Ayurvedic pampering, but the main point of the trip was to spend time in the Rikhiapeeth ashram. I must say I was slightly apprehensive about this.

Since childhood, I'd avoided organised religion and never let the church get its hooks into me. I did once try to do a bit of meditation at Osho's ashram in Pune in Western India but after I'd shelled out a shed load of money for maroon robes, only to be ticked off for wearing the wrong colour of sun hat, I'd found myself rebelliously sticking my middle finger up to a self-righteous German priestess. I'd fled the ashram, concluding, not for the first time, *You're on your own, kiddo.*

But depending on rank, the devotees in Rikhiapeeth wore white, yellow or orange robes, so perhaps things would be different here. I was willing to give it a go.

Our group spent a jolly day, shopping in the town of Deoghar, before we were to leave the world and all its delights for a whole week. We stocked up on oranges, bananas and biscuits, knowing that the monastic food was likely to be frugal.

When we checked in to the ashram that evening, my worst fears seemed to have been confirmed. The one man in our group, a lovely joker called Tim, was separated from us and sent on his own to the men's dormitory. On the women's side, we were greeted with the news that the dorm was only for sleeping and during the day, we were expected to be outside, either sitting in the meditation sessions or doing karmic yoga (work).

"What if someone wants to come in to go to the toilet?" asked an older member of our group and did not get a satisfactory answer.

On top of this, we were warned that we should only go outside the ashram walls in groups of five. Presumably, the higher-ups feared that if we took a little walk, we would be at risk of attack from gang rapists, roaming bandits and crazed Naxalites.

"Why's that?" I asked. "Sounds a bit excessive."

"You don't ask 'why' here," said a young novice in white robes. She told me that, back in Australia, she'd trained as a journalist. Not one of my school, obviously.

That night, I went to my narrow bed feeling very oppressed. All the others in our big, shared room seemed to get off to sleep but I lay awake all night.

At some point in the darkest of the small hours, I found the core of myself. I remembered my uncles, who had been prisoners of war. If they could survive for over three years, I reckoned, I could get through this retreat for one week. I also reminded myself that I was not a captive but a free person who had paid for this experience and while I respected the swamis, I would do what suited me.

Mukti lay in the bed next to me. She was a kind woman, who not only talked the talk but walked the walk of compassion. When we all got up next morning, I told her that I was going to go to the toilet, inside the dorm, during the day, and whenever else I wanted to, and that was that.

"That's fine," she said calmly, and I realised it was only a matter of me asserting myself to some degree.

"I've got some tablets for diarrhea, if you need them," she added.

I must say that throughout, Mukti and Kalika looked after us very well.

That first morning, we all went down to breakfast in the big hall. We ate rice, washed down with sweet tea, sitting cross-legged under a giant portrait of Swami Satyananda.

This is a bit like North Korea, I thought to myself and privately christened the orange swami 'The Big Satsuma'.

Then we heard about our occupational options. We could either spend each day chanting and listening to chants, which was expected of those who hoped to rise in the ashram hierarchy, or we could work. The Australian team had been assigned to water-management duties. I decided to do the latter.

What that meant in practice was that we would be pouring water for thousands of Indian villagers, who would soon be arriving at the ashram to take part in a festival. They were coming in from neighbouring Bihar, one of India's poorest states, to receive gifts and to be fed.

The area was very dry and running water was limited. The villagers, who traditionally ate with their fingers, not knives and forks, would need clean hands before and after their meals. We would ensure optimal and fair use of water by using jugs to scoop it from barrels and pour it over their hands. That was our job. Not a bad one for me, I reckoned, since I am Aquarius, the water pourer.

Things seemed to be looking up. After a day or two of rice, peas and sweet tea at every meal, which made my stomach a bit turbulent, to say the least, a few of us worked out that we could go outside the ashram walls and buy bread and chocolate at Mr. Deepak's little grocery store and, better still, drink coffee at the local chai wallah's stall. And not a Naxalite rapist in sight!

I became a regular at the chai wallah's, where I made friends with a Mr. Jay Ram Singh from Mustafapur village in Bihar. He was a local journalist, a delightful gentleman and a man after my own mind.

Toilets were still an issue, however. Taking it in turns, we were getting up at four in the morning to clean the toilet and shower block, which the higher-ups were then locking, leaving only two lavatories available during the day for dozens of women with increasingly uncertain digestion. Some of the members of our group were, frankly, suffering.

Having cleaned the bogs, singing Russian opera in a loud voice as I scrubbed, I challenged one of the orange swamis about this situation.

"That's just your 'shit' coming up," she said.

What is it about religion and toilets? The Russian Orthodox Church is similarly challenged on the subject.

"No," I said, "I know about my 'shit' and believe me it's a lot darker than what goes down the toilet. No, this is about the basic human right of being able to relieve yourself whenever you need to do so."

"Well, we will have to discuss your complaint at a higher level," she said. (The problem was not resolved in the week we were there.)

By this point, defending my mates from abuse had become my purpose and loyalty to them was the only thing keeping me from walking out of the ashram. I'm grateful to those mates because without them, I would have missed one of the best experiences of my life. I am talking about pouring the water for the Indian villagers.

Their festival was a strange cross between Christmas and a school speech day. The children were receiving books and rucksacks and smart new clothes, all paid for by a generous ashram charity programme. The adults were being given bicycles and even cattle to help them in their working lives. For all its unreasonable rules, the ashram was certainly making a huge difference in the surrounding rural areas.

After they received their gifts, the villagers came to the dining hall for their meals. The girls and boys arrived first, running joyously, shouting and shoving to have their hands washed before they went in to eat. The adults followed, patiently queuing up and holding out their hands for a trickle of water before the food. Some of them spoke a smattering of English. With others, I quickly picked up a bit of Hindi:

'Pani?' ('Water?').

'Ha, Ji' ('Yes, Sir').

'Namo Narayan' ('God be with you').

Over several days, thousands of Indian villagers passed through my hands and every one of them gave me a smile. Some of the older ones took out their false teeth and asked me to wash them before and after they ate. It was such an intimate thing. These were among the poorest people on earth and they had such dignity. It was an unforgettable privilege to serve them.

Coming from the kitchens one day in a state of pure joy, I ran into an orange swami, holding out a basket of chocolates.

"Oooh, can I have one of those?" I asked.

"No, they are only for the people who have been sitting and chanting," she said. She came from Yorkshire; I recognised the accent and the meanness.

"Oh, OK, well I'm not that bothered about getting a chocolate."

"Well, you should be," she said. "This is what you are here for."

The woman actually thought she knew what I was there for.

It was up and down at the ashram but the positive outweighed the negative, so much so that on the last day, I decided to go to the ceremonies and listen to the chanting, which in any case I'd been hearing all week, booming over the loudspeakers. It sounded something like: 'Ein ding

ding, ein ding ding, ein ding ding, swa ha!'

Because I wasn't much good at sitting for hours cross-legged, I got a chair at the back of the ceremonial marquee and sat next to my friend, Joy Taylor. Kalika was somewhere up on the dais, with the more senior orange-clad figures.

The chanting began and I just fell into it. I saw the world as a giant, interconnected tapestry, you know…

Tears streamed down my face. By the end of the morning, I was ready to shave my head and put on the white robes of a novice. I hugged Joy and thanked her and Kalika sincerely for all they had done for me, in India and Alice Springs.

We started to file out, passing on the way a sacred cow that was tied up near the dais. As we approached, a little voice in my head said: *Don't touch it!*

So what did I go and do but stroke it on its flank, from behind? The cow reacted instantly, giving me a mighty kick on the knee. The shock was like an explosion in my brain and the pain was exquisite. As I hobbled away, I thought it was likely I would be crippled for life. But I didn't even get a bruise and the knee has not troubled me at all since.

Miraculously, the cow missed the joint but what it did do was to ground me from my stupid ecstasy.

You, with shaved head, in white robes? Who are you kidding, kiddo? The cow set me back on my own, right-and-proper, lonely path.

The Sixth Voyage
Plan A

"Reminds me of Adelaide," said Vitaly as we drove down the eucalyptus-lined road into Chania in Crete.

"Yeah," I laughed, "remember how we thought everyone in Adelaide was polite?" That was because a fair number of the businesses there operated under the name of Polites. It took us a while to work out that Polites was a Greek surname and that after Melbourne, Adelaide had one of the biggest Greek communities in Australia. With its wineries and olive trees, South Australia felt in many ways quite Greek.

In the summer of 2013, Vitaly and I were on holiday in Greece. We were relaxing on the beaches and trying to put out of our minds the fact that soon we would be standing at a crossroads, with a major decision to make. Our Australian permanent residence was running out and if we didn't go back Down Under by the 30th of January 2014 and put in more time in Australia, we would lose our chance of settling there. It was crunch time.

Vitaly had resumed his staff job in Moscow and was unsure whether he wanted to give that up. He had four grown-up sons in Russia, a factor in his thinking. I still had some work as a journalist in Moscow. In England, my parents were not getting any younger. There was also the question of what to do about my faithful old cat Jack. He looked at me with his yellow eyes and I swear I could hear him saying: 'Choose me, choose me.' But Australian resident status wasn't something you threw away lightly. It was a real dilemma.

Ever since leaving Adelaide, we'd been in two minds. We'd chosen to go back to Moscow in 2010 and thought we were doing the right thing. But then we'd been plagued with doubts that perhaps we hadn't given Australia a long and fair enough go; that we'd blown our big chance. Full of European ambivalence, we prayed in the manner of St. Augustine: 'Dear God, make us Australians but not yet.'

It's difficult to migrate when you're young; harder still when you're in your 50s. The secret of being a successful migrant is your ability to forget the past. The older you are, the more past you have to forget.

In Adelaide, we'd been lucky to get jobs and the local people had been very hospitable. But we'd underestimated the tsunami of nostalgia that was to hit us, making us ache for Russian birch trees where all around were gums; cry for old friends who seemed dearer than new ones.

My friend Sharon Mascall Dare, who herself migrated from the UK, said it was common for migrants to fail on their first attempt to settle. They often went 'home', only to find nobody there was really waiting for them anymore. The second attempt to migrate to Oz was then more successful. These return migrants were known as 'boomerang Poms' – at least that's what the Aussies called the indecisive ones who came originally from England.

With Sharon's insight in mind, Vitaly and I decided we should probably give Australia another shot. So after the Greek holiday, we started to plan our return to Oz. Where exactly should we go and what would we do this time?

For me, there was never any question. The part of Australia that attracted me fatally was the red desert and I always yearned for Alice Springs. But after Vitaly's horrified reaction to desert life, I knew the outback was out as far as he was concerned. For his sake, I was ready to compromise and accept an urban life.

"You could write to the Conservatorium in Adelaide and see if they might have some work for you again," I said to him. He promised to email them. Two weeks later, he had done nothing.

To be honest, I was secretly relieved. I didn't really want to go back to 'the city of churches'. It was nice and the locals had shown us nothing but kindness but my heart didn't flare with excitement at the prospect of living there. And Patrick Power, Vitaly's friend and colleague, had said we needed to 'swim in a bigger pond'.

Sydney then; it was going to have to be Sydney, Australia's biggest and most vibrant city. I began applying for jobs there, online.

The University of Sydney was looking for a lecturer in journalism. That seemed up my street and was certainly a job I could have done, with my 30 years' experience as a foreign correspondent. But it wasn't experience they wanted, rather the letters PhD after my name, which I didn't have. I applied for newsroom jobs instead, but had no better luck.

Vitaly was getting nervous. When we'd gone to Oz in 2009, we did at least have the promise of a job for me, which was something to hold on to. Now we were contemplating a leap of faith and neither of us knew where we were going to land. The void is scary. On top of that, we didn't really have enough money to keep two of us afloat if we were unemployed for long; our savings would only stretch to a trip for one.

Vitaly began to say that the Aussie dream was more mine than his. A part of me felt a bit betrayed by that. Why should it always be me who, in pursuit of a better life for us, had to make the running? We should be going to Oz together. I think a part of him felt guilty that he was letting me down. But neither of us took these feelings to a stupid conclusion. We both knew that if I went alone, he would be playing an equally important part by staying behind and continuing to earn in Moscow until I could get a new life going for us and he could join me Down Under.

There remained the question of Jack Pantera. I went to see my first husband Costya, who had given him to me as a kitten. I thought perhaps Costya might be willing to take the responsibility of looking after Jack but all he said was that he'd ask around to see if anyone wanted a cat.

Then out of the blue, the vet I'd consulted previously in Hungary got in touch to say his family's cat had just died. Very generously, he offered to take Jack and examine him. If he found Jack was too old to make the journey to Oz, he and his wife would keep him as their own pet in Budapest. They could hardly have said fairer than that. It seemed the universe was starting to smile on the new Australia venture.

My hopes were further raised when a British newspaper to which I contributed from Moscow rearranged its Sydney operation and announced it was looking for someone to report on Australian affairs. I immediately put my hand up for that job. It would suit me to go to Oz as a correspondent, writing home to a British readership, rather than as a migrant, struggling to find my way. With a good salary from the paper, Vitaly and I could go together and I would be able to support him until he too found work.

The editor seemed to suggest the job was in the bag. He promised to let me know for definite in a few weeks' time.

Simultaneously, John Vallentine, the round-the-world sailor I had met in Sydney on my last visit and whose cruise down the waterways of Russia I had followed with interest, wrote to say that I had 'firm friends' in Sydney and Vitaly and I were welcome to come and stay at his flat at the Rocks, a most prestigious central location. Suddenly, it was all coming together.

I browsed the pet shops, looking for a clipper cage for Jack. If Vitaly and I were going to Sydney by January, there was only a small window of opportunity before Christmas when the cat could be transported to Budapest. I felt uneasy about the idea of putting Jack on a plane and he certainly wasn't going to like it but needs must.

Then the newspaper got in touch to say they were sorry but they didn't in fact have the budget to send me to Sydney. Everything unravelled. I was not only disappointed but bewildered. All the signs had seemed to point so clearly in the direction of Oz and suddenly they no longer did. Should I go at all then? Was I being stubborn about this whole Oz thing when what I really needed was to forget the kangaroos and settle for the life I had?

One thing was certain. On 31st January 2014, the day after the Aussie visa was due to run out, wherever I was, in Russia, Australia or anywhere else, I knew I had to wake up happy. I couldn't go on torturing myself. If I was content inside myself, then it didn't really matter where I was in the external world.

Friends pitched in with their advice. Western mates said with one voice that of course I should choose Australia. Russians friends said my future was in Mother Russia. *"Kuda ti denishsya?"* they asked, using that terrible, fatalistic Russian expression that roughly translates as 'what choice do you have?' or perhaps 'where can you run to?'

I began to deny Australia. Apart from Oz, I told myself, there were plenty of other nice warm places where I could go to escape the Russian winter and then resume my Moscow life in spring. Take Goa for example.

I phoned my old friend Dima Dashchenko who, like other hippy Russians spends his winters on the beach in India, and asked if I could join him and his family under the palm trees for a few weeks after Christmas. "Sure," he said, "let's discuss it."

He invited me over to his house on the edge of Moscow and on a snowy night, he made a bonfire in the garden. Together we stared at the embers and I told him my Australian conundrum.

"Well, you can come to Goa with us, of course," he said. "You know you're always welcome. But Goa's Plan B, isn't it? Australia's your Plan A. That was your dream."

I knew Dima was right.

I went home and made a list of all the advantages of my life in Europe and it was long. True, living in Russia was getting tougher but from Moscow it wasn't far to the UK, where my parents lived and I had my own house. I listed what I had in Oz – absolutely nothing besides pure potential. It's hard to explain but that blank of potential attracted me more than all that was comfortable and familiar. I had read somewhere that development begins when you step out into the zone of the unknown.

What finally clinched it was a promise from my boss at the Australian newspapers for which I worked in Moscow that she would sponsor me for a new Russian accreditation if things didn't work out Down Under. With that safety net, I decided to jump. I'd be having a winter holiday anyway, so why not have that holiday in Oz? Without further ado, I booked a flight for myself to Sydney, arriving on the 16th of January, with two weeks to spare before the visa ran out.

Vitaly would stay behind, stick at his job and look after Jack. If I managed to find something for us, he would send Jack to Budapest and join me in Oz further down the track.

I fear Vitaly drew the short straw – another winter in Moscow – while I now had the prospect of a vacation in the sun. I would take up John's invitation and stay at his place at the Rocks. I would have a proper look at Sydney, a city I had managed on all previous visits to Oz to transit through and ignore almost completely. Surely Sydney, one of the world's great destinations, deserved some time and attention.

Before that, though, I flew home to England to join my parents in celebrating their Diamond Wedding anniversary on 19 December 2013. It was a lovely family occasion, with a splendid lunch and slap-up tea. Seeing me off at York station afterwards, mum and dad hugged me tightly but didn't hold me back. They were both in their mid-eighties but still as supportive as ever of my need to roam the world.

The Big Burgundy

When suddenly, at the midnight hour,
an invisible troupe is heard passing
with exquisite music, with shouts –
your fortune that fails you now, your works
that have failed, the plans of your life
that have all turned out to be illusions, do not mourn in vain...
Approach the window with firm step,
and with emotion, but not
with the entreaties and complaints of the coward,
as a last enjoyment listen to the sounds,
the exquisite instruments of the mystical troupe,
and bid her farewell, the Alexandria you are losing.
Constantine Cavafy

Christmas saw me at my desk in Moscow, working over the festive season to earn as much money as possible for my approaching trip to Australia. The stories I covered were all about activists being released from jail. Ahead of the Sochi Winter Olympics, President Vladimir Putin was trying to show a human face. He pardoned and freed the dissident oil tycoon Mikhail Khodorkovsky. After that, the two feminists from Pussy Riot came out of labour camp and a group of eco-warriors from Greenpeace were allowed home. I reckoned if these were the last stories I wrote from Russia, it would be a good place to put a full stop.

While I worked, I dismantled my little flat in the suburb of Novogireevo. I gave a lot of clothes and other things away to charity. I wasn't giving up the apartment exactly; I would continue to pay rent on it for a few months in case I needed to return to it. But I wanted it to be as empty as possible if I didn't come back. I honestly didn't know whether I was coming back or not.

Cavafy's poem about Alexandria was in my mind. It's about saying goodbye; losing all you have loved; being ready to bid farewell to life itself. I knew that soon I would have to let go of one vital part of myself, either Russia or Australia. Was Moscow my 'Alexandria' or was it Oz?

I packed a large burgundy-coloured suitcase with considerable thought, aware that I might only need it for a holiday, while on the other hand I might have to live out of it for months. I packed summer dresses and bathers; winter jeans and jumpers; business suits and shirts; and shoes, shoes, shoes.

I also packed some books that my friend Dima had asked me to deliver to a man in Sydney called Maurice. I felt slightly resentful about having to carry the extra weight but Dima had given me good advice and perhaps there was some yet-to-be-discovered meaning in the connection with this Maurice.

And I packed a soft-toy cat that I called my 'travelling panther' and cuddled in lieu of Jack. (In my handbag, accessible when the case was not, I had a small wire-wool cat that I called my 'spirit panther'. As you see, Jack was always with me.)

I locked the case and then locked my flat. I was going to spend my last night before the flight with Vitaly at his place in Balashikha, an hour's drive away, outside Moscow. Jack was moving to Balashikha at this point too.

That evening, in the tradition of Russian cosmonauts who watch a favourite movie before blasting off into space, Vitaly and I watched *Priscilla Queen of the Desert* again together. The ending, when Bernadette, despite being full of uncertainty, decides not to return to Sydney but to give a new desert relationship a go, had me sobbing. I felt I was in Bernadette's high-heeled shoes.

Early the next morning, although I had no appetite for them, I had two hard-boiled eggs for breakfast to set me up for the journey. Jack sat on the kitchen table while I tried to eat. He turned his head to me and kissed me with his nose. Then it was time to set off to the airport.

En route, Vitaly and I were going back to my flat to pick up the big burgundy case.

"Have you got the keys?" I asked Vitaly in the street outside, for the night before I'd given him the keys to my apartment so he could keep an eye on it while I was away.

"No," he said, "I thought you had them." He looked as if he was about to have a heart attack.

We were in time for the flight but had no time to spare. It was a choice between rushing back to Balashikha for the keys to retrieve the case and quite likely missing the plane or going with what I had.

"It's OK," I said, "I've got my rucksack with my computer and I've got my handbag with my passport, tickets and money. Let's go."

Vitaly looked relieved. I felt light as a feather, as we took the red express train out to Domodyedovo airport. I had often advocated that air passengers should travel without luggage. After all, if you can afford a plane ticket, you can afford to buy new tee shirts when you arrive. Now I was going to have to practise this philosophy.

At the airport, I peeled off my winter coat and gave it to Vitaly to keep for me.

"Can't you get rid of that old thing too, since you've decided to travel light?" he asked. "I'll buy you a new one if you come back and need a coat next winter."

So the baggy black garment was laid on a seat in case one of the guest workers who cleaned the toilets fancied it. Then Vitaly took me for a last lunch in one of the airport cafes.

"Find what it is you want for yourself," were his instructions for the trip. We hugged and he waved me off as I headed for passport control. I made it easily onto the flight for Abu Dhabi, where I would have a stopover before continuing on to Sydney.

I thought how deeply Freudian it was that I had left behind the big burgundy, so carefully packed. This could mean only one of two things: either I was leaving my old life behind and would start afresh, from zero, or I'd only be away a short time and would find all the stuff I needed waiting for me on my return.

In the inside pocket of my handbag, I carried the little 'spirit panther'. I fingered it for reassurance as the engines roared and the plane took off.

A Guest in Sydney

John Vallentine met me at Sydney airport, early in the antipodean morning, and took me straight home to his place at the Rocks, where we sat out on the balcony, drinking coffee.

I had arrived in Sydney with almost nothing but the clothes I stood up in. In Abu Dhabi, I had bought an orange swimming costume, so that I could take advantage of the hotel pool, and three shirts, one white, one turquoise and one coral, white and blue. That was the extent of my wardrobe for the Australian summer.

So, although I was jet-lagged, the first thing I did after breakfast was to go shopping for some clothes. I bought Australian basics – bush trousers that could be unzipped to create shorts, strong walking sandals, a little dress and a hat. My hat for this, my sixth voyage, was striped red and white.

I dozed on my bed through the afternoon and went out again in the evening, down to the harbour, which was in easy walking distance of John's house. The full moon hung like a pearl right over the white sails of Sydney Opera House. Of course, I didn't have my camera with me. I just drank in the lovely scene.

The beauty of jet lag is that you are often awake ridiculously early. Before dawn the next day, I walked down to the harbour again. The sun was just coming up and casting a golden light over Cadmans Cottage, Sydney's oldest residential building, built in 1816 for boat coxswains and their crews. It was named after John Cadman, who was transported to Australia in 1797 for stealing a horse. Pardoned by Governor Lachlan Macquarie, he went on to become Sydney's superintendant of boats. The cottage was very sweet and English.

I walked on, round Circular Quay and past the Opera House, to the botanic gardens but it was too early and the gates were still shut. I took some photos of the enormous roots of a Morton Bay fig tree outside the gardens and when I got home again, posted them on *Facebook*. My friend Megg Kelham from Alice Springs 'liked' the post and suggested I look out for the statue of the satyr Pan, sculpted in bronze in 1924 by Frank 'Guy' Lynch. I was to find Pan the next time I went to the gardens, just inside the gate, lolling on his pedestal and looking louche. His hairy, hoofed legs were crossed, concealing his penis, but thousands of visitors before me had found it and rubbed it until it shone.

Again I slept in the afternoon and in the evening John invited me to join him and some friends at a Japanese restaurant, his shout. I must say he was a generous host.

At the weekend, by which time I was starting to get over my jet lag, he took me out to a house party being held by his partner Chris on Scotland Island. We bought a bag of mangoes and licked banana-flavoured 'paddle pop' ices while we waited for the little boat to take us out to the island, in the Pittwater Estuary on Broken Bay, North Sydney.

Chris, who like John worked as a remote area doctor in the outback, loved to come back to Scotland Island to relax. Her beautiful home, with wide verandahs looking out over eucalypt woodlands, was classic Australian good living. The interior was bright with carpets, textiles and Aboriginal paintings.

Gathered round the dinner table were Chris and John's grown up children and their friends. One was a singer in a band; another was a scriptwriter for TV soaps such as *Neighbours* and *Home and Away*. They were talking about how they absolutely had to go to San Francisco that year. Open and friendly, they asked what life was like in Russia. I thought of Vitaly's sons, who had gone through their twenties with the shadow of army conscription hanging over them, and found

I could not begin to answer the question. "It's another planet," was all I could say.

I was glad when John said we would go back to his place at the Rocks for the night. I was enjoying exploring the Rocks area. John's own house, on Argyle Street, was interesting, having been the first butcher's shop in Sydney before it was converted for residential use. I didn't sense the ghost of the butcher but the house had character, with narrow stairs leading up from the front door and old fireplaces in the kitchen and living room. The window of my small room looked out over a thin sliver of harbour water. John said he'd always been attracted to industrial waterfront properties and had been lucky to buy the butcher's shop when it was going cheap. No doubt his house was worth a fortune now.

As I wandered round the Rocks – a district of narrow streets, passages and tunnels, ferns and, yes, rocks – I was in a state of wonder. I had spent so much time in the remote parts of Australia that most Sydneysiders and other urban Aussies never get to visit that it was good, at last, to see the Sydney side of the story.

The nearest pub was the Lord Nelson Brewery Hotel, which claimed to be Sydney's oldest continually licensed watering hole. I had a good steak sandwich there. However, in the area, I soon found other pubs also advertising themselves as Sydney's oldest, so I became a little sceptical of these claims.

To rest from the heat as much as to contemplate, I would go and sit in the Garrison Church at Millers Point, the colony's first military chapel. I have mentioned my interest in Captain James Cook but here I found a memorial plaque to another Yorkshireman who played a role in founding Australia: William Salmon Deloitte, Master Mariner, born Hull 1797, died Sydney 1870.

The Rocks area is the closest Australia comes to heritage and history (if you don't count pre-settlement Aboriginal history), so I could see why locals were up in arms over the building of a giant new casino, the Barangaroo development, just down the road from Argyle Street. They feared the atmosphere of their neighbourhood would be ruined.

John and I settled into a domestic routine. We had Indian takeaways and watched television together. All over the world, TV rots the brain and Australian television is no exception. More or less watchable (with a glass of red wine) was Stephen Fry's comic quiz show QI but I could have watched that in the UK.

However, I must say that I admire Australia's SBS channel, with its slogan 'Your World is an Amazing Place'. Committed to reflecting diversity, it has an excellent programme of world news and good late-night films in foreign languages.

I watched a heartbreaking documentary about Nguyen Tuong Van, a young Vietnamese-Australian hanged in 2005 in Singapore for drug running despite Australian pleas for clemency. Also surprisingly enjoyable was an Aussie film about potato farmer Cliff Young, who in 1983 won the Sydney to Melbourne Ultramarathon at the age of 61.

Cliffie's story inspired me. Because I had come to Sydney at the age of 58, looking for work in the big city, and I guess I was wondering whether I could still hack it or whether it was time for me to be put out to grass. I certainly didn't feel ready to retire and sit in a rocking chair (even if there was 'a sheep or two, a k-kangaroo and a clothesline out the back', to quote Brown and Johnson's offering for an alternative Australian national anthem).

I was grateful to John for the space he gave me to find myself. In Indian religious terms, I was looking for my 'dharma', which I took to mean the work I should be doing in life. What was I born to do? Where was I most useful? I was glad that the decision to stay in Oz or go back to Russia now hinged not on the needs of my parents, or of Vitaly, or of my cat, but on my needs and what I should be doing with my life.

I was conscious that I shouldn't overstay my welcome at John's. I offered to pay him rent but with big heartedness, which I have found typical of Aussies, he brushed off that idea, saying only that I could paint his back door for him, if I had nothing better to do. (I did; in dark red.) I was still applying for jobs online and telling everyone I met that I was in the market for work but I knew it would be a while before any of these seeds sprouted, if at all.

John, who had sailed his yacht Tainui through Russia's inland waterways the previous summer, was preparing to go back to Russia, now in the depths of winter, to do a month's research for a book he was planning to write. He was reading up about the Volga River and by chance I found among his books *Last Boat to Astrakhan: A Russian Memoir 1990-1996* by my old friend and colleague Robert Haupt, who used to work for Australia's Fairfax newspapers in Moscow.

Robert's story was a very sad one. I'd known him as a joker and bon viveur. When he left Moscow, I knew he was writing a book about his experiences. I heard that when he'd put the last full stop to the manuscript and sent it to his publishers, he'd died. And I'd never read his book. At John's, I settled down on the brown leather sofa to read it.

Wherever he is, I thank Robert, because reading his book helped me greatly. As he took me mentally on his last cruise down the Volga, I expected I was going to drown in nostalgia for Russia. In fact I didn't. Reading Robert's memoir made me realise at that moment how very much I wanted a new life in Australia.

I was going to need a miracle to make it happen, though. I had a flight booked back to Moscow on the 9th of March because if by then nothing had worked out for me in Sydney, I was going to have to get back to Russia to renew my work permit and salvage my life there.

If, in January, my task had been to cross the Australian border before my Aussie visa ran out, then now my task was to avoid re-crossing the frontier. I had to miss that flight back and stay in Oz. I had only two months to find a job but I believed in miracles, particularly since a travel webzine with offices right at the Rocks was advertising a senior position. Surely that couldn't be coincidental.

John said that while he was away in Russia, I could have his place at the Rocks to myself, provided I'd made other arrangements by the time he returned. That gave me until the end of February to sort myself out.

"Oh, and while you're here, go to the Sydney Art Gallery. They've got an exhibition of American painting on at the moment," he said to me, as he lugged his case down the stairs and headed off to catch his flight to Moscow.

Tourist Sydney

With all due respect to the Sydney Art Gallery, and its fine collections, it was not at the top of my to-do list but something to save for a rainy day as, to my fresh eyes, Sydney was one giant open-air exhibition. Every street and market, flower and bird, boat and flash of light on water was a picture in itself.

I was keen to find work, of course, but when you're hunting and have laid all your traps, there comes a point when all you can do is wait. I certainly wasn't going to let anxiety about earning a living spoil my holiday but rather make the most of it for every glorious day. 'Pleasant and useful,' was my motto. Until work came along, I was going to enjoy myself to the max.

The harbour was an endless source of interest. I found different ways to approach it and many angles on the iconic Harbour Bridge and Opera House. In the cool of the evening, the ant-like figures of tourists climbing the bridge reminded me of the 'mingas' scaling Uluru, the only difference being that Sydneysiders didn't seem to mind their bridge being mounted while Aboriginal people were upset when visitors showed such disrespect to their sacred site.

In the harbour itself, as well as the little red 'shark' speed boats that gave the tourists a thrill and the green and yellow commuter ferries that plied between Circular Quay and Sydney's various beaches and suburbs, enormous cruise liners came into dock each day. I don't really remember seeing ships like Royal Caribbean's *Radiance of the Seas* and Cunard's *Queen Elizabeth* in Sydney Harbour when I visited in 2001. Certainly, in recent years the cruise business has expanded, with many more liners coming into port.

The liners came in the morning and unleashed their tourists for the day on the shops, markets and cafes of the Rocks area. Hundreds of overpriced tee shirts, koala toys and cream teas were no doubt sold to each shipload of passengers before a booming horn alerted them that it was nearly time for departure, at 5pm sharp. Several times I watched these giant ships slip their ropes and set sail for their next destination. I would wave to the passengers, standing on the decks, taking in their last views of Sydney. Each time I was profoundly moved to think of all those souls – the *Radiance of the Seas* has capacity for 3,360 passengers and crew – heading out into the ocean.

When I wasn't liner-spotting I was watching the street performers at Circular Quay. Every day all kinds of entertainers, from Aboriginal dancers to fire eaters, turned the area into a non-stop circus. For a few dollars, you could listen to music or watch mime acts while enjoying an ice cream or a bag of chips from the kiosks round about.

I saw one 'performer', sitting on the pavement and in a wheedling voice, begging passers-by to stop and watch him, but no crowd was gathering. I approached him and asked if I could use his microphone. "Let me give you a PR tip," I told him. "You've got to give it a bit more punch." And I started ad-libbing into the microphone: "Roll up, roll up for the most amazing show, just about to start!"

Still nothing happened. "By the way, what is your show exactly?" I asked the man. "We have to give the audience a few more details to attract them." He shrugged and I gave up my attempt to promote him.

Afterwards, another artist came up to me. "That was a very kind thing you did to try and help that guy," he said. "But the thing is, see, he makes more money than any of us. He does absolutely nothing and people throw money at him."

I befriended this second artist, who turned out to be a cheerful trick cyclist called Sean Bridges aka Bike Boy. He had peroxide-blond hair and wore glittery shorts for his act, which involved riding a bike on a high trapeze, while juggling and cracking jokes.

"I came originally from Street in Devon, so I am the original street artist," he said one day after buying me a coffee in exchange for some feedback on his show. I suggested he took a less blackmailing approach when encouraging the audience to make contributions but allow his stunts to speak for themselves, for they really were quite impressive. But whether he did, or whether that worked for him, I couldn't say.

I was fascinated by the artists who stood stock-still until someone threw them a coin, allowing them to move. A lot of young, aspiring actors earned money this way, I supposed. One couple, sprayed from head to foot in gold, waltzed whenever they heard the rattle of money in their tin. Another such statue performer was Silver Man, with whom I had a thought-provoking conversation.

I tossed him a coin but instead of moving he said, "Hello." It was a quiet evening and he evidently felt able to break from his work and have a chat; indeed he seemed to want to talk. Through his silver mask, I could see his burning brown eyes.

"I used to be a pianist," he said, "but now I have come to this. I went away to the UK but things didn't work out, so I came back here, because at least it's warm on the streets of Sydney. It's a hard life."

He made me think what Vitaly might do in Sydney, if he failed to get a job in his profession of music. Silver Man also made me think about my own profession.

"What kind of journalist do you want to be?" he asked when I told him I was job hunting. It was a penetrating question because I was applying to all kinds of news organisations, including tabloid papers, while not being entirely sure that I wanted to report on celebrities. Could I really bring myself to write: 'Beyonce Photoshops her Thighs' or 'At 50, Elle Macpherson Still Looks Sizzling in her Undies'?

I thanked the Silver Man, who was both street performer and counsellor. On the way home, I watched the seagulls circling and attacking the tourists eating fish and chips on the benches in front of the Museum of Contemporary Art.

This was Circular Quay, a canvas splashed with vivid colours. If the circus acts and spontaneous chats were not enough, the pavement was covered with quotes from Australian classic literature. One evening, I just wandered up and down, reading the sidewalk.

A quote I found particularly meaningful was by Albert Barnett Facey, farmer, tram driver and author of *A Fortunate Life*. Abandoned as a child, sent to work at the age of eight, injured at Gallipoli in 1915, father of seven and grandfather of 28, he was able to say: 'I have lived a very good life; it has been very rich and full. I am very fortunate and I am thrilled by it when I look back.'

Gratitude was his only attitude and in those first tourist days of going 'wow' at everything in Sydney, it was mine too. I felt so lucky to be in this bright, breezy city, where clivia and aubergines grew on the streets, when back in Moscow, it seemed nothing stirred and the temperature was minus 20C.

I vowed not to waste a minute; day and night I walked around the harbour. In the evenings, especially at weekends, the bars and restaurants were heaving. Snatches of conversations floated out in all the languages of the world. Coloured lights played over the Opera House, turning the familiar white sails turquoise and pink.

One evening, I went inside to hear the Sydney Symphony Orchestra provide live accompaniment to Godfrey Reggio and Philip Glass's new film, *Visitors*. I liked the film but was more impressed by the concert hall itself and the wonderful views out onto the harbour from inside Danish architect Jorn Utzon's avant-garde creation.

When I first arrived in Sydney in 2001, with an old-fashioned box camera, I asked a passerby to take a photo of me, sitting on a ship's mooring bollard, with the Opera House behind me. Now I had a digital camera and was able to take my own blurred selfies against the famous backdrops of bridge and theatre. There is perhaps something rather sad about the lone tourist having snaps taken or taking pictures of themselves. Sydney was so beautiful and I wanted to share it with

Vitaly, my parents, my friends. But I had learnt long ago that some experiences were given to me and me alone. That's both the loneliness and the wonder of life.

I walked for miles each day. I returned to the Royal Botanic Garden that I had glimpsed on my first morning and went deeper and deeper into the extensive grounds. I loved the mixture of familiar European plants and exotic tropical vegetation; of buddleia on the one hand and on the other, giant tree magnolias. Spikey orange and yellow canna lilies thrust up against the background of the skyscrapers in the CBD (central business district). Round the corner were peaceful pools with lotuses.

Australian native plants were well represented, of course, and I started to understand why the Aussie national colours are green and gold. The words on the plaque were originally by Monty Python but the Australians have adopted them as their own:

This here's the wattle,
The emblem of our land,
You can put it in a bottle
Or hold it in your hand

I sat near some beds of lavender and echinacea, trying to work out what was the thin vibrating sound I could hear; some strange Australian bird or insect? Eventually I traced the source of the tremulation to a bower where a Chinese child was practising her violin – ah, so it was the lesser Cantonese bower bird then.

The real bird life was shocking to my European eyes and ears. Huge white cockatoos screamed blue murder as they flew from tree to tree while on the lawns sacred ibis, with their big curved beaks, dug for what I supposed must be worms (the mind boggled at how fat those antipodean worms might be). To the Aussies, the ibis are common pests, like pigeons, but I knew back in Moscow Vitaly's son Cyril, who is crazy about birds, would love the ibis, so I posted photos of them on *Facebook*.

Near the café, I saw a large brown spider in a web that stretched between two bushes. "Is it a funnel web?" I asked nervously. "No, it's quite harmless," said a gardener. Apparently, the spiders that scuttle near swimming pools are the ones to watch out for.

Apart from the living things, there were some interesting sculptures in the gardens – a cairn of white stones that tilted but didn't collapse; a wirework confection in the shape of a nut; a dramatic Polynesian figure in wood; and a number of rhinos, from a herd of 125 dotted all over city as part of Taronga Zoo's campaign to raise awareness of the threats of poaching and habitat-loss facing rhinos in the wild.

It started to rain and I unfurled my umbrella. Down by a small lake, I heard a young man say in Russian: "Oh, pancake (the polite way of swearing), rain, and we only have one day in Sydney."

I don't normally intrude into other peoples conversations but couldn't help approaching and surprising him by saying in his own language: "Don't worry, the sun will soon come out again."

He chatted with me for a while before saying, rather formally, I thought: "Well, thanks to this kind Mary Poppins. It was nice to talk to you." Suddenly I noticed more young people with video cameras on the other side of the lake. I realised I had walked into a film they were making. They turned out to be a Ukrainian TV crew, making a travel programme, in which I suppose I might briefly appear as one of the charming oddities you can find Down Under.

Since it was still raining, which the succulents in the Succulent Garden were no doubt glad of, I slipped into the Maiden Theatre, showing the works of the winners of the International Garden Photographer of the Year competition. I passed a pleasant half hour, looking at wood anemones in a Polish forest and mist over cotton grass in the Netherlands, before I went outside again to discover the brash Aussie sun was back.

Whichever way one walked in the botanical gardens, there was something to delight. The aria 'Where E'er You Walk' by Handel came into my mind. One path would take you to the Palm House and Camelia Garden; another led via the herbs and roses to the Conservatorium of Music, its gatehouse resembling a castle.

If you went up through the Domain and past the must-see-but-still-to-do Sydney Art Gallery, you came to St. Mary's Cathedral (Catholic) and Hyde Park. I did this one day, drawn by the sound of an orchestra playing Tchaikovsky's 1812 Overture. They were rehearsing for a performance in the park, as part of the annual Sydney Festival.

Near the Archibald Fountain, I watched a man entertaining children by blowing giant bubbles that hung prettily in the air. I saw a possum trying to steal the lunch of a woman sitting on a bench. Without any sentimentality, she aimed a kick at the marsupial. Then I walked up the allée of fine trees to the war memorial and also took in the statue of Captain James Cook. Standing on his pedestal with outstretched arm, he appeared, like the thousands of Lenins all over the former Soviet Union, to be hailing a taxi.

Hyde Park was getting too close to the city for comfort, so I doubled back into the botanical gardens, which I found more restful. I reckoned I'd earned a croque monsieur and quite possibly a chocolate pie in the café, with my favourite flat white coffee, of course.

I devoted several days to the gardens, studying them in detail. I was interested not only in the visible but the invisible. The Cadi Jam Ora or 'First Encounters Garden' gave a hint of what was missing from the surface picture. Belatedly, it honoured the Cadigal people, indigenous to the area that was to become Sydney.

The Cadigal were one small clan among a number of tribes living in the bay. The arrival of white seamen and convicts was disastrous for them. Shortly after landing with the First Fleet in 1788, Governor-designate Arthur Phillip estimated the indigenous population of Sydney district at 1,500. A smallpox epidemic in 1789 wiped out about half of them and by 1791, there were said to be only three Cadigal people left, although some archeologists say survivors may have moved elsewhere.

Before Cadi Jam Ora was created, the information panel said, 'nowhere was it apparent that the site of this modern-day botanic garden once supported native plants and animals in a natural balance, providing food, shelter and building materials, as well as carrying the spiritual meaning of an indigenous culture for thousands of years'.

White culture is certainly more obvious in the gardens. If you keep going around Farm Cove, past the open-air cinema and the Fleet Steps, you eventually come to Mrs. Macquarie's Point and Mrs. Macquarie's Chair, a bench carved out of sandstone by convicts as a seat for Governor Lachlan Macquarie's elegant, muslin-clad wife. Apparently, she was fond of sitting at this spot and watching the ships come in from England. Now the tourists flock there to park their bums and munch on sandwiches.

I went a number of times to the point to watch the turquoise waves lapping on the orange rocks and caressing the dark seaweeds. Then rounding the point one afternoon, I came upon – oh, joy of joys – the Andrew (Boy) Charlton Swimming Pool and that was it. From then on, all I wanted to do was go swimming every day.

The facilities were fantastic. True, the large main pool did rather feel like a bath of testosterone, as tanned and toned Aussie blokes scythed up and down the lanes, as if they were training for the Olympics. But I soon discovered that I could swim in the children's pool, which was the size of a regular pool in Europe, and blessedly empty of children. (Perhaps they were all down in the gardens, watching *Toad of Toad Hall* at the outdoor kids' theatre.)

After swimming, I would go and have a snack in the pool café. I was good and chose lentils over cake. The pool was right down at the waterfront and from the café verandah, I could see the ships moored in Woolloomooloo Bay. One enormous, bright-red vessel particularly attracted my attention. It was there every day through January. Only weeks later, when I saw a picture of it in the papers, did I realise what I'd seen was the Australian Navy's *Ocean Shield*, which took part in the Indian Ocean search for missing Malaysia Airlines flight MH370.

All this I saw and more – a bi-plane looping the loop over the harbour and spelling out the words 'Jesus Loves You' with its vapour trail; a visiting Russian folk troupe, with balalaikas, dancing outside the Opera House. But I didn't did get to see The Sydney Art Gallery – the problem was, there was never a rainy enough day.

Liveable City

I began to live in the liveable city that is Sydney. I hopped on the buses, rode the double-decker trains and found out where the ferries might take me. True, in Monocle's Quality of Life Survey for 2013, Melbourne came second and Sydney only ninth in terms of world livability but for my money, Australia's biggest city was still streets ahead of gridlocked and bad-tempered Moscow.

I say 'Australia's biggest city' and that is still true of Sydney but I have read reports that Melbourne is set to overtake its rival by 2040. After the gold rush in the 19th century, Melbourne not only outgrew Sydney but became the richest city in the world. The tables were turned in the 20th century but now again Melbourne is on the rise.

Apparently the reason for this is Melbourne's superior urban planning and transport infrastructure, making it more desirable for businesses and generally an easier place in which to live. Sydney's CBD extends back from the habour but most of the city's population lives out in the western suburbs, from where they struggle to commute into work. Oh, the dreaded southwestern suburbs... I heard quite a lot about them from Sydneysiders and they didn't sound at all appealing.

Luckily my dinner date was in gentrified Glebe. I had been invited by my old friend Geoff Winestock, who used to be editor of *The Moscow Times*, and his wife Louise Newey to visit them at their home. I had seen Geoff for a coffee on one of my previous transits through Sydney but I hadn't seen Louise since we'd been together in Moscow in the 1990s. The last time had been at a party where, I remember, she wore a stunning electric-blue dress.

Entering their house, which like many Sydney dwellings had a modest frontage but opened out beautifully once you were inside, I immediately sensed a bit of a Russian influence. There was a 'Russian room', with a piano and paintings, including a portrait of Louise in her Moscow days, looking elegant in an understated way. As she welcomed me, I saw Louise had hardly changed but still looked fresh and lively.

The difference was that Geoff and Louise's children had grown up. They'd been babies in Moscow but now Josh and Zelda were teenagers, both musically talented. After a delicious dinner, Josh, who played various instruments and composed music, gave me a little private recital on his tuba. For some reason, it made me think of *Mrs. Carey's Concert*, a wonderful Australian film about a school music teacher who inspires her pupils and takes them to perform on the stage of the Sydney Opera House. I was sure Josh had a future on a concert platform somewhere.

When the youngsters went up to bed, Geoff, Louise and I took our chamomile teas out onto the verandah and reclined on sofas under the stars. Geoff and Louise reminisced about Moscow, saying the years they'd spent there, in politically fascinating times, had been some of the most exciting of their lives. I asked why they'd left.

"There came a point," said Louise, "when it all just got too heavy – swaddling the children up when they were small and in winter, endlessly carrying them into and out of cars." How well I understood her.

"Do you think you'll stay in Sydney?" Geoff asked me.

I wanted to, very badly.

"I reckon you'll get a job eventually," he said, "if you give it three to six months."

But I didn't have that time. I needed a breakthrough on the job front rather quicker than that.

The travel webzine based at the Rocks had turned down my application to become its content producer. Its 'talent acquisition consultant' wrote to me, saying: 'I've had a good look over your CV and whilst you have some really great experience, you've unfortunately not made the shortlist. I want you to know this is not a reflection on your skill set, but due to the fact that we've had some really strong applicants apply who were more closely aligned with what we are looking for.'

I wasn't unduly bothered. I had other irons in the fire at various newspapers. What I needed was for some potential employer to see me in person. Online was all very well but face to face, I could be so much more convincing.

Meanwhile, I decided to go and see the one boss I did know, the editor who every year gave me a letter of endorsement so that I could renew my accreditation to work in Moscow. She was kind, as ever, and gave me the piece of paper that would open the door back to Russia. *Well, good to have it but let's hope I won't need it,* I thought to myself.

"Your roots are in Europe," she said to me quietly as we parted.

Leaving her office, I walked through Darling Harbour, Sydney's other harbour, and made my way to the Chinese Garden of Friendship, where I sat and watched a cormorant on a rock in the lake and wandered among the pagodas, dragons and bamboo. Then I went into Chinatown and had custard-filled dumplings in a little dim sum bar that I had discovered.

On my way home to the Rocks, I paid a visit to the Museum of Contemporary Art. At the entrance was a fresco, showing parrots and kangaroos and Aboriginal tribesmen living in an unspoiled idyll and row boats arriving, carrying white, pneumatic figures that looked like the Michelin Man. The white figures had mouths but no eyes. It was rather disturbing.

Inside was a visiting exhibition of work by Yoko Ono, which personally I could have lived without, but the permanent collection was interesting. I sat mesemerised for ages by a desert collage by Imants Tillers, whose Latvian father had gone up into Central Australia and lost himself in the Never Never.

On another floor, a whole wall was covered with Aboriginal bark art, contrasted with some rather mediocre modern daubs and chandeliers hung at odd angles. The Aboriginal stuff was treasure – if only it had been spaced out for better appreciation and juxtaposed with some worthier contemporary examples.

As I left, I found myself thinking that the best things in the whole museum were the glass lifts and the big glass windows, offering splendid views out over the harbour. So that just goes to show you how much I know about art.

While I was down at the harbour again, I checked the ferry times because the next day I was planning a trip to one of Sydney's famous beaches. I'd been to Bondi in 2001 and found it rather seedy, although the waves and lifesavers were obviously impressive. This time I was considering Manly, 'seven miles from Sydney and a thousand miles from care', to quote the publicity slogan of the old Port Jackson and Manly Steamship Company. When my old Moscow friend Lindy Sinclair contacted me to say that she was over from Europe for two weeks and staying with her parents in Manly, well, that settled it. We agreed to meet where the main street joined the promenade in time for morning tea.

The ferry ride over to Manly was exhilarating. I stood at the rail, watching the CBD, the Harbour Bridge and the Opera House fade into the distance, but found myself needing to sit and take some deep breaths when the swell increased as we went out through the Heads. Once we landed, it was a quick walk from the ferry terminal to the place of rendezvous with Lindy.

I hadn't seen dear Lindy for 20 years and yet, when we met up again, it was as if we'd been together only yesterday. That's what I call friendship. Without her that day, I would probably have walked back and forth along the main beach, maybe paddled a bit, and then eaten in the most obvious café before heading back to Sydney. But Lindy knew the place; this was the stamping ground of her youth.

She took me beyond the main beach to a little bay called Fairy Beach, where the water was shallow and the waves gentle. She knew I'd got into difficulties in the currents near Coffs Harbour on my last visit to Oz and that I was a little nervous of the sea as a result. Here it was safe for the smallest kiddies and I swam joyfully while Lindy sat on the sand.

Afterwards, we took a walk, spotting an eastern water dragon (grey lizard) among the rocks and bushes of bottlebrush. I admired the manmade seawater pools, cut out of the rock right down by the water's edge, where you could swim safe from rips and sharks, yet feel you were in the sea. I made a mental note that I was going to give those a try at the earliest opportunity.

"I had to get away from this place," said Lindy, who after Moscow had moved to London and now also had her own farm in France. "I used to see this woman on the bus, reading romantic novels. I left Australia for a while and when I came back, there she was, still on the same bus, reading the same books."

I understood. What was exotic to me had been stifling for Lindy; she no doubt thought my 'boring' birthplace of Yorkshire was brilliant.

Fish and chips we had in common, though, and Lindy treated me in a fishery down by the ferry terminal. (I got my revenge with ice creams later in the afternoon.) Then she took me along another path, away from the open ocean, on the more sheltered side of the peninsula.

What Lindy showed me that day was so marvellous that I went back on my own another day for a second look at Manly. I retraced our steps along the Manly Scenic Walkway, sniffing the frangipani and photographing the aloes and hibiscus.

Back at home, I posted photos of Manly on *Facebook*, misspelling Australia's second most famous beach as Manley. Geoff Winestock was not an editor for nothing and he gently picked me up on the mistake, elaborating that Captain Arthur Phillip had named the place after an incident in which an Aboriginal elder had speared him in the shoulder.

Phillip ordered his men not to retaliate but said of the indigenous Guringai people, 'their confidence and manly behaviour made me give the name of Manly Cove to this place'.

Unfortunately, not all my friends on *Facebook* noticed Geoff's correction but went on repeating my mistake, which sent him into an apoplexy of frustration. So here for the record, it is MANLY.

After the ecstatic feelings I experienced at Manly, I sank into a dip of depression for a day or two. I noticed a recurring pattern in my emotions – I would be in love with the light and freedom and ease of life in Oz and then suddenly, I would have a wave of homesickness for old Europe, bringing with it a sense that Down Under I was in exile.

Aussies, who are well travelled and always seem to be planning their next trip overseas, speak of the 'tyranny of distance', for this country is so far from anywhere else. The nearest major foreign city is Singapore, if you don't count Auckland, which is also Down Under. A Russian friend who lived for years in New Zealand said life there was like a 'picnic on the roadside'; nice, but you weren't going anywhere. An English friend living in Sydney told me this ache for Europe – this feeling that *there* you had been 'in the heart of things' – never quite went away.

I imagined how hard it must have been for the convicts, transported to Australia without hope of seeing the old country again. On the other hand, having no choice, they had to make the best of it. My problem was I had options.

I wasn't low for long, however, because Max was taking me out.

Max Vlasov was one of my students in Moscow. I coached him in English to help him pass the necessary language test for migration to Australia. He settled successfully in Sydney and got a good job in IT.

From his home in the southeastern suburb of Sutherland, we were going to drive to the Royal National Park or 'Nasho', as Sydneysiders affectionately call it. Just 20 minutes in a car from Sutherland and you are in Sydney's 'beautiful big backyard', to quote the park publicity, with 16,000 hectares of bush, perfect for hiking, cycling, picnicking and whale watching (in season).

It was hot, so our first stop was at Bundeena beach, where Max erected a small shade tent before we both waded into the exquisite turquoise water. The sea was calm and shallow, perfect for a safe swim. We bathed, snacked on nuts and berries in the tent, and hit the water again. I couldn't tear myself away from the place.

"Perhaps we should have a walk down the beach?" Max said eventually. I followed him, lazily picking up shells, until we came to a little creek, easily crossable as the water was only knee-high. We sat on the far bank, poking the sand with sticks like children.

From Bundeena, we drove through the park in companionable silence. The eucalypt woods on either side of the road were thick enough to get lost in. We came out at the start of the Grand Pacific Drive, a coast-hugging highway that would have taken us all the way to Melbourne if we'd kept going. Instead, we stopped in a lay-by and bought mango ice creams from a van. The view of the ocean was spectacular.

On the Sea Cliff Bridge, I took a photo of Max with the Pacific in the background. He told me he'd grown up in Vladivostok and that his father had been a submarine commander. He said he felt more at home in Oz than Europe. "Europe's beautiful but it's not mine." I guess he had the Pacific in his blood.

We finished up in Wollongong, 50 miles south of Sydney, where we watched the surfers and looked across to Port Kembla in the distance. The coal terminal's famous 49-year-old chimney was clearly visible and we must have been among the last to see it. (A few days later, it was demolished in a crowd-drawing controlled explosion.)

An hour later, we were back in Sutherland, drinking tea with honey from Max's own beehives. His flat was a five-minute walk to the station and a half-hour train ride into the CBD, yet all the beauty of the national park was right on his doorstep. This is what I mean when I say Sydney is a liveable city.

Year of the Horse

The Aussies were barbequing their steaks and sausages. In the evening, there would be fireworks over the Opera House. It was Australia Day again and, by happy coincidence, my birthday. I felt sure there was some mystical meaning in our sharing of 26th January. This was my fourth Australia Day among the Aussies and I felt one of them.

That didn't mean I was joining the boozy crowds, or painting a flag on my face. I was conscious that for Aboriginal people, it was 'Invasion Day'. Indeed, on the 26th of January 2012, there had been a demonstration in Canberra, during which the then prime minister, Julia Gillard, had been confronted by angry indigenous rights protestors and lost one of her pretty high-heeled shoes as she fled.

I wasn't looking for dramas. Rather, I intended to spend the day peacefully, in my own way, enjoying my right to individual freedom, which is Australia's greatest gift. I was meeting Maurice Gelbert, the friend of my Russian friend Dima Dashchenko, to whom I was supposed to be delivering a parcel of books – except that they were packed in the big burgundy suitcase I'd left behind in Moscow.

I phoned Maurice on the number Dima had given me.

"I'm a friend of Dima's. I'm supposed to give you something but I'm afraid I've arrived empty handed," I said. "I don't suppose you would like to meet me anyway?"

To which the open and friendly Maurice responded by inviting me for lunch.

He picked me up in his big silver car and took me to a non-descript area of small streets. He did say where we were going but I forgot the name of the district. It was perfect because it was very quiet, away from the partying masses, and we ate in a lovely little café that did good vegetarian food.

It was relaxing in Maurice's company. I didn't know him at all but he seemed to be a gentle, calm kind of guy. He'd met Dima through yoga classes, in India or Moscow or somewhere. He told me he was a lawyer, a defence barrister for criminals in the poorer suburbs of Sydney.

After lunch, he suggested a walk and chose the rather dull Centennial Park, again because it was likely to be relatively quiet compared with the more obvious beauty spots on Australia Day. We spent a good couple of hours, sitting on the benches and walking on the grass. We had much in common, as it turned out.

The books I should have delivered were Russian grammar books. Maurice, although born in Australia and not really speaking much Russian, was Russian on both sides of his family. In middle age, he had started to feel the need to explore his roots and started visiting Russia and now he wanted to master the language. We mirrored each other in an interesting way – he an Aussie of Russian background, me Russian-speaking and almost half Russian after spending nearly 30 years in Moscow but English by birth and increasingly Australian in my heart.

A friendship was born that day. I knew I would see Maurice again.

"Perhaps you would like to meet my mother Tanya. I'll call you," he said before dropping me off back at the Rocks.

My birthday celebrations extended into the next day when Anna Masyakina, another young Russian whom I had taught in Moscow and prepared for migration to Australia, invited me to a restaurant for lunch. She lived in the suburb of Kogarah, not far from the famous Botany Bay, where Captain Cook made his first landing in 1770. It's now a multi-ethnic district, with Greek and Chinese restaurants. Anna chose a good pizzeria for our reunion.

Lovely Anna, she was one of my star pupils. She didn't speak very much English when I first met her but she worked hard, devoted many hours to further education and, after settling in Sydney, got a prestigious job as a business analyst at a top bank. I was very proud of her.

She'd been my student but now in Sydney she took me under her wing and in a way became my guide and teacher.

Laughing, I told her how I had left my suitcase in Moscow. My wardrobe was still pretty limited, as the fashion shops around the Rocks were very expensive and I had only been able to afford one pair of trousers and one dress when I first arrived.

"Oh, you should go to Chatswood; it's on the yellow line going north," she said. "There's a decent shopping centre there, with plenty of cheap shops, like Millers and Target."

This was good, practical advice and I decided to go the very next day. Before we parted, Anna took me back to her flat and gave me some of her own clothes, so I got a few fitted blouses that I might not have had the imagination to choose for myself but that actually suited me fantastically and made me look younger.

Even more generously, Anna said I was welcome to stay with her whenever I wanted, for as long as I needed. I thanked her, saying that I was OK for the time being but might well take her up on the offer when my time at the Rocks ran out.

The next day, I followed Anna's tip and went to the shopping centre. In Target, I bought a load of stuff that made me feel I had sartorial options again. I started to understand why people drag big suitcases across the world. It takes time to build up a wardrobe of clothes you like and feel comfortable in, something that's not easy to replace overnight.

The store was still decorated with green and gold balloons for Australia Day. On the wall near the checkout, I noticed a sign. It said: 'EVERY AUSTRALIAN HAS A RIGHT TO FEEL SMART, AT AFFORDABLE PRICES'. Now that was slogan I could relate to – nothing pompous, nothing overly patriotic but the essence of the Aussie ideology that everyone should have a 'fair go'.

Over the next few days, the carnival atmosphere continued. I began to see a lot of brides and grooms down at the harbour, having photographs taken after their weddings. The couples were mainly Chinese and while many of the brides wore Western-style white meringue dresses, a few were in their traditional scarlet silk. It was an auspicious time for these marriages because the Chinese New Year was approaching.

I had high hopes that it would be a good year for me because, according to my Chinese horoscope, I would be saying goodbye to the difficulties of the outgoing Year of the Dragon and riding the stallion of success in the New Year of the Horse.

Playing around on the internet with horoscopes, as you do when you are going through a period of uncertainty, I also asked for a free reading from *Astrology Answers*, an American zodiac site. Soon I got a message in my mailbox:

'Flash Alert! Aquarius, you simply cannot afford to ignore this! Soon a major transit will occur in your sign, bringing amazing new opportunities. For years, something has been blocking you from reaching your true potential. Despite periods of success and happiness, a 'fog' has been pursuing you, practically since childhood. All this is about to change. The good news is that something very positive and special is about to happen in your life. In order to help you navigate this transition and make the most of what the stars have in store for you, we offer you a full reading for only $60.'

I decided that I would navigate the transition for myself, thank you very much, and ignored the message, after which I was bombarded with repeated emails, offering me bigger and bigger discounts on the full reading. At the risk of missing my great life chance, I ignored them all. Perhaps I had achieved some wisdom in my 58 years.

And then I had a bit of a breakthrough. My mates Joy and Kalika from Alice Springs were in town for a few days and we met for drinks at the Sydney Theatre's 'Bar at the End of the Wharf'. The next day Kalika took me to meet a friend of hers who was involved in yoga. She had a large house with a swimming pool in the garden. She was an established Sydneysider, very well connected.

I went to see this friend of my friend to talk about my private interests in yoga and alternative healing but to my surprise, I came away with the promise of an introduction to a very big shot in the world of journalism. I was going to be fixed up with a meeting with this celebrity reporter and columnist. At last I would have a foot in the door at a national newspaper and a chance to charm someone who was only a few phone calls away from Rupert Murdoch himself.

The guy's name was Ralph. The necessary networking was evidently done because when I emailed him, he knew who I was and responded immediately with an offer to see me in mid-February. Things were looking up.

Meanwhile, it was the eve of Chinese New Year, 30th January, the day my Australian visa would have run out if I had not returned to Oz. I had given myself the task of waking up happy on 31st January – happy once and for all, secure in the knowledge that I was always and forever in the right place, at the right time, for the right reason, because the universe was taking care of me and had my best interests at heart. In other words, no more worrying or complaining, ever.

It was rather daunting. What if I woke up and discovered that I was still my crappy old self? But I didn't. I woke up, feeling blessed, as if I had cheated death. My visa should have run out but here I was, still in Australia, with everything to play for.

After that I went to see the Chinese New Year parade that went from the Town Hall to Cockle Bay Wharf in Darling Harbour. The floats were colourful and imaginative – there were winged horses, illuminated horses and a little Chinese girl riding a giant rocking horse. Police on real horses let the children in the crowd stroke the muzzles of their mounts.

It was all about the horse, of course, and yet the other animals of the Chinese zodiac were represented, reminding the onlookers that other years belong to the rabbit, the goat and the ox. The crowd was mainly

Chinese but not exclusively so. I saw plenty of European Australians and Muslim families, their women distinctive in headscarves. Security was minimal and the event was joyful and peaceful, an example of Australian multiculturalism at its best.

Tasmanian Interlude

While I waited for the meeting with Ralph at the newspaper, I decided to leave Sydney and have a long weekend in Tasmania, which I'd visited once before and found very beautiful. Most internal flights in Oz are fairly affordable and for 300 dollars, I was able to jet away to the island that is distinctly different from mainland Australia.

Aussies use the naughty expression 'map of Tasmania' to refer to the pubic triangle and joke unkindly that 'inbred, sheep-shagging' Tasmanians have two heads. In answer, Tasmanians produce maps that blow up the size of their island to continental proportions and show the mainland as a dot of irrelevance to the north.

Tasmanians flying from Hobart to Sydney speak of 'going to Australia', as if Tassie were not part of Oz, which of course it is, politically. With it mountains and forests, Tasmania is perhaps physically more like New Zealand than Australia. But it's not New Zealand either. Tassie is Tassie; Tassie is unique. And when you land there, the air is so fresh you could eat it with a spoon.

I was going to stay with my friend Farida Khawaja, with whom I had developed a very close connection since she first gave me a dragonfly when we met in Alice Springs. She was now working in Accident and Emergency at the hospital in Hobart, together with Sonia Twigg, another doctor whom I had known in Alice. Joining us for the house party was Megg Kelham, the historian from Alice Springs who, like me, was having a short break in Tasmania.

I have noticed there is a strong link between Central Australia and Tasmania. A lot of Alice Springs people seem to choose Tassie when, for whatever reason – education, career or retirement – they leave the desert and move down South. Although the geography and climate are very different, the societies are polarised in similar ways, both having on the one hand rural populations who might be called 'rednecks' and on the other, alternative types that the 'rednecks' would call 'do-gooder lefties'.

Tasmania, or Van Dieman's Land as it was known, was a prison within a prison in convict days, reserved for the most hardened English criminals, who were sent not to the penal colony of mainland Australia but to the 'inescapable prison' of Port Arthur. (One inmate called George 'Billy' Hunt did try to hop away by disguising himself under a kangaroo pelt but, when the guards shot at him, thinking he was edible, he surrendered and received 150 lashes.)

At the same time, some of the worst atrocities against indigenous people occurred on the island; as a result of a genocide, no full-blood Aboriginals live in Tasmania anymore. Somehow the legacy of these dark days lingers in present-day Tassie which, along with its idyllic landscapes, has its fair share of social problems.

Farida said the island was divided by something the locals call 'the flannelette curtain' – not an iron curtain exactly, but a deep split between the disadvantaged (who wear cheap flannelette shirts) and the better-off and trendy. As in Alice Springs, many of the unconventional and socially aware (or 'hairy, feral, lefty lesbians') are in the caring professions, picking up the pieces of damaged lives.

They tend also to be into organic food production and green issues, which are big both in Alice and Tasmania. The United Tasmania Group was one of the first green parties in the world and Tasmania remains at the forefront of environmental politics, not only in Oz but globally.

I'd come to Hobart but here I was, hanging out with the Alice Springs set again. Farida had met me off the early morning flight and taken me in her car straight to MONA or the Museum of Old and New Art, where Sonia and Megg were already wandering among the exhibits. The four of us planned to spend the whole day at MONA, as there was plenty to see.

The museum's founder, David Walsh, has described himself as a 'misfit child' and someone 'internal to the point of autism'. He made millions by gambling and acquired a private collection of over 400 artworks. He opened MONA in 2011 and the 'world's most far-out museum' instantly began attracting visitors, putting Tasmania more firmly than ever on the tourist map.

MONA is in the Moorilla Winery on the Berriedale Peninsula. You can reach it overland or by ferry. Once inside the museum, your eyes pop at a thought-provoking mixture of the exquisite and the confronting. Images and objects of a sexual or violent nature are juxtaposed with things of delicate loveliness to make you question: what is art?

The inaugural exhibition in 2011 included Wim Delvoye's *Cloaca Professional*, a machine that turns food into excrement, and Stephen Shanabrook's *On the Road to Heaven, the Highway to Hell*, the remains of a suicide bomber, cast in dark chocolate. Yet alongside this, you could also see such wonders as a carving of a peach from ancient Persia.

When Farida and I joined up with Sonia and Megg, we repaired to the café for a late breakfast of quiche and coffee. Thus fortified, we went to try out the 'death machine', which offered visitors an experience of euthanasia. Sitting on a leather sofa, we clicked various buttons on a computer screen to confirm that we chose lethal injection and understood the consequences. Then we sat there, imagining what it would feel like to have only three minutes left to live.

Another hall was set up with armchairs and TV sets, on each of which ordinary people from around the world were speaking about their lives. I found this fascinating and, had I had all day for this one room, could have sat in every chair and listened to every interview, so much richer were these accounts than the usual fare of television.

Farida and I also stood entranced, watching a giant, wind-powered pen drawing random strokes on a piece of paper, depending on the strength of the breeze. And there was a waterfall that spelt out words.

You didn't have to look at the pictures of child abuse, although they were there. An uplifting alternative for me was Sidney Nolan's *Snake*, a giant mural of the sacred Aboriginal Rainbow Serpent, made of 1,620 individual paintings.

As with British stately homes, where the gardens are often as rewarding as the interiors, so in the case of MONA I discovered the grounds had a lot to offer. There were a number of outdoor pavilions, including a chapel or small mosque – it was hard to say which, because it had both Christian and Moslem features. Made of lacey, deliberately rusted metalwork, it stood down by the water. Coloured light from the stained-glass windows played on the floor and the acoustics would have delighted equally a chorister or a muezzin.

MONA hosts regular craft markets on its lawns, as well as the annual Museum of Old and New Art: Festival of Music and Art or MOFO for short, a festival of contemporary music, dance and theatre. In winter, there is also the so-called Dark MOFO, with bonfires and light shows to relieve the chill and gloom of Tasmania in June.

Our day at MONA flew by and before we knew it, it was time to go. Farida and Megg left by car while Sonia and I took the ferry to Hobart. We giggled as we sat astride models of sheep on the deck, which replaced conventional bucket seats. (Perhaps there was something to that sheep-shagging joke after all.) Once back in the city, the four of us went to the Me Wah Chinese restaurant, where we had a tip-top evening meal.

Farida's house, where Megg and I were staying, was just above the famous Cascade Brewery, in the foothills of Mount Wellington. There were beautiful views of bush and mountain from every window and balcony. When I woke up the next morning, Megg was still sleeping but Farida was already outside in the garden, in wellington boots and rubber gloves, digging up potatoes.

Her garden was a gorgeous mixture of vegetables and flowers. We stood in the lavender patch, contemplating the sight of the mist in the valley, before picking fresh salad nibbles to add to the luxurious spread of cereals, yoghurt, berries and almonds already laid out for breakfast.

Megg joined us at the table, her curly hair unruly from bed. Already she was offering a view on some topic or other. She tended to be voluble – some might even have said an opinionated Fury – but I have always found her stimulating.

"Have you got a pair of knickers I could borrow, darling?" she asked me as we polished off the discussion and the coffee. "I've run out of clean underwear." I went and got her a pair, apologising for their faded bagginess, and thought nothing more of it.

After that, we went to the hairdressers and had smart new haircuts. We went bushwalking, ate fresh fish down at the harbour and took in a movie at the cinema. We had a wonderful women's weekend, during which we talked about everything under the sun and gave each other measureless support.

I couldn't believe it was already Sunday and by evening I would be flying back to Sydney. On that last morning, we had breakfast at the town market. Tasmania is a well-known paradise for foodies and the variety of stalls, selling everything from cheeses and meats to salads and pastries, matched anything you could find on a French farmers' market.

Sonia, who had been on the night shift at the hospital, joined us again, as did Nadine Kessler and Joshua Santospirito, two more friends with links to Alice Springs. Nadine was a designer and Josh was also an artist, although he had started out in mental health and worked as a psychiatric nurse in Aboriginal communities around Alice Springs.

He gave me a book he had just illustrated called *The Long Weekend in Alice Springs*, which showed in cartoon form how Aboriginal people live in 21st century Australia. He drew them around their camp fires, with their blankets, dogs and cans of beer; their ancient dreamings and modern nightmares. The book looked brilliant and I put it in my bag to study properly on the plane.

From the market, we drove out to Oatlands, a 'historic' village on the shores of Lake Dulverton. It had a mill and some pretty little cottages with roses in the gardens. I left the girls at the mill visitor centre and wandered off by myself for a while. I don't know why but always in Australia, if I was feeling any ennui, it was strongest in the places that were trying hardest to be like England. I walked down Gay Street and found a Masonic lodge in a building that looked like a garage.

The mood passed and I returned to the mill. In the gift shop, I found a postcard that I thought would make Megg laugh. It was a Victorian-era sketch of protesting women at the Cascades Female Factory, the workhouse for women convicts in Van Dieman's Land, pulling down their bloomers and showing their bums to the governor. I decided to wait and give it to her at the airport.

Before I disappeared into the departure lounge, we said our goodbyes and I pulled the card out of my handbag with a flourish. Farida had got the same card for Megg and Megg had bought one just like it for me, which just went to show how our great and gloriously dirty minds thought alike.

A Migrant in Sydney

Returning to Sydney felt like going home. I let myself in at John's place at the Rocks and put the kettle on. When I sat down to read my emails, though, I saw my internet access had run out. It was a reminder that it was time to pack up and leave this comfortable pad. Luckily, I had somewhere to go. I was moving in with my former student Anna, who'd kindly offered me a flat-sharing arrangement. No longer a guest or a tourist in Sydney, I would now be a migrant in the suburb of Kogarah.

Before leaving, I cleaned John's flat, putting a few goodies on the kitchen table for him to find when he got back from Russia. Then I set off with my rucksack and computer case for Kogarah, only a 20-minute train ride south from Circular Quay but another world from the up-market location I had been enjoying.

Everyone knows the superior suburbs in Sydney are to the north, fine waterfront districts like Neutral Bay and Cremorne, where the starting price for swanky properties is a million dollars and the sky's the limit. But going south, you're still hugging the coast, getting the benefits of sea air and reasonable access to beaches, even if the houses and flats are more modest.

"The main thing," said Anna, "is to avoid the western suburbs. They're so far from the sea that you might as well be in the outback and the crime's so bad they have to put bars on their windows."

Apart from its relative proximity to the sea, another advantage of Kogarah for Anna was its ethnic mix of Chinese, Arabs, Greeks and Macedonians. "I could have gone to Hurstville," she said, "but that's much more predominantly Chinese."

Anna, newly promoted at work, had only recently moved to Kogarah. There were beds in each of the two bedrooms of her flat but not much other furniture. She sat on a purple beanbag in the living room to watch television and a camping table and chairs did for dining. The apartment was lovely and light, though, with obvious potential.

Anna was very busy and most of the time, I hardly saw her. She left the flat early, wearing smart black or black and white dresses, the uniform of office staff in the CBD, and after work she went on to night school, so it was often eleven or midnight before I heard her key in the door lock. "Help yourself to whatever's in the fridge," she said on the first morning when she left me home alone.

To begin with, I didn't quite know what to do with myself. I didn't have any work and it was a while before I was due to meet Ralph at the newspaper. I began to understand how Anna must have felt when she first came to Australia and went through a period of unemployment until she found her feet.

I opened the half-closed blinds and fly-screen door in the main room and discovered that outside Anna had a fabulous balcony. She wasn't using it, because she didn't have the time, and I could see that the tiles were grimy. Good; now I had a job that would occupy me, at least for a day.

I left the block of flats and walked through streets of bungalows, with frangipani trees in their gardens, until I came to Kogarah High Street. Here I found a shop of household wares, run by Chinese migrants who barely spoke a word of English. "Brush," I said hopefully, "mop and bucket." Eventually, by pointing, I managed to buy the items I needed.

Back at the flat, I scrubbed and mopped the balcony. Now what I needed were some plants to brighten it and attract Anna out. I returned to the high street but despite wandering up and down several times, past bakeries and bookmakers, banks and shops with second-hand clothes, I couldn't find anyone selling plants or flowers. My surprise for Anna would have to wait for another time. I went home and closed the blinds, hiding the balcony from view.

After lunch, I took myself for a walk in the opposite direction from the high street. Within 20 minutes, I came to Botany Bay. Captain Cook had landed here and given such a promising description that those who followed in the First Fleet, bringing convicts to Australia, also entered by the bay before discovering that Port Jackson (present-day Sydney Harbour) was actually a better anchorage.

On a workday afternoon, the beach looked rather desolate. A few Muslim women in headscarves sat looking out to sea. Across the water, planes were taking off and landing at the airport. A part of me wished I was catching one.

Instead, I studied the long list of names on the memorial to those who arrived with the First Fleet, many of them in chains and effectively sentenced to life imprisonment for offences as minor as stealing food. I wondered if there was a Womack among them but couldn't find one. Of course these days, those Sydneysiders who can trace their ancestry back to a convict consider themselves Australian aristocracy.

And then it came on to rain; in fact it bucketed it down and soon I was soaked from head to toe, as I ran through the puddles in my sandals. I lost my way back to Anna's place; the streets of bungalows all looked the same. I started to need the toilet, desperately.

Almost out of my mind, I knocked at a house. The woman who opened the door would have seen a total stranger, looking like a drowned rat and begging for a wee. To her credit, she let me straight in. After I'd visited her facilities, she showed me on a map how to get home to Green Street. The Aussies are amazingly trusting and friendly; I can't think of many other countries where you would receive such unquestioning help.

So ended my first day as a migrant. I reckoned I'd made enough of an effort and deserved an evening of mindlessly watching television. I was half asleep when Anna came home, exhausted after her day.

The morrow brought bright sunshine and as soon as Anna had left for work, I put my mind once more to the business of doing up the balcony. If I couldn't find plants in Kogarah, then I would take the train down to Cronulla and go shopping there.

In its way, the southern resort of Cronulla is just as attractive as the snobbier northern beaches. Before starting the search for plants, which I would have to carry, I had a lovely morning, walking on the sands and watching the junior surfers. The sea was turquoise and there were the same ocean pools for safe swimming that I had seen at Manly.

I was touched to notice The Seed, a sandstone memorial to seven women from Cronulla and the surrounding Sutherland Shire who were among the 202 victims of the Bali bombing in 2002. It was a dreadful attack on innocent holidaymakers in which 88 Australians lost their lives and it profoundly shocked Australia's easy-going society.

In The Best Little Bookshop in Town, I bought a book on the workings of the brain and promptly applied my own to the matter of lunch. Delicious aromas were wafting from a pie shop that proclaimed the pie to be an Australian icon. Back in Russia, I was used to icons of the Virgin Mary and St. Nicholas but if icons could also be pies, that was fine by me. The choice of spicy vegetarian or lamb with mint was impossible, so I ordered both. Afterwards, I felt it was only fair to Cronulla to sample the local frozen yogurt as well.

Finally, I found a plant shop, where I bought some red and yellow peppers and basil and parsley in pots. These I carried on the train back to Kogarah, attracting approving glances from Chinese housewives riding with me in the middle of the afternoon. Decorated with the plants, the balcony looked much nicer and was ready for when Anna wanted or had the time to start lunching and lounging outside.

Two days spent in the suburbs were fine but on the third, I felt a need to go into the city, so I caught a train up to town. Sydney was preparing for its famous Mardi Gras parade and all the branches of the ANZ bank, which was a sponsor of the event, had converted their ATM machines into GAYTMs by covering them with leopard skin or leather.

What a fabulous and witty city!

I crossed the bridge over Cockle Bay, festooned with balloons, and came into Darling Harbour. At Pyrmont Wharf, I saw something called the Welcome Wall, attached to the Australian National Maritime Museum. Listed on bronze were the names of thousands of migrants from all over the world, who had come with hope of starting new lives.

'In one of history's great migrations, more than six million people have crossed the world to settle in Australia. Was your family among them?' asked the museum, offering migrants the chance, for 105 dollars per person, to add their names to the growing list and briefly tell their stories for an online archive.

There were quotes from people from Malta to South Korea, from Ireland to Italy, who had battled homesickness and separation to settle in the Southern Hemisphere's version of the Promised Land. In its way, this welcome wall was a wailing wall, because it spoke of suffering as well as achievement. I began to see that with the convicts' experience added to the migrants' struggle, not to mention the tragedy of Aboriginal people who lived on the continent for at least 40,000 years before white settlement, the whole history of Australia was a layer cake of suffering. Only recently had Sydney become one giant, non-stop, swinging party.

Still reflecting on this, I decided to drop in at a TAFE (college of technical and further education) on my way home and see if they might need an English teacher for students of migrant background. I have a Cambridge University qualification to teach English as a foreign language but at the school, they told me the level of my certificate was only good enough to teach foreigners temporarily studying in Oz, not permanent migrants, and in any case they didn't have a vacancy. *Back to journalism then,* I thought.

Maurice Gelbert, my new Russian-Australian friend, phoned to ask how I was getting on and I told him of my musings about migrants.

"Ah yes," he said, "the first arrivals were dumped here, then after the war people came seeking asylum and now migrating to Oz is something to aspire to; you have to pass the points test."

He might have added that, until as recently as 1970, the 'white Australia policy' was aimed at encouraging European migrants and keeping Asians out.

"So what are you doing, then?" asked Maurice. "Busy?"

"Not really."

"Would you like to come and meet my mother Tanya?" I was thrilled to receive the invitation.

A couple of days later, Maurice picked me up in his car to take me out to Fairfield, about 20 miles west of the city centre. At last I was going to see the dreaded western suburbs.

I didn't doubt that commuting back and forth might be tedious on mornings when there were heavy traffic jams but the town itself seemed pleasant enough. *Frightful Fairfield?* I thought to myself. *They haven't seen Balashikha in Moscow region.*

I wanted to buy a gift for Tanya, so we went first to the market, a multicultural hub with Arab, Vietnamese and Polish traders. Among the counters of dates and noodles and sausages, I had no trouble finding a flower stall and chose a bunch of red gladioli.

Tanya's house was a bungalow, built in the 1960s, I would guess. But it certainly didn't have barred windows. On the contrary, it was open and spacious and there was a fine garden at the back, with orange trees.

"I'm afraid the weather's been dry for gardening," Tanya said. "We haven't had any rain for weeks." So it was true that the absence of the sea made a difference and an area only 20 miles from where Anna lived had quite another climate. Still, I wouldn't have called it the outback.

Tanya led us to a table on the verandah, spread with all the *zakuski* (starters) of a traditional Russian meal. She had made *blini* (pancakes) and there were dishes of fish and beetroot salad.

Looking considerably younger than her age, Tanya was sharp-minded and elegant. She told me she'd come to Australia with her mother after the war. Neither of them had spoken a word of English when they arrived but somehow they'd adapted.

Her mother had been a singer who happened to be on tour in the Belorussian capital of Minsk when it was overrun by the Nazis. With Tanya, just a small child, in tow, she'd been taken away to Germany. At the end of hostilities, she'd sung in the British-controlled sector of Berlin. After that, migration to Australia had been the best option.

"Did you and your mother not want to go back to Russia?" I asked Tanya before realising I'd been tactless. They'd no doubt wanted to go back very much; they were true patriots who loved their country. But innocent people in their position were considered traitors by Stalin. Yes, Australia had definitely been the best option.

"I've had a good life here," Tanya said quietly. "I've raised my family in peace and been content."

We had dessert and coffee then, and a little while later Maurice drove me home.

I found the visit to Fairfield very inspiring. I hatched an idea about writing the various stories of migrants; they were inexhaustible and could be told in a regular newspaper column. It could be called something like 'Melting Pot'. Yes, 'Melting Pot' was a good title.

My meeting with Ralph was approaching. To be honest, I was in two minds. On the one hand, I wanted a job; any job. On the other, I wasn't sure, with all my experience, that I could shrink myself to do something ridiculously junior. And I wasn't certain that I could stand the idea of going back into an office, nine to five or longer, five days a week.

After having covered Kremlin intrigues, I found Australia's parochial politics didn't really grab me. I was slightly better informed than Bill Bryson, who had trouble remembering the names of Aussie prime ministers, and I did know that the PM was a Liberal (conservative in Australia) called Tony Abbott, famous for wearing tight-fitting swimming trunks called 'budgie smugglers'. But that was about the extent of my knowledge, or interest.

The only major news story I'd seen on my latest visit to Oz – one significant enough to merit filing for overseas readers – was the scandal of Manus Island in Papua New Guinea, where asylum seekers who tried to reach Australia illegally by boat were being held in a detention centre. There was a disturbing case in February 2014 when an Iranian would-be refugee called Reza Barati was killed and 60 others injured in a riot at the camp. I could see myself writing on subjects like that. But I couldn't kid myself that I cared what expletive the education minister had used when he insulted the leader of the opposition or what Mr. Abbott's daughters were doing. Would Ralph understand?

When we finally met and drank coffee in the reception area of the newspaper, I was relieved to learn that he understood my mixed feelings and concerns exactly. "You're obviously a senior writer and you need a special role," he said.

I suggested my idea of doing 'Melting Pot' and he loved it.

"That's brilliant," he said. "I'll put it to the editor-in-chief and we will get back to you soon." At that, he gave me a firm handshake and showed me out of the building.

I ran down the street, punching the air with excitement. I sent an SMS to Anna, telling her the news. This looked like the breakthrough I'd been waiting for. I remembered reading that the explorer John McDouall Stuart had made five unsuccessful treks across the desert before, on his sixth attempt, hacking through the mangrove swamps, he'd reached the Timor Sea. How ecstatic he must have felt. It seemed I'd similarly burst through the urban jungle into the cool of Sydney society. And I wasn't going to have to start at the bottom, like the poor Thai immigrant women who stood on George Street, with placards advertising massage services.

In Kogarah, I began looking in the windows of real estate agencies. I reckoned if Kogarah suited Anna, it might be a good place for Vitaly and me as well. But there was only any point in us uprooting ourselves from Moscow if we were going to something better. I discovered that for 700 to 1,000 dollars per week, I could rent us a good flat or a house, with a garden or swimming pool even. That would be my minimum requirement, then, when I started to negotiate a salary.

Ralph emailed to say that the editor-in-chief was keen to meet me but could only manage an appointment in a fortnight's time. Fine, I thought, and arranged a short trip up to Alice Springs in the meanwhile. I had a wonderful week in the desert with old friends, returning to Sydney with just a day to spare before the interview.

Walking in the streets of Kogarah, I had another of those episodes when a certain heartsickness crept over me. I found myself thinking: *Sydney's just a big Adelaide.* In Balashikha, I survived by regarding the cardboard boxes in which we all lived as a temporary samsara to which I need not cling. Suddenly it dawned on me that the boxes in Kogarah, while being much nicer, of course, were also a temporary samsara, an illusion of home.

The day of the interview came. On my way there, I dropped in to St. James' Church, an inner-city Anglican church dating back to 1824 which, with its architecture and lunchtime recitals, reminded me of St. Martin-in-the-Fields in London. I gazed at the gold arch behind the altar and didn't know what to ask for.

I continued on my way to the newspaper. I was almost outside the building when I got a text message from Megg in Alice Springs: 'Wearing your knickers for you today, darling, and wishing you the best of luck,' she wrote, God love her.

I reported to reception just as the editor-in-chief came down in the lift, recognised me and said: "Let's go out to a café." For some reason, I sensed that us going out rather than up to his office meant I was not going to be taken on and so it turned out.

The boss told me he was sorry but he didn't have the budget to hire me. With Vladimir Putin poised to annex Crimea, I would probably be better off going back to Russia, he said. Why had he bothered to meet me at all, only to tell me that?

Deflated, I went back to Kogarah and changed out of my smart interview clothes into something more casual. I had tried so hard to change my life – my life and Vitaly's – for the better and I had failed. I walked down to Botany Bay and strolled on the beach, kicking the sand and staring out at the horizon. I felt empty.

The Natty Little Turquoise

This outcome was inevitable. Like every other experience I had in Oz, I set it up and drew it to myself. 'Thou knowest, Lord, the secrets of our hearts…' Deep in my heart, I already knew I was leaving; the migrant dream was over. I'd defeated myself by my own ambivalence.

The week before the job interview, I'd flown to Alice Springs to see my beloved red desert for the last time and say goodbye to friends there. I was losing Alexandria. I was going to have to be brave and bid her farewell, this 'Alexandria', which in my case was the little town of Alice.

I stayed with Maya Cifali in her comforting house, with the Egyptian blue verandah and oasis garden, where green-eyed Momo padded among the plants. On my first morning I swept the backyard, glad to tend again this place I had 'house-sat' and loved when Maya had been away. This time the owner was home and for a whole week, I had the pleasure of her hospitality and company.

It was an incredibly intense seven days. At breakfast, Maya and I would already be discussing the French Revolution or talking about writers from E.M. Forster to Lawrence Durrell. It was exhausting for both of us but like me, Maya loved a good intellectual workout.

In particular, Maya reminisced a lot about her childhood in Egypt, for it was Maya who had literally had to leave Alexandria. On one of my previous visits, she had said that I belonged in Alice Springs but it was Maya who belonged in Alice, the town of palms, eucalypts and camels that had compensated her for the loss of the Middle East.

Maya and I had some grand outings that week. On a rare desert day when dark rain clouds massed over the MacDonnell Ranges, we drove out to Simpson's Gap and sat like two Buddhas on separate rocks on either side of the steep gorge. A group of noisily chattering Indian visitors, obviously touring to a timetable, swept in and swept out again before silence returned, broken only by the sounds of insects and birds.

Maya and I drove on to Standley Chasm but it was too wet and muddy to walk into the chasm, so we had meat pies in the café instead. I recalled the lines of a Barry Humphries poem I had seen inscribed on the pavement at Circular Quay in Sydney:

I think that I could never spy
A poem lovely as a pie,
A banquet in a single course,
Blushing with rich tomato sauce.

Maya laughed and asked the waitress to bring ketchup.

On another day, we had a splendid lunch at Chiffley Resort, sitting by a shimmering swimming pool that brought to mind the paintings of David Hockney in his Los Angeles period. We both ordered barramundi – Maya's came with almonds and mine in a coconut crust – and we fell uncharacteristically quiet as we tucked into our respective platters.

Maya had said that I could have a party for all my friends at her place at the end of the week and we were planning what food and drink we would need to buy. Before the party, I was also trying to see each of my Alice friends individually.

My mate Barry Skipsey, the photographer and musician, and his wife Cathy, an outback nurse, were unfortunately away but I chatted to Barry on the phone. I loved the Skipseys. They'd gunned for me and wanted me to fulfill my Australian dreams. We joked it was a good thing Barry was going to miss my 'girly party', as my women friends had never been too keen on his True Blue Aussie style of singing.

The local historian Megg Kelham invited me to dinner – dear, mettlesome Megg, with whom I'd sparred so often, yet never fallen out. We'd become closer than ever and she'd worn for me the knickers of sisterly solidarity.

Denise Grieshaber, my friend the social worker, made a lovely lunch for me and then for dessert, we went to Bunnings, a new DIY and furniture megastore that had just opened and was proving quite an attraction in the small town. Over coffee and chocolate pies in the store's café, we talked about Denise's plans to visit my home in the UK. I was intensely happy that afternoon. It sounds daft but such a simple treat in good company is all you need to walk on air.

The café was closing and fresh cakes would be delivered the next day, so the waitress gave us the rest of her stock of chocolate pies to take home, free. They came in handy when another friend, Kate Lawrence, my dear doppelganger, so often mistaken for me, dropped round for tea on Maya's back verandah later that afternoon.

Maya had things of her own to do while I was staying with her. One day she attended the funeral of a young Aboriginal man, who'd had mental problems but been released back into the community. A member of his own family had then seen fit to kill him.

This was one of those cases where words failed. I felt great sorrow about Aboriginal suffering but had come to understand that indigenous business often wasn't any of my business, and I should simply respect it and leave it alone.

Continuing to see friends, I went swimming with Meredith Campbell in the Olympic-sized town pool; bliss. Swimming together was a tradition for Meredith and me, along with picnicking and bush camping in the pink swag. Joined by her husband Richard Brady, we also floated around in the little pool in her back garden.

Appropriately, it was in the Olive Pink Gardens that I caught up with fellow journalist Dave Richards, who is an expert on the life of Ms. Pink, botanist and campaigner for Aboriginal rights. Dave refused to take my farewell to Alice seriously. "You'll be back, you duffer," he said.

I saw clever and creative Mary Menotti, acupuncturist, patron of the Wearable Arts and driving force behind Alice's own nude calendar; also Joy and Kalika, Metta and Robyn and Liz and Maureen, friends with whom I'd shared both classical and rock music and much more; and Noel and Katie Ferry, artists and educators, who had taught me many things but most of all to love the Greek poet Contantine P. Cavafy.

Amid this social whirl, I knew I had to find a moment for myself; a breathing space when I could carry out an act of ceremony and magic.

From her extensive library, for my bedtime reading, Maya had given me *King* by John Berger. The story of homeless people, told from a dog's point of view, interested me only up to a point. But one paragraph I found particularly relevant to my own situation. It spoke of a bird that had accidentally flown into a room and was flapping at the windows – beating itself, bloodying itself against the windows – in a desperate attempt to get out.

Then, during the next last frantic circling, a miracle. It mistakes the window it is aiming itself at and flies through the one that is open. The bird knows immediately – before its tail has crossed the window frame – that it is back in the sky.

I went up onto Anzac Hill, from where, 13 years earlier, I had stared at Heavitree Gap and aimed myself like an arrow flying through that narrow gap and willed for myself the possibility of staying in Australia. And I looked through that same gap in the ranges and I asked Australia – Alice Springs in particular – to free me.

I had read somewhere that a person can have anything he or she wants but can't have everything. An Indian story tells of a monkey with his hand stuck in a jar. If only he would let go of the sweet inside, he could free himself but he holds on until the hunters come to kill him. I was like that monkey, wanting both my Moscow and Australian lives and I obviously couldn't have both. I had to let go of one of them.

Afterwards, I walked down into town and bought for myself a small turquoise suitcase. If I was going to stay in Sydney and live out of a suitcase (a future in which I already didn't really believe), then let it be a good case. Otherwise, I would have some natty new luggage for my journey home to Europe. I also bought a good-quality, striped cotton shirt in a cowboy outfitter's closing-down sale, as a gift to myself from the outback.

Why did I beg for release from the place I loved so much; where I felt at home? Because I knew that even if it was a good place for me, it wasn't suitable for my loved ones. And although Vitaly had said I should do what I wanted, when you are interconnected with someone, you cannot be happy, knowing they are unhappy.

Vitaly, at 54, still had something of a career in Moscow. But it wasn't so much about Vitaly, a grown man able to make his own choices, as about my cat Jack, 16 years old, devoted and dependent. I knew if I got the job in Sydney, I would have to give instructions for him to be put in a cage and flown to Budapest. However kind and competent his new owners would be, I would be sending him in his old age into the hands of strangers. The very idea broke my heart.

On the Friday night, we had the party at Maya's place. The guests contributed a variety of dishes. From the buzz of the conversation, I think they all enjoyed themselves. For me, the event passed in a blur. I formally thanked everyone for their friendship and said I couldn't begin to tell them what Alice Springs had meant to me. Amanda Worrall, like me originally from Yorkshire – and with whom I'd enjoyed choir practice and pickled egg parties – said I'd touched the lives of many people in Alice.

Afterwards, Amanda and I sat and dangled our legs in Maya's little spa pool. I cried and told her that the 'Distinguished Talent' visa, making me feel that I had to do something special to live up to it, was becoming a burden to me.

"Amanda, do you think I can finally go home, with honour?" I asked. She hugged me and said of course I could.

The next day I was flying back to Sydney. In Russia, before a journey, people sit together for a moment to collect their thoughts. Maya had another tradition. She poured me a glass of water and said: "He who has drunk from the Nile will drink it again." I thought to myself that since I was saying goodbye, that was perhaps unlikely.

The goodbyes were getting too much. I wanted to be off to the airport. But Maya insisted on taking me to the Telegraph Station to see her 'meditation spot'. In a rather agitated state I went with her. We sat on a bench by a waterhole that the telegraph engineer Charles Todd had named after his wife Alice, hence the town's name of Alice Springs. The indigenous Arrernte people call it Mparntwe. I fell into a trance. Suddenly I didn't care if I missed the plane. I could have stayed forever.

In fact, we made it to the airport with time to spare. Richard and Metta were there to see me off. Once in the plane and up in the air, I took photos out of the window of the vast expanse of the red desert below; the great Australian emptiness, a landscape for which I would always ache.

Back in the city, the night before the job interview, I went to bed, holding the little wire-wool cat that I called my 'spirit panther' in my hand for comfort. If I got the job, I would have to sacrifice Jack. I rather hoped that like Abraham, ready but not keen to give up Isaac, I would be let off the hook.

Bright and early the next morning, I donned my new striped shirt and went to see the editor. I did my best to secure a job in his Sydney office. And as I've said, he had nothing to offer. He told me that with my Russian skills, I had better chances of finding work back Moscow. I went away, slightly disappointed and mightily relieved. It was what I wanted, wasn't it?

Except that a couple of days later, it began to sink in that I would be leaving Australia and when I crossed the border on the 9th of March,

I would lose my permanent residence. What started as a light sadness soon turned into the pain of someone who has had a limb amputated. I wanted to howl.

"Don't give up on your dreams," Anna said to me. "Perhaps you will come back to Australia and you know you are always welcome to stay with me." I thanked her profusely for her kindness.

Over dinner with John Vallentine, the yachtsman who had given me a roof over my head while he was away in Russia, I got the kick in the pants I needed. "Get off your arse," he said. "While you're still on Australian territory, go and see the immigration people. You've got nothing to lose."

It was my very last day in Sydney, a Friday. I had an appointment in the morning and would only be free by about two in the afternoon. At that late stage in the game, with zero hope, I went to the immigration department's offices on Lee Street and stood in the queue.

Chinese and Indian migrants were lining up to see case officers behind a long desk but one officer was walking up and down the queue to see if he could give quick answers to people and save their time. I thought it was very well organised.

This officer, whose name tag identified him as Guido, spoke to me and I explained my problem – that I had not put in enough time in Australia and now work was taking me overseas again and I would lose my permanent residence. I said I was needed back in Russia to cover the crisis over Crimea, which was true.

Kindly, Guido took my passport and went into a back room. He came back and confirmed that indeed, I had not met the time criteria for getting an extension of the permanent residence. But then he surprised me by saying that if I was serving Australia by working abroad for an Australian employer, there was a good chance I would still be eligible to return to Oz, not as a tourist but as a resident. And as long as I had residence rights, Vitaly would have them too, as my spouse.

I wanted to hug him. "You have made me very happy," I said.

"That's what we like to think we're here for," he replied.

Instantly I sent SMSs to my friends in Alice to tell them the news. 'Who says you can't have your cake and eat it?' Liz Archer texted back. How come I had forgotten that philosophy, by which I had always lived in my confident youth?

I skipped to the Westpac bank and discovered from a friendly customer adviser called Helen (she was a Greek Helen) that I didn't need to close my account but could keep it open without incurring any fees.

And finally, passing a cinema, I noticed that Robert Redford's new film, *All is Lost*, was starting in the next five minutes. I bought a ticket and walked in.

The film is about a lone yachtsman, whose frail craft starts to sink after being rammed and damaged by a loose cargo crate. The sailor bails out the yacht, only to be hit by a storm. He transfers to a life raft, only to be hit by another storm. He sends out flares to passing ships but they ignore him. At the end of the film, when the sailor has set fire to his dinghy in a last attempt to attract attention and is overboard and drowning, a hand reaches out to rescue him.

John, a real sailor, dismissed the movie as crude and ludicrous. In another frame of mind, I might have been inclined to agree with him. But I had just had an unmistakable sign from the cosmos and was open to the idea of salvation.

The point is the divine hand would not have appeared if the sailor had lost hope and failed to take any of the small steps to help himself of which he was capable until he had reached his limit.

I was at my limit. A hand had reached out to save me. In the dark of the cinema, I broke down in floods of tears.

I spent my last night in Sydney at the waterfront home of my old ABC friend and colleague Deborah Snow and her screenwriter husband John Collee. They gave me a good Thai meal and put me to bed in their boathouse. I fell asleep to the gentle lapping of waves on Sydney Harbour. It was magical.

Then I was off to Kingsford Smith Airport to catch my long-haul flight to Abu Dhabi, with an onward connection to Moscow. Without any illusions that I could become Russian or settle in Russia, I would continue to do my professional job there, as long as my strength allowed.

I would go back to my mean little flat but get to keep Jack, which was a plus. Vitaly, who I'd missed, it goes without saying, would meet me and we would resume our lives, essentially happy if it were not for Putin's repressive policies and our lack of prospects for housing. Long ago, I'd realised that despite, or rather thanks to, our ups and downs, he was my muthabadah (man) and I was his udjerlah (woman). Each of us was whole but we could be doubly powerful together.

On the return journey, I was travelling light, carrying only the small turquoise suitcase, packed with the few clothes and other possessions I had acquired during my sixth voyage to Oz. I understood the grace of God is infinite and the universe always surprises us with a slightly different outcome from the one we expect.

In the turquoise case, like Pandora, I carried hope; hope of further voyages. If I still called Australia home, perhaps Australia would go on calling me one of its own. And in time Vitaly and I might find the window of antipodean possibility not shut after all, but letting in a gentle breeze.

Postscript

Back in Moscow, I applied for an Australian Resident Return Visa. Twelve Australians who knew me in various capacities supported my application. To my surprise, within two weeks, the visa was granted.

In July 2015, the Russian Foreign Ministry refused to extend my accreditation as a journalist. It was not an expulsion exactly, as I was not declared *persona non grata* and could always return as a guest or tourist, but the bureaucrats of Mother Russia were showing me the door.

One door was closing while another remained open. It's a long way to Australia; we all know that. It's not just the long-haul flight but above all, it's a long emotional journey.

I put my cat Jack in a soft travel bag and carried him on the plane from Moscow to Budapest. Aged 17, he travelled for the first time in his life, on pet-friendly Aeroflot, and went to stay with the vet's family in a house by the Danube. Vitaly remained at his job in Moscow, waiting to see how things unfolded.

I was going to Australia again. With my husband in Russia, my cat in Hungary and myself heading for Melbourne, I was unsure how the scrambled Rubik's Cube of my life would resolve itself. Would I find work and stay in Australia for good this time, or would I simply visit old haunts and friends before returning to Europe?

Aussies who'd kept in touch with me over the years lamented that, with the global migration crisis and right-wing government, Australia had become a less welcoming society than the generous country I'd always known. That was a shame, if true.

But however things turned out, I had the bonus of a seventh odyssey to Oz and intended to make the most of it. I guess I wasn't searching for myself so much anymore, knowing that wherever I went, I was a constant. Mindfully, I packed the big burgundy suitcase, the one I'd left behind in Moscow, and this time I didn't forget to take it with me.

Arriving in Oz, I went to stay in a place called Healesville in rural Victoria and woke on a spring morning to the sound of kookaburras laughing.

Healesville, October 2015

Acknowledgements

Thanks to all the real people named in this memoir for their generosity and hospitality. Special thanks to Bill Bryson, Barry Skipsey, Megg Kelham, Tarla Kramer, David Oakes and Linda Wells, who gave permission for me to quote their writing, and to Robyn Grey-Gardner and Maya Cifali, who allowed me to tell their stories at length.

Thanks also to the first readers of the manuscript, who spotted mistakes and made useful comments: Glenn Morrison, Jill Fairley, Coralie McGrath, Miranda Ingram and Jean Abbott. And finally, thanks to Ben Kay for his meticulous editing and to cover designer, Hannah Belcher, for the artwork.